TABLE OF CONTENTS

Foreword	Page 4
Chapter 1: Practical Realities	Page 9
Chapter 2: The Call of the Segrada Familia	Page 15
Chapter 3: On the Nature of Judgment	Page 19
Chapter 4: Straight Out of Purgatory	Page 25
Chapter 5: All Apologetics. No Apologies	Page 40
Chapter 6: What John the Baptist Taught Us	Page 44
Chapter 7: The Serpent's Legacy	Page 47
Chapter 8: Jesus In the Wilderness	Page 51
Chapter 9: The Lord's Prayer	Page 55
Chapter 10: Releasing Tradition's Grip	Page 59
Chapter 11: Creationism and the Science of Denial	Page 63
Chapter 12: Why the Easier Path Leads to Difficulties	Page 71
Chapter 13: Lessons in Bad Theology	Page 77
Chapter 14: Playing God and Imposing Tradition	Page 80
Chapter 15: The Corrupting Influence of Repression	Page 92
Chapter 16: In Originalism We Cannot Trust	Page 97
Chapter 17: Echoes of Manifest Destiny	Page 110
Chapter 18: Cause and Effect	Page 116
Chapter 19: Scriptural Inventory	Page 127
Chapter 20: Religion from Earth	Page 130
OF EARTH AND OURSELVES	Page 130
THE DEATH OF THE WILDERNESS	Page 133
THE EARTH IS THE LORD'S	Page 137
THE SPEECH OF GOD	Page 144
OUR PLACE IN CREATION	Page 148
JESUS AND THE ECOLOGICAL CRISIS	Page 152
THE COSMIC CHRIST	Page 158
PROPHETIC JUDGMENT ON OUR WAYS	Page 161
THE SEED OF THE FUTURE	Page 169
A WAY OF RETURN: ST. FRANCIS OF ASSISI	Page 173
THE WAY OF WISE MANAGEMENT: ST. BENEDICT	Page 179
SALVATION	Page 182
OF PURPOSE AND REASON	Page 186
Chapter 21. Reconciliation	Page 192
Bibliography	Page 207
Acknowledgments	Page 236
About the Authors	Page 237-8
Map of Legalism in Christianity	Page 239

Honest-To-Goodness:
definition: not fake, false, or artificial: real

"God writes the Gospel not in the Bible alone, but also on trees, and in the flowers and clouds and stars." —Martin Luther

Foreword

Our high school's Youth For Christ (Campus Life)[1] program drew many of its counselors from a religiously conservative Christian college in the Chicago suburbs. During group discussions, I'd sometimes defend secular views, such as the theory of evolution, that did not agree with the Bible-based worldview favored by the leadership. Halfway through the school year, I was pulled aside by one of the counselors who warned, "You know, if you keep asking questions and talking about these ideas, you'll never be a Christian."

That admonishment was not entirely unexpected. The pastor in our 8th-grade Confirmation class also collared me for asking questions about religious beliefs. My purpose was simple. I wanted to know why people embraced traditions that turned people away from other forms of truth.

Higher education

After graduating from high school, I attended Luther College[2], a Christian liberal arts school in Decorah, Iowa. All students were required to take religion classes, yet critical thinking was highly encouraged. That's when I first heard the phrase "the unexamined faith is not worth having," a quote partially credited to American writer and editor John Meacham.

With that thought in mind, I enrolled in a Philosophy of Existentialism class. We read books such as The Plague[3] by Albert Camus. The plot and theme of that novel forewarned the challenges faced in the present-day Covid-19 pandemic. "The townspeople of Oran are in the grip of a deadly plague, which condemns its victims to a swift and horrifying death. Fear, isolation, and claustrophobia follow as they are forced into quarantine. Each person responds in their way to the lethal disease: some resign themselves to fate, some seek blame, and a few, like Dr. Rieux, resist the terror."

We also read the Jean-Paul Sartre play titled No Exit[4] in which three people are locked together in a room for eternity. At any given point, two of the occupants in the room do not get along with the third. It all

> The vast majority of people walking away from Christianity in America are not rejecting the person and work of Jesus.
>
> They are rejecting faulty biblical interpretations that lead to bigotry, oppression, and marginalization.
>
> This rejection isn't unchristian.
>
> It is Christlike.

Julius Lumsden · 2h
Creative
4d · Edited

America is the only nation that wants to arm to the teeth all it's citizen's with weapons of death , then claim they are Christian .

The culture is so fear based that you need a gun to go the grocery store, then claim you are free.

No other nation lives like that.

America is not a Christian nation, it is fear based and that is not a powerful position, rather the opposite .

Americans are obsessed with guns , not life, then claim that in name of Jesus Christ . What a disgrace to Christianity

The Democratic Coalition
182,534 followers
8h

Trump's comment comes as Marjorie Taylor Greene calls herself a Christian nationalist and Lauren Boebert says the church should direct the government.
...see more

Trump says 'Americans kneel to God, and God alone' as support for Christian nationalism grows among Republicans
businessinsider.com

Many voices* are speaking out against the corruption of the Christian religion for purposes of power, wealth, and political control. Truth is starting to rise up.

This book is about how to make the changes necessary to return Christianity to an honest-to-goodness understanding of its purpose in this world, and beyond.

*You'll find more compelling samples as we go along.

♥ John Pavlovitz liked

John Fugelsang @JohnFugelsang · 7h

Creationism is the belief that God could create the world in 6 days but couldn't find 2 naked people hiding in a garden.

💬 83   ⟲ 381   ♥ 2.9K   ⬆

To Bill whoever —
A man of great faith
and good works

1

Honest-To-Goodness:

Why Christianity Needs a Reality Check,
and How to Make It Happen

©Copyright 2022, Christopher L. Cudworth

All rights reserved.

No portion of this book may be reproduced by mechanical,

photographic or electronic process, nor may be stored

in a retrieval system, transmitted in any form or otherwise

be copied for public use or private use without written

permission of the copyright owner.

Cover Design, Illustrations and Layout by Christopher Cudworth

Printed in the United States of America

For more information, contact:

Human Nature Publishing

Christopher Cudworth https://www.christophercudworth.com/

cudworthfix@gmail.com

comes down to a harsh conclusion, "Hell is other people."

It ultimately struck me that there were parallels between Christian and existentialist philosophy. I saw parallels between the story of Adam and Eve in the Book of Genesis and the fate of characters in Voltaire's book Candide[5], where people caught up in a series of chaotic events arrive at a resigned and pragmatic conclusion: "We must cultivate our garden."

That sounds much like the fate of Adam and Eve following their banishment from the Garden of Eden. God tells the couple they'll be forced to "cultivate their garden:"

> 17 To Adam he said, "Because you listened to your wife and ate fruit from the tree about which I commanded you, 'You must not eat from it,›
>
> Cursed is the ground because of you;
>
> through painful toil you will eat food from it
>
> all the days of your life.
>
> 18 It will produce thorns and thistles for you,
>
> and you will eat the plants of the field.
>
> 19 By the sweat of your brow
>
> you will eat your food
>
> until you return to the ground,
>
> since from it you were taken;
>
> for dust you are
>
> and to dust you will return."
>
> --Genesis 3: 17-19

Despite the seemingly different source of their origins, there are striking similarities between religion and existentialism. Both acknowledge the existence of free will. Each recognizes the need to deal with the consequences of our actions and seek to answer important questions about the human condition, such as: "What is the meaning of life?" and "Where do we go from here?"

The material world

As a young man interested in nature I took science courses in high school and college to learn more about the material world. In Earth Science class, we learned about the theory of plate tectonics[6] and how the continents moved across the earth's surface. In combination with the theory of evolution,[7] these branches of science converged to explain how new species emerge when ecosystems changed as continents separated or volcanism produced entirely new land forms. Most notably, the timescale of geology, plate tectonics and evolution work in perfect accord. It all made sense and provided a perfectly rational way to describe the material world and how life evolved and changed over time. But the scientific narrative was not popular, I grew to understand, with certain conservative religious groups.

Natural revelations

Beyond college I continued studying natural history and became a wildlife artist and environmental writer. I reconciled what I learned about the material world in context with my faith upbringing because I never saw the need to treat science as competition with religion. Instead, I saw the value of religion in the expression of love for others and an appreciation of creation. That seemed like the ideal way to reconcile my belief in God with study of the natural world.

To find out what other people thought about these subjects, I delved into the history of the Christian religion, including books by authors from all perspectives; conservative, liberal, traditional, and radical. I especially wanted to know how Christianity developed its scriptures and how they came to be used over the centuries. It took time to pore through the Bible for clues about its origins and learn about the many kinds of literature contained within.

At the church my late wife and I attended from the early 1980s through 2012, we participated in a Read the Bible in 90 Days program. That involved reading twelve pages of scripture a day. It took discipline to keep up and stay on course. As a longtime distance runner, I treated that project like I was training for a marathon, logging the "miles" as we traveled through the Bible. We also engaged in group discussions, taking notes, and compared our beliefs to others. I stumbled on a few (indeed many) scriptural surprises along the way. I was stunned, for example, to find out King David was denied the chance to build a temple to honor God because he'd been too good at fighting wars and committing genocide. Upon learning of David's plan to build such a temple, God told him, "No, you have too much blood on your hands."[8]

While David was known for promoting the cause of Israel, he also committed some of the most egregious sins imaginable. Not only did he order the killing of women and children in military campaigns, he also stole another man's wife by sending her husband off to be killed in the war. That's likely another reason why God did not want David to build a temple in his honor. The ends do not always justify the means when it comes to finding favor with God. That realization made me think about other ostensibly righteous acts carried out by religious figures in history. It didn't take much digging to learn that for centuries the Christian religion persecuted Jews for the killing of Jesus, and that anti-Antisemitism continues to this day.[9]

During my historical digging I also learned how the Bible was used to justify slavery, promote racism, suppress women's rights, and persecute gay people deemed "sinful" according to certain views of scripture.[10] The more I read, the more it was apparent that the list of human rights abuses committed by Christianity on the basis of scripture was so long it was hard to tally them all. That included inquisitions, torture, political subterfuge, religious wars, and genocide committed in the name of God.[11] Piled on top of all these was the exploitation of natural resources under the guise of "dominion over the earth."[12]

The more I read about how Christianity exploited the world, the more I wanted to figure out what caused a faith with so much potential for good to become toxic. Scripture clearly shows that Jesus warned us about the dangers of religion corrupted by political power. He challenged the legalistic brand of religious authority wielded by self-righteous hypocrites.[13] We also know that Jesus fell prey to their political calculations and self-righteous defense of tradition. What's that supposed to teach us? It taught me that there is often a harsh cost of standing up to religious authority. Those who do are often persecuted or killed. Holding religion accountable is a dangerous job, and in this book we'll talk about some of the brave people willing to take on that kind of work. And just like as we should follow the example of Jesus in loving others, so should we stand up to abusive brands of religious authority. If we don't, history repeats itself and the cycle of legalistic damage continues.

The roots of resistance: The Genesis Fix

When I was forty-three years old and working as an editorial writer for a leading newspaper, I started work on a book about what I saw wrong with certain aspects of Christianity. The project started with an essay titled *How the Earth Was Forgotten Since Creation*. Seven years later I completed **The Genesis Fix: How Biblical Literalism Affects Politics, Culture, and the Environment**. The book caught the attention of Dr. Richard Simon Hanson, a Professor of Religion (Emeritus)[14] at my alma mater Luther College. He filled his copy of *The Genesis Fix* with encouraging comments and sent it back to me. A few months later he mailed me a thick manila envelope with a manuscript inside. It was titled **Religin From Eearth.** "If you write another book," he wrote, "Feel free to use any or part of this."

Encouraged by support from a scholar that I greatly respect, I embarked on a new round of research to examine the historically conflicted nature of the Christian religion.

The book you are reading is about how the Christian religion frequently gets it all wrong by trying to prove itself right about every subject under the sun. We'll examine how scripture too often depends on anachronistic sources[15] selectively chosen to achieve a specific, often selfishly motivated agenda. That presumptive worldview deserves to be challenged when it leads to harming other people and creation. Only then can we help Christianity find its honest-to-goodness place in the world. We'll begin by examining some of the practical realities we all face.

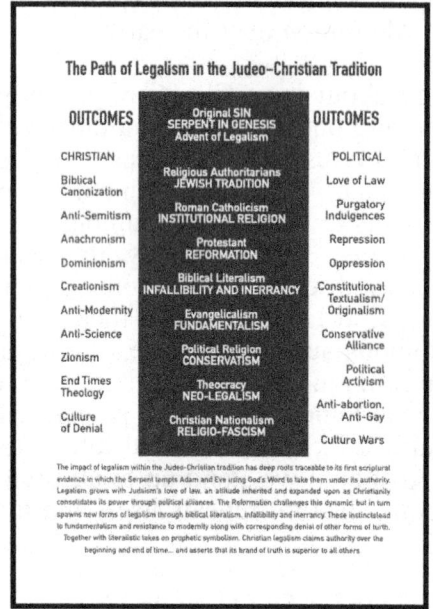

The Path of Legalism in the Judeo-Christian Tradition

OUTCOMES (CHRISTIAN)		OUTCOMES (POLITICAL)
	Original SIN / SERPENT IN GENESIS / Advent of Legalism	
Biblical Canonization	Religious Authoritarians / JEWISH TRADITION	Love of Law
Anti-Semitism	Roman Catholicism / INSTITUTIONAL RELIGION	Purgatory Indulgences
Anachronism	Protestant REFORMATION	Repression
Dominionism		Oppression
Creationism	Biblical Literalism / INFALLIBILITY AND INERRANCY	Constitutional Textualism / Originalism
Anti-Modernity	Evangelicalism FUNDAMENTALISM	
Anti-Science		Conservative Alliance
Zionism	Political Religion CONSERVATISM	
End Times Theology	Theocracy NEO-LEGALISM	Political Activism
Culture of Denial	Christian Nationalism RELIGIO-FASCISM	Anti-abortion, Anti-Gay
		Culture Wars

The impact of legalism within the Judeo-Christian tradition has deep roots traceable to its first scriptural evidence in which the Serpent tempts Adam and Eve using God's Word to take them under its authority. Legalism grows with Judaism's love of law, an attitude inherited and expanded upon as Christianity consolidates its power through political alliances. The Reformation challenges this dynamic, but in turn spawns new forms of legalism through biblical literalism, infallibility and inerrancy. These instinctualead to fundamentalism and resistance to modernity along with corresponding denial of other forms of truth. Together with literalistic takes on prophetic symbolism. Christian legalism claims authority over the beginning and end of time... and asserts that its brand of truth is superior to all others

To view a map of how legalism migrated from Jewish tradition through the advent of Christianity to the modern era, please turn to page 239 at the back of the book. It will be helpful in understanding the path and its impacts on religion and the world.

Chapter 1

Practical Realities

Some secrets in this world seem destined to remain hidden. Others exist out in the open, relying on the irony of the obvious to obscure their existence. Unfortunately, neither of these is an honest approach to the pursuit of truth. The open secret of the Christian tradition is that early in its history[1], the simple faith that began with disciples spreading the word two-by-two transformed into the one thing Jesus most despised, an institution wielding scriptural legalism[2] to gain political status and economic power. That great sin flourished despite many efforts over the centuries to free Christianity from the grip of corrupt traditions. Even the tremendous changes wrought by the Reformation[3] did not rid the Christian religion of the toxic and dishonest influence of legalism. Instead, the Protestant[4] tradition formed its own brand of legalism around the concepts of biblical inerrancy[5] and infallibility[6]. These in turn are anchored in scriptural literalism.[7] These tactics fuel an inherently legalistic tradition called apologetics,[8] which constitutes a wall of ideology specifically designed to defend the narrow worldview it protects.

The first practical concern is that Jesus decried legalism and its ardent claim to scriptural authority long ago. His teaching methods differed greatly from people chained to scripture as the source of absolute, literal truth. He shared spiritual lessons in a much simpler fashion than the legalistic religious authorities he criticized for demanding that everyone behave according to their version of the letter of the law. Instead, Jesus taught using parables[9] based on events from everyday life and the world around us. That was an honest-to-goodness approach to encouraging people to think about God in new ways. He invited us to engage with God through a mind open to connecting human lives, creation, and the spirit within us. There's nothing complicated about that, nor does it require any kind of apologetic hairsplitting to explain it. Jesus trusted that when people encountered the truth in its earthiest form, they would recognize the truth of God in it. That doesn't happen when the truth of God is buried under layers of rules and laws. The lessons taught by Jesus had far fewer rules than the controlling traditions favored by religious authorities[10] whose strict control over scriptural interpretation granted them power and position in life. Instead, Jesus preached that the meek should inherit the Earth.

The website theologyofwork.com[11] published an interesting treatise examining what it means to be "meek" or to "inherit the earth," as it appears in Matthew 5:5. "The third beatitude puzzles many people in the workplace, in part because they don't understand what it means to be meek. Many assume the term means weak, tame, or deficient in courage. But the biblical understanding of meekness is power under control. In the Old Testament, Moses was described as the meekest man on Earth (Numbers 12:3, KJV). Jesus described himself as "meek and lowly" (Matt. 11:28-29, KJV), which was consistent with his vigorous action in cleansing the temple (Matt. 21:12-13)."

"Power under God's control means two things: (1) refusal to inflate our self-estimation; and (2) reticence to assert ourselves for ourselves. Paul captures the first aspect perfectly in Romans 12:3:

> "For by the grace given to me, I say to everyone among you not to think of yourself more highly than you ought to think, but to think with sober judgment, each according to the measure of faith that God has assigned."

That assessment by theologyofwork.com accurately describes where religious authority so often goes wrong. It is easy for people in positions of power to get caught up in their own significance and mistake (or claim) their position in service as an excuse to exert control over others. That is the problem Jesus saw in the religious authorities of his day. It is still a problem that corrupts religious authority to this day.

If Jesus showed up in the present era, he would undoubtedly tell the religious legalists, political power brokers, wealthy televangelists, and purveyors of End Times[12] theology, "You've got this thing all wrong. The Kingdom of God is not something you own. It is something you create and appreciate in this world through the honest-to-goodness extension of grace, love, and care. God empowers us to do these things."

Though Jesus originally sought to cure religion of the toxic effects of legalism, that item on his wish list was not fulfilled in any generation to come. Even during the first century A.D., squabbles broke out between supporters of Jesus' legacy.[13] These included the apostles, Jesus' relatives, and also the inspired (self-designated) representatives of the Christian faith, such as Paul. Outside that sphere, many more groups argued about who Jesus was and what Christianity would become.[14]

Many of them were fated for destruction once the Christian religion consolidated with Roman authority[15] under Constantine. Canonizing the books of the New Testament relegated competing factions of Christians to the sidelines, or worse. Gnostic[16] and other versions of scripture were banished. Emboldened by this rush of power after centuries of persecution from the Romans and other cultural opponents, the Christian religion turned its ire against all that opposed its doctrines.

That righteous fury fueled a long line of Popes, kings, religious leaders, and zealous laypeople wielding the Bible as a weapon against perceived enemies and detractors. In its most egregious actions, the church, while claiming to act in God's name, conducted murderous inquisitions, torture, and genocides. None of this was what God or Jesus intended for the institution that would become the Christian church.

Worldly efforts

Getting Christianity back on the right path today is a difficult task because many believers refuse to admit that the Christian religion has ever been wrong about anything. That is why it is so hard to help folks comprehend that religion is capable of causing real suffering in this world. The track record does not lie. Christianity has been used to block civil rights,[17] brand love between two people sinful,[18] and denigrate useful science[19] based on a biblically literal interpretation of scripture. And that's just the start of the list.

None of that negative behavior serves God in any useful way. Yet, these are some of the highest priorities among legalistic Christians determined to "win" what they term a Culture War.[20] We must ask: What kind of worldview works so hard to deny obvious material truths and block equal rights to people deserving of them? The answer is that Christian legalism needs to aggressively protect its worldview because it does not necessarily stand for truth. That is why scriptural legalists defend their biblical views from any sort of objective analysis or criticism, lest any errors or contradictions be exposed.

The central tactic is for Christian apologetics to claim that "scripture can only be tested with other scripture."[21] That's better known as tautology, "a statement that is true by necessity or by virtue of its logical form." Yet any religion dependent on strongly defensive tactics is inherently susceptible to an "ends justify the means" psychology to protect its doctrine and authority. It's not hard to find evidence of this approach in recent headlines covering the relationship between religion and politics in the news.

A 2019 Los Angeles Times story[22] titled "Evangelicals Stand Firm with Trump" shares a revealing quote about defending religious support for Donald Trump. "God always chose people that had flaws," said Bob Love, a Newport Beach real estate developer. "I feel people are people — nobody's perfect." That apologetic missive could apply to a long line of ostensibly Christian politicians eager to exchange policy promises for voter support. That is the type of self-fulfilling prophecy that covers all kinds of sins. It also reveals the lengths Christian apologetics will go to avoid accountability for corruption and hypocrisy in their cultural relationships.

It's easy to excuse morally conflicted behavior by making the claim that people exhibiting lousy behavior are still "doing God's work." That's the "end justifies the means" approach, and it aids all sorts of quid pro quo alliances between religion and politics. That's exactly the pattern of morally twisted, politically-motivated religion Jesus intended to depose.

And yet, that tradition persists because so many people care more about personal power and claiming self-righteousness than carrying out the meek and honest work of God on Earth. That means we have a right to ask, "Who gets to make the claim that they're doing 'God's work?'" Too often in human history, it is religious authoritarians making such claims, and when those objectives are combined with authoritarian political ideology, we wind up with a form of religio-fascism. The United States of America is dealing with that specific situation right now.

The alliance of American Christian extremism with nationalistic instincts and fascism was addressed in a March 27, 2022 Chicago Tribune editorial written by the Rev. Pamela Cooper-White, dean and professor of psychology at Union Theological Seminary in New York. She observed, "But as Putin grows more and more isolated on the world stage," she commented, "he's retaining one surprising base of support: far-right American Christians." She continued, "As Delaware Republican Laureen Witzke, a U.S. Senate candidate, recently said at the Conservative Political Action Conference: "Russia is a Christian nationalist nation…I identify more with Russians,' with Putin's Christian values than I do with Joe Biden's."

Cooper-White shares that American Christian nationalists actively embrace Putin's anti-LGBTQ stance because it parallels their own judgments about those communities. She also notes that the Christian nationalist instinct harbors racist instincts centered around the idea that God favors the white race and the accompanying belief that Christians "deserve" to run the country because they claim to have originated it. "Christian nationalists…" she observes, "look for the restoration of what they see as a white patriarchal way of life."

That tribal desire for control of the homeland is why Christian nationalists also identify with Vladimir Putin's efforts to take back Ukraine. His goal is restoring the authority of the Russian Orthodox Church to unify his vision of the "motherland" that was once the Soviet Union.

That's part of the motivation behind the Russian attack on Ukraine. It is chilling to realize that Putin's instincts directly parallel the goals of Christian religious zealots and their political allies working to turn the United States into a "Christian nation."

The irony is that the Republican Party and most American Christians once ardently opposed the Soviet Union (or Russia) with its communist system of government. But that's not the case any longer. In an article published in the same March 27 issue of the Chicago Tribune, New York Times reporters Sheera Frenkel and Stuart A. Thompson collaborated to write "How Russia, US right-wing converged on war." The piece chronicles the broader dynamics at work in the relationship between right-wing America and the Russia propaganda machine. "When Putin insisted he was trying to "denazify" Ukraine, Joe Oltmann, a far-right podcaster, and Lara Logan, another right-wing commentator, mirrored the idea."

We can surmise that either the messaging is coincidental, indicating like-mindedness, or the viewpoints are shared, suggesting a form of collaboration at work. "People are asking if the far right in the U.S. is influencing Russia or if Russia is influencing the far right, but the truth is they are influencing each other," said Thomas Rid, a professor at Johns Hopkins University who studies Russian information warfare. "They are pushing the same narrative. Their intersecting comments could have far-reaching implications," the authors note, "potentially exacerbating polarization in the United States and influencing the midterm elections."

Strong evidence exists that Vladimir Putin and the Russians successfully infiltrated the United States electoral process using social media to spread propaganda criticizing political candidates with hopes of dividing the country in two.* The original goal was to foment political debate as an "us vs them" dynamic and push the country toward the authoritarian leanings of Donald Trump, whose relationship with Russia with business ties was already cozy. That Russian objective was easily achieved in a nation with deep-seated authoritarian leanings stemming from the "follow your orders" doctrine of the Religious Right. And, it continues.

It hurts to even admit how successful these tactics were in garnering right-wing support for a President exhibiting zero qualities identifiable with the more wholesome aspects of Christianity such as human compassion, forgiveness, and humility. Trump was the opposite of all that, but evangelicals triumphantly crowed that he was simply a flawed human being carrying out the Lord's work. Never mind that he hung out with porn stars, committed fraud with his own Trump University, mocked disabled people in his speeches, and consistently belittled veterans and war heroes for suffering wounds and torture in their line of duty. The

* https://www.brennancenter.org/our-work/analysis-opinion/new-evidence-shows-how-russias-election-interfer-

deeper that Trump lowered the bar with his distasteful remarks and behavior, the more evangelicals crawled through cultural mud to worship at his political feet. Many seemed to regard their fealty to The Donald as a holy duty as if supporting Trump was a welcome form of persecution on behalf of Jesus the Christ.

Exploitation for God

Along with its perverse propensity for seeking political power above all else, the Christian religion also needs to account for its long record of siding with economic and political interests willing to despoil the Earth for the short-term gains of material profit.[25] That's ironic when we look at the Bible's obvious reverence for nature as a source of eternal truth. All the most important symbols in scripture come from nature, starting with the Garden of Eden, running all the way through the organic parables of Jesus to the apocalyptic imagery found in Revelation.[26]

Rather than take this organic scriptural connection for granted, we should take seriously its deeply spiritual significance. That means it is our calling to respect the Earth by placing its welfare at the forefront of everything we do. The organic roots of scripture are the original evidence that God entrusted stewardship to humanity. Crushing creation beneath the selfish aims of people with no eye for the future and no genuine respect for God is neither an honest or sustainable way to live. It clearly has not worked to claim that creation is the "67th Book of the Bible"[27]. Instead we need to recognize that creation is indelibly woven into the DNA of all scripture. It is inseparable from God's Word. Nature is the component that makes God's Word symbolically whole. Ignore that core principle of organic symbolism and foundations of scripture are lost.

We should never allow that foundation to be smothered by scriptural literalism, caged by inhumane brands of anachronistic legalism, or wasted in fatalistic fits of self-fulfilling prophecies about the End Times. Recognizing organic truth is the most honest way to approach the Bible is a key reality check. Yet the Christian religion has indulged in the psychological drugs of politics and power for so long it lives in a haze of denial about the true roots of God's relationship to this world. That malaise is addictive, and it is hard to break through. Therefore, it is helpful to look at the work of people who followed the example of Jesus in celebrating the organic symbolism found in all of scripture. To do that, we commence with the beautiful work of Antonio Gaudí,[28] a Spanish architect who celebrated the organic truth of scripture in all its glory. His inspiring work began one hundred years ago and continues to this day. Perhaps we should ask the question: how well does the world listen to his example?

CHAPTER 2

The Call of Sagrada Familia

The Spanish words "sagrada familia" mean 'sacred family.' That concept is the central motif across the many tall towers forming the Sagrada Familia basilica in Barcelona, Spain. Construction of the massive structure began more than a century ago.[1] It is scheduled for completion in the year 2026. That culminates the plans originated by late Spanish architect Antonio Gaudí, whose organic style of architecture fuses symbols of Creation's glory with God's spiritual transcendence as symbolized through the Sacred Family.

A time.com[2] article describes how Gaudí developed his masterwork, explaining that the architect had a grand concept in mind: "It didn't take him long, however, to transform the Sagrada Familia's original plans into an extraordinarily ambitious undertaking: a structure that would combine natural forms and Christian symbolism into a temple that, as Faulí puts it, "expressed meaning not only through the sculpture and other decorations but through the architecture itself." Gaudí was not a practicing Catholic when he received the assignment. But he became increasingly devout as he worked on it, eventually coming to see the very structure as a vehicle for Christian evangelism."

An earnest and down-to-earth description on the website Culture Trip[3] outlines the practical aspects of its design: "The central tower in the middle will reach 170 meters tall. Despite having a powerful height, Gaudí believed that nothing human-made should ever be higher than God's work. It is no coincidence that the ultimate height will be one meter less than Montjuïc, the mountain in Barcelona, which is also the city's highest point. There are tons of symbolism in each part of Gaudí's structure. Aside from the religious symbols, there are two you should look out for. First, the interior pillars resemble trees, and when you look up at them, their shapes constantly change, as real trees appear to do. There is also a tortoise and turtle holding up these pillars, representing both the earth and the sea."

Standing before the Sagrada Familia and wandering its interior spaces is an immersion in natural symbolism. Yet, the sacred family still resides within the theme. It is that balance of wonder and appreciation that makes the experience so unique and meaningful.

Gaudí's celebration of Creation through architecture mimics the methods scripture employs by using natural metaphors to portray spiritual concepts and principles.[4] In the Bible, symbols such as the Tree of Life, the River of Life, and Living Water depict the relationship between God and Creation. The same holds with the Rock, the Dove, and the Lamb, symbols for the Trinity. In scripture, we also find God appearing through thunder, lightning, clouds, and smoke. Meanwhile, humanity takes on prosaic forms, such as frail blades of grass or a humbling pile of dry bones. These, too, are organic symbols, signifying the transient nature of our fleshly lives while calling us to live as fully as we can.

The role of scripture's organic symbols should be respected. They create a bridge between our spiritual and material lives and teach us how to appreciate God's will "on earth as it is in heaven." Yet, some people refuse to look at scripture that way. They insist that biblical literalism as applied to the Book of Genesis and its creation narrative represents the absolute and only path to truth. That approach typically aligns with the claim that scripture is infallible and inerrant in every respect and never changing. Combined, these are the foundations of religious legalism, defined as "excessive adherence to law or formula."[5]

Old habits and new regimes

In that regard, today's religious legalists share ancestry with the religious authorities[6] who resisted Jesus because he was not respecting or obeying the scriptures in the strictest sense. They attacked Jesus for breaking their laws,complaining that his earthy parables lacked authority and integrity. The religious leaders also regarded his association with lowly and disenfranchised people as signs of an unclean spirit.[7]

Jesus, in turn, deemed their long list of laws and punishments as unnecessary, sometimes cruel, and often corrupt.[8] He sought to restore the rights of everyday people to engage directly with God and indicted the religious authorities for setting up stumbling blocks[9] to that relationship. Jesus also found it disturbing that those in control of the religious system grandly profited while neglecting the needs of everyday people, even to the point of exploiting them. But Jesus had a warning for them:

> 13-14 You Pharisees and teachers of the Law of Moses are in trouble! You're nothing but show-offs. You lock people out of the kingdom of heaven. You won't go in yourselves, and you keep others from going in.[b]

Jesus set out to rid the world of religious legalism and hoped that people following his example would avoid mistakes made by religious authorities who corrupted the Kingdom of God through an obsession with law and tradition.[10] He offered a radical alternative to the power structure of the day, and beyond. His most frequent instructions were to sacrifice the benefits of wealth, position, and even family ties if necessary to seek the Kingdom of God. These actions ran counter to everything that religious authorities at the time believed about the role of their tradition. Jesus provided the original Reality Check.

Consolidation of religious power

The Christian religion that emerged after the earthly life of Jesus should have known better than to imitate the brand of religious authorities that resisted and ultimately conspired against him. Yet by the time Christianity merged with the Roman Empire in the 4th Century A.D.,[11], it became a religion consumed by legalistic tradition, driven by political jealousy, and possessed of an insatiable appetite for power. As its reach expanded,[12] the Christian church changed from a persecuted minority into a predator of competing ideologies, wiping out even.The empowered church met any type of resistance with fury and engaged in conversion campaigns, inquisitions, wars, even genocide against those who stood in the way of Christian dominance.[13] The liberal invitation of the Great Commission to "make disciples of all nations" (Matthew 28:16-20) became an authoritarian commandment to "convert or die."

To question the authority of religious tradition in those days led to accusations of blasphemy, heresy, and judgments of many kinds. The calling in Titus to "rebuke with authority"[13] was carried out with dire fury in the hands of a consolidated Christian religion. Jesus would neer have approved of that approach to belief and accountability to God. His focus was far more practical in helping people understand spiritual, moral, and cultural outcomes. He encouraged people to be honest about their lives and focus on God's judgment of their hearts and behavior rather than worry about the opinions of those around us.

> **Shane Claiborne**
> @ShaneClaiborne
>
> Jesus wasn't white.
> He didn't speak English.
> He wasn't a Republican, or a Democrat.
> He carried a cross not a gun.
>
> The flag is not a Christian symbol.
> The national anthem is not a worship song.
>
> The Bible doesn't say "God bless America" - it says, "For God so loved the WORLD."

> "Religious freedom ends when it becomes an excuse to harm other people."
>
> -Pete Buttigieg

> Hard to believe
>
> How sad it must be - believing that scientists, scholars, historians, economists, and journalists have devoted their entire lives to deceiving you, while a reality tv star with decades of fraud and exhaustively documented lying is your only beacon of truth and honesty.
>
> — @christophurious —

CHAPTER 3

On the Nature of Judgment

"For if you truly amend your ways and your doings, if you truly act justly one with another, if you do not oppress the alien, the orphan, and the widow, or shed innocent blood in this place, and if you do not go after other gods to your hurt, then I will dwell with you in this place, in the land that I gave to your ancestors forever and ever."

Jeremiah 7:5-7

The words of Jeremiah provide an important reality check when it comes to the priorities of God in relation to human culture and conduct. The instructions are simple enough. First, respect and take care of others. Don't hurt or kill people. Don't run off to worship other gods. Take care of creation, and it can be yours forever and ever. Those are the honest-to-goodness virtues of faith.

Following the ways of God would be easy if the obligations and temptations of life never got in the way. But when selfish interests become our God, we tend to forget about the needy and oppressed in this world. It is far too easy to chase after the next shiny object or inviting situation that crosses our path. It is also true that these seemingly innocent pursuits can lead us into actual sin and scandal. That is why scripture seeks to be a stabilizing influence in our lives. It helps ground us in a world where wayward thoughts or actions can quickly lead to trouble. That is the practical value of scripture.

God knows it can be hard to stay on track. That is also why it is essential to ask forgiveness when we fail ourselves or others. In that same context, scripture also warns us not to be too quick in personally judging others.

> 1 "Do not judge, or you too will be judged. 2 For in the same way you judge others, you will be judged, and with the measure you use, it will be measured to you.3 "Why do you look at the speck of sawdust in your brother's eye and pay no attention to the plank in your eye? 4 How can you say to your brother, 'Let me take the speck out of your eye,' when all the time there is a plank in your eye?5 You hypocrite, first take the plank out of your eye, and then you will see clearly to remove the speck from your brother's eye.
> –Matthew 7:1-5

That all seems clear enough. The allegory of the plank versus the speck in the eye illustrates the problem with judging others when you're not perfect. But there's another layer of insight offered by scripture about judgment as well, especially as it concerns institutional judgment:

> 8 Jesus returned to the Mount of Olives, 2 but early the next morning he was back again at the Temple. A crowd soon gathered, and he sat down and taught them. 3 As he was speaking, the teachers of religious law and the Pharisees brought a woman who had been caught in the act of adultery. They put her in front of the crowd.
>
> 4 "Teacher," they said to Jesus, "this woman was caught in the act of adultery.5 The law of Moses says to stone her. What do you say?"
>
> 6 They were trying to trap him into saying something they could use against him, but Jesus stooped down and wrote in the dust with his finger. 7 They kept demanding an answer, so he stood up again and said, "All right, but let the one who has never sinned throw the first stone!" 8 Then he stooped down again and wrote in the dust.
>
> 9 When the accusers heard this, they slipped away one by one, beginning with the oldest, until only Jesus was left in the middle of the crowd with the woman.10 Then Jesus stood up again and said to the woman, "Where are your accusers? Didn't even one of them condemn you?"
>
> 11 "No, Lord," she said.
>
> And Jesus said, "Neither do I. Go and sin no more."

This passage offers an essential insight into how Jesus regarded religious authority and its potential to produce hypocrisy in this world. By defending the woman from punishment, Jesus was not seeking to demonstrate her innocence. Instead, he tried to show that the traditions favored by the religious authorities pitted people against each other in a system of personal judgment and competition for God's favor. That was not the path to the Kingdom of God. It does not lead to goodness on any account. Yet while the woman's accusers walked away in possible contrition, the teachers of religious law and the Pharisees were left wondering what the whole thing meant. Did they ever figure it out?

Likely not. Because when Jesus bent down to write in the dust with his finger, he was redirecting their attention to make a point: "Your traditions do not mean that you own the Kingdom of God or its authority."

Time for a change

Jesus was warning the religious authorities that while the laws they embraced were sufficient concerning the history of their elders and traditions, it was time for a change. The people of God deserved better than living by rules and rituals that had nothing to do with finding spiritual fulfillment or seeking goodness in this world—or beyond—as in heaven. Jesus wanted to bring the Kingdom of God to life, not choke it to death by holding so tightly to tradition that people had no room to breathe. Unfortunately, the religious authorities that Jesus confronted were more concerned with adherence to moral law. That is better known as legalism. Here's a definition to be clear about its meaning.

Legalism, def: noun *excessive adherence to law or formula. As used in THEOLOGY dependence on moral law rather than on personal religious faith.*

Jesus made it a top priority to free the kingdom of God from the repressive and oppressive grip of legalism. Did he succeed? He did not. We learn from scripture and history that legalism's proponents do not quickly let go of that authority. We all need to understand the reasons why religious people still cling to systems of authority based on a top-down model. For example, Wes Macadams of Radically Christian[1] insists, "Jesus never once taught his disciples to turn over tables, because they did not occupy the same position of authority he occupied."

Macadams is being selective in his interpretation of scripture here. Turning over tables a political statement just like Jesus instructing his disciples to ignore the phalanx of rules installed by religion at the time. Men like Macadams like to parse the truth with judgments like these to people under control of their own doctrine because it profits their own sense of authority. Even his website title is a gaslighting oxymoron. He may view himself as a heroic and "radical Christian', but it's all a ruse. He's another authoritarian in disguise.

The same dynamic was at work among the religious authorities that refused to listen to Jesus. They loved their tradition and felt a need to protect it, but it was also practical and selfish concerns that blocked their will to change. They were rightly concerned about losing their positions of authority and the status it conferred upon them. That's why they reacted to Jesus with such religious ire and self-righteous recriminations. Their fear of Jesus exposes an uncomfortable truth about the nature of religious authority. The folks standing behind protective walls of tradition are often just as insecure about their beliefs as anyone else.

Not about the Jews

Let's be infinitely clear about something critical to our understanding of the clash between Jesus and the religious authorities of his day. The problems Jesus saw in those religious authorities had nothing to do with their specifically Jewish[2] heritage. After all, Jesus was Jewish. He certainly would not have recommended killing Jews in revenge for the conspiracy against him. His own words on the cross exonerated all those involved when he said, "Father forgive them, for they know not what they do."[3] Jesus taught us that we should love our enemies, never persecute or kill them.

The sad truth is that rather than learn from what Jesus sought to teach the religious authorities of his day, the Christian church ultimately chose a legalistic and calculating path quite like the religious authorities of Jesus' day. It began by casting literal blame on the Jews for killing Jesus,[4] an approach that won favor with the Roman state[5] because it was politically expedient to excuse its own sins. That opened the door for the Christian religion to claim power for itself. Armed with political and religious authority, the Christian church rushed down a vengeful path of destructive behavior, conducting campaigns against all those who opposed its legalistic aims.[6]

To this day, the good works committed in the name of God and Jesus do not compensate for the churn-and-burn mentality of Christianity's too often feverish pursuit of dominance in human affairs. The tragic outcomes of religious force in action are too many to count. Even creation suffers under the legalistic notion of human dominion[7] over the world. All that legalistic Christianity seems willing to say about its sins is that Jesus will return someday to fix it all.[8] That's the supposed Get Out of Jail Free card of legalistic Christianity.

End Times prophecies

We can easily identify where some Christians get the idea that Jesus prophesied his return. Luke 21:25-36 appears to be a literal prediction of that event: "There will be signs in the sun, the moon, and the stars, and on the earth distress among nations confused by the roaring of the sea and the waves. People will faint from fear and foreboding of what is coming upon the world, for the powers of the heavens will be shaken. Then they will see 'the Son of Man coming in a cloud" with power and great glory. Now when these things take place, stand up and raise your heads, because your redemption is drawing near." If we leave it at that, the story does seem to conclude with a warning that Jesus will return in literal fashion.

Luke goes on to explain the situation in somewhat different terms. "Then he told them a parable: "Look at the fig tree and all the trees; as soon as they sprout leaves you can see for yourselves and know that summer is already near. So also, when you see these things taking place, you know that the kingdom of God is near. Truly I tell you, this generation will not pass away until all things have taken place. Heaven and earth will pass away, but my words will not pass away."

This passage defies a literal interpretation of the term 'generation' because many hundreds of human generations have passed without the return of Jesus in any sort of physical or empirical fashion. What has come true is the message of the highly symbolic parable in which he notes that the kingdom of God is symbolized by the annual renewal of leaves on a tree. The generation in which Jesus lived did spout new leaves, and Christianity has followed suit in every generation since. That is the renewal of spirit that Jesus predicted, and it is what brings the kingdom of God near.

Yet a stubborn faction of Christianity insists that Jesus needs to return through some grand physical event to make scripture come true. That same faction systematically avoids blame for the sins that it commits or the suffering it has caused humanity. Instead, these legalistic branches of religion love to point fingers at other traditions or the secular world for the problems either causes or ignores.That's better known as gaslighting,[9] accusing the other side of you are most guilty.

Denying Christ

The most massive conspiracy in all human history sits in plain sight: Christianity gaslights the world to cover up its conflicted history and protect its authority by denying legalistic behaviors that Jesus would to this day condemn. The goal of this deception is to direct the cultural narrative to its advantage. This brand of controlling behavior is damaging to any relationship, be it personal or institutional. The website NBCnews.com[10] describes it this way: "Psychologists use the term "gaslighting" to refer to a specific type of manipulation where the manipulator is trying to get someone else (or a group of people) to question their reality, memory or perceptions."

We have a choice to make. We can allow religion's worst instincts and traditions to maintain power, or we can resist this gaslighting by calling its bluff. That means standing up in the name of Jesus to break Christianity free from its addictive association with legalism.We must engage in that pursuit even knowing that the toxic influence of legalism will never completely go away. There will always be evil in the world, but religion must be held culpable for any evil it creates. Our job as Christians is to confront the brands of religion that breed evil, willful ignorance, and false judgment in this world.

Beginning with genuine apologies

The best way to restore the honest-to-goodness legacy of Jesus Christ is to demand that Christianity account for its past transgressions and its current abuses, and change its ways. In some quarters, that process has begun. A July 25, 2022 story in the Chicago Tribune documented the journey of Pope Francis to apologize to Canada's Indigenous people. "The gesture set the tone of what Francis has said is a "penitential pilgrammage" to atone for the role of Catholic missionaries in the forced assimilation of generations of Native children—a visit that has stirred mixed emotions across Canada as survivors and their families cope with the trauma of their losses and receive a long-sought papal apology."

That's one step toward healing some of the hurt caused by abusive brands of religion. But getting legalistic Christianity to admit to its sins is a difficult confessional to bring about. That's because many people are convinced that their version of the Christian religion cannot be flawed because it ostensibly emanates directly from God's Word in the Bible.[11] That perspective leans on the notion that biblical literalism and its close cousin legalism translate the Word of God inerrantly. We'll address that claim by demonstrating how many ways that has been proven untrue.

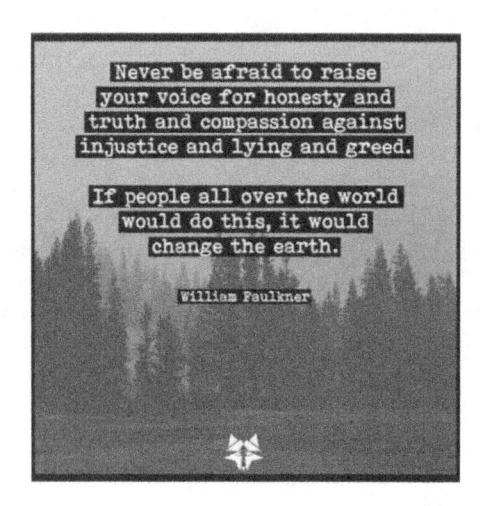

> Never be afraid to raise your voice for honesty and truth and compassion against injustice and lying and greed.
>
> If people all over the world would do this, it would change the earth.
>
> William Faulkner

CHAPTER 4

Straight Out of Purgatory

One might ask, on what evidence do we assert that a corrupt brand of legalism still infests this world and that it migrated from the tradition of the Jews to the orthodoxy of the Christian world where it has spread through nearly every denomination of the Church?

One of the most high-profile examples of transactional legalism was the invention of purgatory.[1] The concept of purgatory migrated from the ancient Jewish belief[2] that soul purification requires suffering. The Catholic Church took this legalistic belief straight from Jewish tradition and turned it into a prodigious form of commerce. To some, that tradition still holds merit, as this 2018 excerpt from a post on the website Catholic.com[3] illustrates:

"The doctrine of purgatory, or the final purification, has been part of the true faith since before the time of Christ. The Jews already believed it before the coming of the Messiah, as revealed in the Old Testament (2 Macc. 12:41–45) as well as in other pre-Christian Jewish works, such as one which records that Adam will be in mourning "until the day of dispensing punishment in the last years when I will turn his sorrow into joy" (The Life of Adam and Eve 46–7). Orthodox Jews to this day believe in the final purification, and for eleven months after the death of a loved one, they pray a prayer called the Mourner's Kaddish for their loved one's purification.

Jews, Catholics, and the Eastern Orthodox have always historically proclaimed the reality of the final purification. It was not until the Protestant Reformation in the sixteenth century that anyone denied this doctrine. As the quotes below from the early Church Fathers show, purgatory has been part of the Christian faith from the very beginning."

The author of this piece pulls references from Jewish tradition to defend purgatory as a naturally inherited aspect of the Christian tradition. He treats this holdover piece of legalism as if it were a necessary "hand-me-down" or desirable indicator of true faith from ancient days. Then, he has the nerve to complain that the upstart claims of the Reformation unnaturally ended the supposedly respected tradition of purgatory. The author seems oblivious that the Catholic invention of purgatory exemplifies the kind of legalism and commercialization of religion that Jesus most ardently resisted. As we've already noted, Jesus physically attacked the commercial interests of the temple with its taxing authority and marketing of goods and services to an indoctrinated public.[4]

The temple tax and associated enterprises were funding the material operation in question.Likewise, the Catholic Church sought to pay for capital expenses and saw a big opportunity in charging people for the release of souls from purgatory. The payment system called "indulgences"[5] drove these transactions. The fear of purgatory poured money straight into the overstuffed belly of the Church. To seal itself from criticism, the Church conveniently became both "judge and jury" and the sole arbiter of who stays in purgatory and who gets to leave.

The entire concept of indulgences was a big, fat, legalistic lie. The church cut God entirely out of the process. It was a scam so unworthy of the true Christian faith that a Catholic priest named Martin Luther[6] called the Catholic Church to account. He was not the only one that had grown sick of the specious methods of the church. The pursuant Reformation came about through resistance to the Catholic Church. It was a reality check of the highest order, an attempt to restore the Christian religion to an honest-to-goodness state of affairs.

With thanks to Martin Luther

We can thank Martin Luther and others for trying to dispense with the legalistic nonsense of indulgences. In so doing, they followed the examples of John the Baptist and Jesus in challenging the institutional corruption they saw. It was Luther's goal to pull the Christian religion toward a faith founded on grace[7] and the love of God. But the resistance he met from the Catholic hierarchy was severe.

As the website European Reading Room[7] notes:

"On October 31, 1517, Martin Luther posted his Ninety-five Theses against papal indulgences, or the atonement of sins through monetary payment, on the door of the Church at Wittenberg, Germany. Within less than four years, the Catholic Church would brand Luther a heretic, and the Holy Roman Empire would condemn him as an outlaw. These were the early years of the Protestant Reformation, a turning point in history that would transform not only the Christian faith but also the politics and society of all of Europe."

The reaction by the Catholic Church toward Luther was nearly as aggressive as the approach religious authorities took toward Jesus. Luther was fortunate not to be tortured or executed because the Catholic Church was not above using those tactics to punish its perceived enemies.

With no thanks to Martin Luther

While Luther was a great reformer in challenging the legalism of the Catholic Church, he never wholly erased his penchant for hardline theology, embracing the ugliest form of legalism known as anti-Semitism.[8] Initially, he worked to convert Jews to Christianity. However, over time he became frustrated, as shown in the words he shared with a Jewish reformer asking his help to reconcile the Jewish people to Christianity:

"I would willingly do my best for your people, but I will not contribute to your [Jewish] obstinacy by my kind actions. You must find another intermediary with my good Lord."

To his credit, Luther recognized that attempts by Christians to convert Jews were mostly ham-handed and awkward. He once wrote:

"If I had been a Jew and had seen such dolts and blockheads govern and teach the Christian faith, I would sooner have become a hog than a Christian. They have dealt with the Jews as if they were dogs rather than human beings; they have done little else than deride them and seize their property. When they baptize them they show them nothing of Christian doctrine or life, but only subject them to popishness and monkery ... If the apostles, who also were Jews, had dealt with us Gentiles as we Gentiles deal with the Jews, there would never have been a Christian among the Gentiles ..."[9]

Luther's addiction to anti-Semitism led to intolerance, dismissal, and exasperation toward Jewish people. In that regard, he was one with the disturbingly common attitude of the Christian religion. His views matched millions of people blaming Jews[10] for the death of Jesus, an accusation used to persecute Jewish culture and religion for thousands of years. That literalistic brand of hate echoed through history until it found expression in one of the evilest men in all human history, Adolf Hitler,[11] the despot that fused legalistic religious authority and politics into a hateful whole.

Hitler's brand of Christianity

The Christian legacy of persecuting Jews gave Adolf Hitler a ready focus for his hatred. In a March 2019 ChurchandState.com[12] article, author James McDonald shares two telling quotes linking Hitler's Nazi tactics with the longtime Christian persecution of Jews:

"The Catholic Church considered the Jews pestilent for fifteen hundred years, put them in ghettos, etc., because it recognized the Jews for what they were …. I recognize the representatives of this race as pestilent for the state and for the Church…"

—Adolf Hitler, April 26, 1933

"Without centuries of Christian anti-Semitism, Hitler's passionate hatred would never have been so fervently echoed."

—Robert Runcie (1921-2000), Archbishop of Canterbury (1980-1991)

For all his angry words, Hitler also knew how to "talk the talk" and sound like an apologetic Christian to win over hearts and minds. In this example of one of his calculating rants,[11] Hitler mimics the confessional language so valued for Christian approval:

"In this hour I would ask of the Lord God only this: that, as in the past, so in the years to come He would give His blessing to our work and our action, to our judgment and our resolution, that He will safeguard us from all false pride and all cowardly servility, that He may grant us to find the straight path which His Providence has ordained for the German people, and that He may ever give us the courage to do the right, never to falter, never to yield before any violence, before any danger.... I am convinced that men created by God should live following the will of the Almighty... If Providence had not guided us I could often never have found these dizzy paths.... Thus it is that we National Socialists, too, have in the depths of our hearts our faith. We cannot do otherwise: no man can fashion world history or the history of peoples unless upon his purpose and his powers there rests the blessings of this Providence."

-Adolf Hitler, in a speech at Wurzburg on June 27, 1937

Hitler ardently claimed the Jesus of religious authority while rejecting the Jesus of compassion and love. That's the legacy of legalism when it is unleashed on the world. In the face of such righteous-sounding religious language, the world knew not what to make of Hitler or the Nazi Party[13] and its claims to the Will of God. That's why so many at first did so little to resist the power of Hitler. This confusion is described in an article on Counterpunch.com[14] titled "Christian churches, the master race, and American exceptionalism,"

> "The silence of most Christian leaders allowed Hitler, with his Aryan, "Master Race" ideology, to turn six million Jews — and Gypsies, homosexuals, black persons, Communists, political dissidents, and even disabled German citizens — into The Other and persecute, deport and murder them."

Rather than admit the direct connection between the original forms of right-wing Christian theology and the Holocaust, apologists for the Christian religion eagerly blame other causes, especially science and the theory of evolution,[15] as the supposed force of mind behind the Holocaust. That accusation lumps evolution together with discredited racist theories such as eugenics[16] to blame science for Hitler's notions of Aryan supremacy.[17]

Given that conservative Christian religion has a long history of disputing material science,[18] it's proved convenient to blame the Holocaust on evolution rather than acknowledge the Christian tradition of persecuting Jews. That's called scapegoating,[19] a term drawn from the Book of Leviticus:

> "On the Day of Atonement a live goat was chosen by lot. The high priest, robed in linen garments, laid both his hands on the goat's head, and confessed over it the iniquities of the children of Israel. The sins of the people thus symbolically transferred to the beast, it was taken out into the wilderness and let go. The people felt purged, and for the time being, guiltless."

Science does not deserve to be scapegoated for the religious prejudice responsible for persecuting and slaughtering millions of Jews. It also has no responsibility for the fact that Hitler chose to cherry-pick aspects of evolutionary theory to bolster his political claims of an Aryan and superior race. The far more damning cause of the Holocaust is the direct connection between centuries of Christian anti-Semitism and the cultural impact on Jews that continues to this day.

Looking back, we can see that what Adolf Hitler wanted from Christianity was permission to act with impunity toward the Jewish people of the world, a tradition that Christians had built up over centuries. He treasured the institutional authority of the religion and borrowed the anti-Semitic portion of Christian tradition as an excuse to kill Jewish people. It is true that he ignored the true purpose of Christianity in the process, but that does not exonerate the religion from the centuries of sick behavior that ultimately fueled his instincts. He cynically and slickly sought to exonerate those actions while trying to recruit the Christian religion to his cause.

He stated [20]:

"My feeling as a Christian points me to my Lord and Savior as a fighter. It points me to the man who once in loneliness, surrounded only by a few followers, recognized these Jews for what they were and summoned men to fight against them and who, God's truth! was greatest not as a sufferer but as a fighter. In boundless love as a Christian and as a man I read through the passage which tells us how the Lord at last rose in His might and seized the scourge to drive out of the Temple the brood of vipers and adders. How terrific was his fight against the Jewish poison. Today, after two thousand years, with the deepest emotion I recognize more profoundly than ever before the fact that it was for this that He had to shed his blood upon the Cross. As a Christian, I have no duty to allow myself to be cheated, but I must be a fighter for truth and justice. And as a man I must see to it that human society does not suffer the same catastrophic collapse as did the civilization of the ancient world some two thousand years ago—a civilization which was driven to its ruin through this same Jewish people."

Hitler misappropriated Jesus' fight against legalism and conveniently dismissed the compassionate call of Christ to love all people. Instead, he repackaged the Christian tradition of persecuting Jews into an appeal to support the Nazi Party as represented by a twisted cross[21] of self-righteous fury. He understood the cultural power of literal and legalistic threats against the Jews for the death of Christ, a brand of hate heightened by claims of blood libel[22] and other malicious characterizations of Jewish people.

Amid all the cultural debate and political conflict, one theologian wrestled with how best to handle Christianity's role in fueling Nazi aggression and subjugation of innocent people. That man was Dietrich Bonhoeffer.

Calling religion to account In the face of such dire threats to human civilization, German theologian Dietrich Bonhoeffer[23] still hoped to avoid politics in his Christian life. However, when he saw the level of evil emerging under the rule of Hitler, his conscience demanded that he speak up against the corruption of the Nazi regime. As devoted as he was to the Christian religion, Bonhoeffer arrived at a somewhat startling conclusion about what should be done about Christian legalism and its dire effects on the world.

As described on Britannica.com,[24] "Reviewing the history of secularization in the West since the Renaissance, Bonhoeffer asked whether humanity's increasing ability to cope with its problems without the hypothesis of God might not indicate the obsolescence of the "religious premise" upon which Christianity had hitherto been based. Rather than looking for gaps in human knowledge or accenting human weaknesses as a basis for apologetics, he asserted, the Church ought to affirm man's maturity in a "world come of age." The stripping off of "religion," in the sense of otherworldliness and preoccupation with personal salvation, Bonhoeffer suggested, would free Christianity for its authentic this-worldliness per its Judaic roots. The Church should give up its inherited privileges to free Christians to "share in God's suffering in the world" in imitation of Jesus, "the man for others."

Bonhoeffer realized that religion was the cause of many of the world's problems. He recognized that wherever its premises were not already compromised by the perverse human instincts of prejudice and persecution, it was too often and eagerly leveraged to justify worldly wealth and power. The cure, Bonhoeffer ultimately proposed, was returning Christianity to its most basic premises by casting off the armor of religious authority and tradition to adopt the more vulnerable truth of Jesus Christ. He wanted Christianity to undergo an honest-to-goodness intervention and get back to its roots.

Bonhoeffer understood that the ultimate judgment of earthly behavior was God's to make. Yet he determined that we should not sit idly by while evil characters take over this world. That was the struggle he embraced. He confronted the calculating madness of Hitler and the Nazi regime, a courageous act that cost him his life. Like so many martyrs for Christ, he did the right thing knowing that he might not win in the end.

Echoes of Nazi ideology

It is sad to realize that the themes of hatred instigated by the Nazis persist in society today. In a January 27, 2021 interview[25] on NPR, Mikey Weinstein, Founder of the Military Religious Freedom Foundation and a graduate of the Air Force Academy, observed that the Hitleresque memes of the past live on in extreme forms of evangelical Christianity to this day.

For example, in talking about the January 6, 2021, insurrection at the United States Capitol, Weinstein observed: "Well, you saw people carrying large crosses. You saw people wearing shirts saying "Camp Auschwitz," massively giving homage to one of the worst concentration camps that the Nazis had. You saw the Proud Boys stopping in Pennsylvania to pray to their version of Jesus Christ. The Mother Ship of homophobia, transphobia, misogyny, anti-Semitism, and hatred of the Constitution is this form of fundamentalist Christianity, which is known as Dominion Christianity."

These factions of a warped and corrupt brand of Christianity are all a result of the religion's refusal to be honest with itself about its deeply conflicted and legalistic history and tradition. The long practice of literally blaming the Jews for the death of Jesus is now frowned upon in polite Christian circles, yet the religion largely refuses to deal with these and other toxic beliefs when they rear their heads.

Zionism

Another reason why Christianity has never fully confronted its anti-Semitic traditions is the complicated issue of Zionism,[26] the belief that Jews either politically or religiously deserve their state or have a role to play only as it benefits Christians. In a May 14, 2018, CNN article[27] titled "For many evangelicals, Jerusalem is about prophecy, not politics," Commentator Diana Butler describes the mindset of Zionists as it relates to Christianity: "When I was young, our pastor insisted that Jerusalem had an important role to play in these end-times events. When the Jews rejected Jesus as the Messiah, he explained, God chose the Church to accomplish his mission. Soon this "church age" would end with the rapture of true believers.""But God still loved the Jews, he told us and wanted to redeem them. Thus, absent the Church, the Jews would experience a great religious rebirth and rebuild their Temple in Jerusalem. Of course, this would spark a series of cataclysmic events culminating in the Battle of Armageddon, the last war of humanity. But it would also cause the Jews to accept Jesus as their savior finally. After all, this occurred, Jesus would return in glory and God's kingdom – a thousand-year reign of peace. And it would begin in Jerusalem."

This theology, a literal belief that all these things must happen before Jesus returns to reign on Earth, is called "dispensational pre-millennialism." It is not the quirky opinion of some isolated church. Although most Christians do not share these views, versions of dispensational pre-millennialism dominate American evangelicalism."

"It originated as a small movement in the 1840s, but by the 1970s, millions of evangelical and fundamentalist churchgoers had embraced some form of it. Dispensationalism was popularized in a best-selling book called "The Late, Great Planet Earth" by Hal Lindsey; and later, in the 1990s, it reached an even larger audience through the "Left Behind" novels by Tim LaHaye and Jerry Jenkins. The theology spread via Bible camps and colleges, through theological seminaries and revival meetings, in films and videos, by Sunday school materials, and in daily devotional guides – all teaching that the end of the world was near, and that Jerusalem was the physical place where this apocalyptic drama would unfold."

Sacrificial roles

The conflicted nature of Christianity's attitude toward Israel and Jerusalem requires an intervention of its own. Shockingly, many Christians interpret scripture to mean that Jews play little more than a sacrificial role as keepers of Zion until the day that Jesus returns to crush all those who don't fall in line. That narrative reads more like the plot to a superhero flick or a science fiction movie than a discerning grasp on the spiritual meaning of scripture. People that eager to grab salvation and claim eternal life block out all else. They are bolstered in this pursuit because guilt over such dismissive beliefs is buried under centuries of pious claims that devotion to Jesus justifies such a dismissive ideology. The truth of the matter is that End Times theology is in many ways just another form of Anti-Semitism cloaked in literalistic prophecies.

That explains why even mainstream Christian leaders fear talking about the real reasons why Jesus confronted the religious authorities of his day. They avoid such topics for fear of being labeled anti-Semitic. The irony here is that today's Christian zealots bear great resemblance to the religious authorities Jesus confronted over their love of legalism and embrace of tradition above all else. That means there are multiple layers of hypocrisy at work. The authoritarian wings of the Christian church desperately want to maintain institutional authority despite the damning evidence of its longstanding prejudices and outcomes. In so doing the church acts much like the religious authorities that Jesus to admonished for their legalism.

These are the ugly truths that many in the Christian Church prefer to avoid. Meanwhile, mainstream Christian denominations are busy trying to retain membership levels in the face of shrinking church attendance[28] and the corresponding loss of funding. These are difficult challenges for Christianity to face in an increasingly secular society, so most avoid any sort of self-critical analysis, lest it cast a negative light on the religion.[29]

While millions of people love the Christian Church and choose to support it right or wrong, there are also millions more that do not trust a church that refuses to address the abuse of its authority in religious, civil, political, and environmental matters. That leaves the Christian religion in a state of reverberating conflict over what its ultimate role should be. Unfortunately, the only segments of the Church that seem to be growing in America are denominations that boldly ignore any mention of the religion's conflicted history and its hypocritical recreation of authoritarian tradition. It is far easier to claim perfection in God while baldly denying any personal or institutional flaws. That proves an adage that Mark Twain once said about such puffery, "All it takes is ignorance and confidence, and success is sure."[28]

Perhaps the Christian Church honestly lacks the will to confront these issues from an institutional perspective. In that case, the world of lay-Christians and even the secular world is called upon to conduct an intervention and help the Church find its way back to a more sustainable, honest-to-goodness approach to Christian leadership.

Social media theology

The argument over who owns the authority of Christianity these days plays out not just in churches but on social media, where groups troll each other mercilessly with a terse mix of Bible quotations and unconcealed insults.

In late January 2021, the Facebook Group PROGRESSIVE CHRISTIANITY[30] posted a meme that read,

God cares infinitely more about making sure everyone has food, shelter, and healthcare than "accepting Jesus Christ as your personal Lord and savior."

The trolling responses from ardently legalistic Christians filled the comment sections immediately. They all bore a similar theme in claiming that Christians should be much more concerned about eternal salvation than doing good works in this life. One writer commented:

"It doesn't matter if you have food, shelter, and healthcare if you're going to hell for eternity. We need Jesus Christ more than those earthly comforts.

Another wrote:

And then those people you helped die warm with full bellies were eternally condemned. Works mean nothing without the gospel.

One writer compared eternal salvation to a cheeseburger:

"So, he cares more about your mortal body than your soul? He cares more about the thing that is dying than the thing which is eternal? OK, this is just not OK to teach. God came so whoever believes has ETERNAL LIFE. He didn't die, so we could eat, drink, have a bed, and a doctor. He rose with all power giving us power over our flesh, but he much rather (sic) us accept his son Jesus Christ for salvation than give us a nice home and a cheeseburger." A Progressive Christian advocate pushed back a bit with this comment:

"We're dealing with a group of people who believe in the Left Behind series more than they believe in the Bible. It's honestly impossible to describe the horror this raises in my heart."

Another shared this perspective:

"There will still be those that think preaching the so-called word of God is more important than doing as Jesus commanded. We make our hell here on Earth and have the ability to change other's hell to a better life not with silly acceptance of Jesus as savior but with real actions. Good people who by their actions toward others do have eternal life because their goodness and example live on."

At some point far into the thread, having read dozens of trolling comments about the importance of seeking eternal life over helping others in this life, I posted a statement that read:

"What good is it to let other people die to preoccupy yourself with the afterlife selfishly? Recall the tale of the Good Samaritan, in which the self-righteous priests passed by the "unclean" man beaten and left for dead in the ditch because they did not want to soil themselves spiritually, lest they suffer in some mysterious way. But the Good Samaritan, recognizing that humanity reflects the grace of God, tended to the nearly dying man and paid for his lodging until he was well. And Jesus said, "There is a righteous dude, right there."

From this kind of debate, we can see how certain brands of Christians still refuse to recognize what Jesus did in holding religious authorities accountable for their devotion to tradition and law over showing love to others. Today's "salvation" advocates would rather ignore clear instructions by Jesus to care for the poor and hungry to instead focus on the business of claiming salvation for themselves. Let's call that what it is: "salvation greed." The term describes Christians so eager to gain entrance to heaven that they cease to care about bringing the Kingdom of God to life here on Earth.

That form of greed is worse in many ways than an obsession with earthly wealth, as identified in 1: Timothy 6:10, which reads:

> "10 For the love of money is a root of all kinds of evil. Some people, eager for money, have wandered from the faith and pierced themselves with many griefs."

Instead, the profound message to care for others spiritually and materially as advocated by Jesus is summarized here:

> "The King will reply, 'Truly I tell you, whatever you did for one of the least of these brothers and sisters of mine, you did for me.'-- Matthew 25:40

What these exchanges illustrate is that some 'salvationists' find it convenient to focus on the afterlife because it frees them from having to apologize for anything that they, or their religion, does in this world. Granted, the Bible tells us the store up treasures in heaven rather than here on earth. But that does not mean coveting salvation above all else and letting the rest of creation and all the people in it suffer whatever fate befalls them. That is nothing more than spiritual greed. Even if salvation is the ultimate spiritual goal, that does not excuse people to 'check out' and cease caring about how they conduct business in this world.

Today's brood of vipers

Much of Christianity still acts like the religious authorities whose defense of tradition involved lashing out at anyone who questioned their right to impose their beliefs and laws with no questions asked. Evenmore cynically, today's legalistic religious authorities seek to impose religious law and belief on society by claiming "religious liberty" as their cause. Their chosen weapon is taking complaints about so-called religious liberty to court.

One case revolved around a matter in which a professed Christian baker refused to make a cake for a gay couple's wedding.[31] Another centered around offering birth control in a health care plan offered by a religious institution.[32] The irony of so many 'religious liberty' lawsuits is that in seeking to claim religious freedom for an individual or institution, ther legal actions quite typically involved denying others' fundamental human or civil rights.

The difference between maintaining religious liberty and imposing one's religion on other people is distinct. To put a finer point on the issue, the Constitution grants religious people and their institutions the right to pursue their beliefs, but not to the point that those beliefs infringe on the civil rights of others, especially to the point of discrimination or persecution. Unfortunately, some religious liberty advocates regard those limits as unfair to their interests, and cry "persecution" whenever their religious beliefs can't be imposed on society. This brand of religious self-victimhood makes good content on conservative media feeding on and fueling outrage in America. Does anyone reading this watch Fox News?

Poor track record

The ugly truth about so-called "religious liberty" lawsuits is that the legalistic tenets of Christianity have a cataclysmically poor track record when it comes to supporting fundamental human rights and even expecting basic morality out of the heroes they choose to represent their cause. Going back in history, the legalistic wings of Christianity have been used to slavery[33] and to justify genocide of Native Americans.[34] Racist groups still claim Christian support for their cause to this day.[35] In advance of the 2016 presidential election,[36] Christian evangelicals eagerly dismissed the well-documented sins of sexual abuse, financial fraud, serial adultery, and mean-spirited intolerance in their candidate of choice. All these actions prove that the concept of "religious liberty" takes on perverse tones in the hands of Christian legalists, and even leads to crimes against humanity. The real problem with Christianity in America is not a lack of religious liberty. It is the liberties taken with religion to satisfy selfish aims that cause harm in society. .

The authors of the United States Constitution understood the risks of giving religion too much power and specifically sought to prevent religion from corrupting the nature of democracy. That is the purpose of the section of the Constitution characterized as the Separation Clause, a specific ban on the institution of a state religion. The nation's founders wisely prevented the forces of religion from taking over the country or dominating the republic. As quoted in Forbes.com:[37] "When Benjamin Franklin was asked after a session of the Constitutional Convention, "What kind of a government have you given us?" he replied, "A democracy if you can keep it." Legalistic and fundamentalist religious beliefs remain one of the greatest threats to American democracy. A well-known (from a seemingly anonymous source) accurately predicts: "When fascism comes to America, it will be carrying a cross and wrapped in a flag."[38] Whether any specific person is responsible for the phrase, we may never know. What we do know is that the claim is coming true.

In the wake of the post-Trump Presidential era and investigations into the strategies behind the January 6, 2021 insurrection, we're seeing clear evidence of the religio-fascist belief system that fueled attempts to overthrow America. One of Trump's close allies and former national security adviser is Michael Flynn, a convicted perjurer that received a pardon by then-President Donald Trump. On Saturday, November 13, 2021, Flynn called for America to be united under one religion.[39] "If we are going to have one nation under God, which we must, we have to have one religion. One nation under God and one religion under God."

The website Business Insider the next day observed, "Flynn made the remarks speaking at a far-right "ReAwaken America" event in San Antonio, Texas. Flynn, who has embraced QAnon supporters in the past, has pushed his Christian faith in recent months, perhaps partially to rebut a QAnon conspiracy theory that he's secretly a Satanist."

The Christian religion needs to own up to these competitive instincts and fully admit to the cultural damage caused by conflicting sources of Christian ideology. That should include a long-overdue institutional apology for the abuse of religious authority throughout history.

Calling for an apology

By way of a good example in making an apology, we should consider the words of German President Fran-Walter Steinmeier while speaking in Poland about the sins of Germany and its conduct during World War II.[40] Steinmeier spoke to Poland's top leaders with U.S. Vice President Mike Pence present during the 80th anniversary of Germany's invasion of Poland in 1939. Steinmeier said, "I ask for forgiveness for Germany's historical debt. I affirm our lasting responsibility." That's how a person of honesty and integrity apologizes for the sins of the past. Admitting errors and asking forgiveness is the first stage of repentance. That is an attitude deserving of forgiveness and representatively Christian at its core. The President's admission to 'lasting responsibility' indicates a will to account for past mistakes and commit to positive change in the future. The German President shows us how to do it right. Though it is a secular apology, it still demonstrates the heart of humility found in Jesus. It also proves the power of vulnerability to communicate real strength.

His public apology does raise questions about others in attendance at the ceremony. Did the American Vice President Mike Pence sense any need to confess the sins of his own country or his religion? He likely did not. It is no coincidence that he hails from the unapologetic side of a Christian theocracy that believes that religion, and America by proxy, can do no wrong.

Granted, the United States has done much to promote and protect freedom in this world. Yet its formative years were stained by slavery and the genocide of Native Americans to achieve its destiny. Much of that was done under the banner of Christian dominion[41] and the doctrine of Manifest Destiny[42] that emerged from it. That is a nation with some apologizing still to do. Christianity is not the only belief system that could benefit from a reality check. The United States of America could use one as well. The myth of American Exceptionalism is rotting before our eyes.

Many people reject the idea that assuming responsibility for the sins of their ancestors or events in the past is a good idea. But when the attitudes and traditions leading to those sins remain apparent in a culture or nation, it is vital to bring them into the light for consideration. That is the main reason to issue an apology. It is a constructive way to illustrate problems from the past that affect us in the present or future.

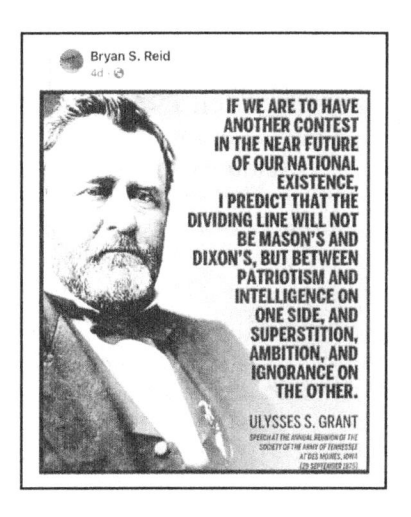

CHAPTER 5
All apologetics. No apologies.

It appears that many Christians remain secure in the belief that their religion is an infallible product of their tradition. It bears repeating that the religious authorities who conspired to put Jesus to death felt the same way about their religion and tradition. They refused to admit anything was wrong with their legalistic worldview or its love of rites and rituals as portals to God. It was that transactional system of worship that led to the corruption and commercialization of the temple.[1] Religious tradition had come to honor a desire for control and power over a faith anchored in humility.

These parallels between religious authorities of the past and those in the present are apparent and disturbing. That is exactly why the legalistic wings of Christian religious authority choose to ignore them. No one wants to be associated with the brand of legalism that denied Jesus.

It is therefore unlikely that heartfelt apologies will emerge for past and present sins from the legalistic side of the Christian world. Rather than apologize, the so-called "Christian Right"[2] and its evangelical power base seek to aggressively protect its position through apologetics,[3] "a branch of theology devoted to the defense of the divine origin and authority of Christianity." That is fancy language for a worldview that calculatedly denies the deeply conflicted roots of religious legalism within the Christian tradition. In truth, the apologetic (or apologist) approach reflects the same type of defense that religious authorities threw in the face of Jesus while protecting their control of the scriptural narrative and tradition.

We can imagine how Jesus would respond to today's religious authorities claiming that their traditions of biblical inerrancy and infallibility are immutable. He would tell them they are defending God from a faulty human perspective.

Moody zealots

One of the best-known institutional sources for Christian apologetics is the Moody Bible Institute.[4] The organization's mission and philosophy are mapped out in uncompromising terms in a Doctrinal Statement that serves as a bulwark against any form of knowledge deemed challenging to their assumed authority:

"The Bible is without error in all it affirms in the original autographs and is the only authoritative guide for faith and practice and as such must not be supplanted by any other fields of human learning."

These claims of scriptural perfection and superiority by Moody seem absolute and confident in their clarity, yet they ignore facts about how the "books" of the Bible were assembled in the first place. The Doctrinal Statement infers the clean transfer of scriptural texts from early Christian "autographs" to the scripture we know today. The truth is far messier than that. For example, the Bible suggests there were a few grand fights between James, the reputed brother of Jesus, and Paul, whose letters form much of the New Testament. They argued about how the religion named for The Christ was to be managed.[5] All of that took place before the Gospels were even written down. In some respects, the New Testament is a reactionary document, a response to controversy over what Jesus really represented.

There were prolonged debates among other sects and factions of "Christians" about who Jesus was. For the first three hundred years after the earthly life of Jesus Christ, there was little agreement as to which teachings represented his life and ministry, much less which "books" or letters belonged in the final canon. The International Bible Society describes the process this way:[6]

"The 39 books of the Old Testament form the Bible of Judaism, while the Christian Bible includes those books and also the 27 books of the New Testament. This list of books included in the Bible is known as the canon. That is, the canon refers to the books regarded as inspired by God and authoritative for faith and life. No church created the canon, but the churches and councils gradually accepted the list of books recognized by believers everywhere as inspired."

It was not until 367 AD that the church father Athanasius first provided the complete listing of the 66 books belonging to the canon. He distinguished those from other books that were widely circulated, and he noted that those 66 books were the ones, and the only ones, universally accepted. The point is that the formation of the canon did not come all at once like a thunderbolt but was the product of centuries of reflection."

This perspective, written by a conservative Christian organization no less—admits that the formation of the scriptural canon was a long and inexact process. We can certainly appreciate the dedication it took to gather and preserve the foundations of scripture, but by no means was the process infallible, inerrant, or perfect in any way.

These issues do matter. The facts come out most when people try to hide them. Michael J. Kruger,[7] president of the Reformed Theological Seminary, seeks to defend the notion that the Bible as we now know it somehow represents the "original autographes" without flaw or error. In this method, he parallels the contentions of the Moody Doctrinal Statement. He also fails to provide a convincing argument. Even Kruger is forced to admit that scripture passed through a gauntlet of intentional and unintentional changes over the centuries, and the outcome is unsure.[7]

"Of course, there are more substantive textual changes (much fewer in number) that do affect the meaning of the text. But these changes would only be a problem if we could not identify them as changes. Or to put it differently, these kinds of variants would only be a problem if we could assume that every one of them was as equally viable as every other. Thankfully, textual scholars can determine, with a relative degree of certainty, which of these readings were original and which were not. There are still some gray areas, some instances where a choice between variants is unclear. But we can have confidence that the words we read are the words of the original authors."

Kruger's stumbling defense rests on the generous use of relativistic terms such as "generally speaking" and "with a relative degree of certainty" to make the case for biblical inerrancy and infallibility. He classically avoids issues of outright contradiction between Gospel texts and within even single accounts from Genesis and other books. From this apologetic it is apparent there is no such thing as absolute fidelity to the "original autographes." The flatly obvious reason is that the original autographs no longer exist. All that Christianity owns are copies of copies made tenfold over the centuries. That explains why the Moody Bible Institute tries to hide behind a legalistic statement: "The Bible is without error in all it affirms in the original autographs…"

The phrase "in all it affirms" is a specious attempt to justify claims of biblical inerrancy and infallibility. The reason for this anxious claim to purity is obvious. That supposed standard of perfection in the Word delivers a form of control to its claimants. From that position of supposed perfection, the self-righteous are free to judge others' perspectives or opinions on scriptural matters. The legalistic proprietors or religious apologetics like it that way. It also gives them the right to judge humanity on behalf of God. That is an active form of tautology and a self-fulfilling prophecy. But mostly, it's just selfish.

It is not hard to figure out what Jesus would think of these tactics, or the position taken by religious zealots seeking to create a theocracy around the idea of biblical perfection. He'd place their assertions about "moral law" in the same category as the age-old religious strictures governing unclean behavior, ritualistic hand-washing and the close-minded habits of ritualized religion favored by religious authorities two thousand years ago. Jesus would urge today's religious authorities to search their hearts and confess their institutional sins past and present. What we need more than ever is an intervention, a Christian reality check, to differentiate between which aspects of scripture honestly lead to the goodness of God and which laws don't do anything but make life miserable for people based on age-old customs and prejudices.

Given the fact that Jesus is not here to direct this process, we are the folks expected to confront the forces of religious legalism with its often-mean-spirited traditions. To do nothing is to deny God's intentions in this world and ignore our calling to resist the corruption of religion in His name.

Let scripture guide the way

Having looked at some of the ways corrupt religious authority impacts the world, we can proceed to do something about it by looking for better examples in scripture to lead our way. The Bible provides insights on people with the courage to speak truth to power and confront corrupt forms of religious authorities. You may know a few of them, but the real question is how well do you appreciate why they acted as they did?

> Bishop John Shelby Spong
> 12h
>
> NAKEDPASTOR
>
> "A HERETIC IS JUST A PERSON WHO TELLS THE TRUTH TOO EARLY"
>
> - SARAH KENDZIOR

CHAPTER 6

John the Baptist taught us much.

When it comes to legendary figures in biblical history, there are few more compelling characters than John the Baptist, the counterculture figure who hung out in the wilderness, wore animal skins for clothing, dined on locusts and honey, and saw nature as a legitimate portal to God.

John lived in the wilderness because he didn't like what he saw back in town. In his view, power corrupted the religious authorities at the temple. They marched around as if they owned the entire city and behaved like a gang of religious cops trying to catch people doing bad things. John was sick of the rules they made and how they ran the temple like a money-making business. He decided to do something about it.

Rather than marching into town to make a scene and risk getting snagged in the net of the law, John employed a more creative approach. Artfully, he took on the role of a "voice crying out in the wilderness," aligning himself with the prophet Isaiah's prediction about the one who was to prepare the way for Messiah:

"I am the voice of one calling in the wilderness, 'Make straight the way for the Lord.'"[1]

John also separated himself from the trappings of civilization because he wanted to avoid competing on the same turf as the priests in their expensive robes lording their positions of status and wealth over others. So, John ignored their strict dietary and hygiene rules. Instead, he replaced all that with a simple lifestyle and a call to baptism and repentance. His message appealed to people hungry for spiritual care and willing to change their ways. There was no admission price or cost of ownership. No need for turning scripture into law. People could own it for themselves as an honest-to-goodness faith, refined to its purest form.

John's invitation was reasonable and sane in contrast to the high maintenance brand of religion being preached and practiced at the temple. John the Baptist was a leader in rescuing religion from the grips of scriptural legalism. He provided the original reality check.

Sparks of rebellion

While John's approach to ministry was remote by nature, it didn't cease its influence outside the city limits. Like all good prophets, he made sure his voice resounded within the temple walls, railing against the hypocrisy of the country club lifestyle led by authorities within the temple while people suffered in the streets. He branded the religious leaders and factions vying over scriptural control a "brood of vipers" for lashing out like a den of snakes when questioned about their traditions. John used what we might call 'guerrilla tactics' to "make straight the way for the Lord." He was the ultimate outsider.

Of course, his criticisms drew anger and scorn from the religious authorities[2] he targeted. His accusations posed a threat to their reputation and job security. Some likely feared that a full-blown rebellion[3] could erupt from John's wilderness movement. But, of course, that was all part of John's plan. His calling was to make the self-righteous and entitled feel anxious over the falsehood of their authority. It worked because there is nothing more daunting to the self-acclaimed elite than a truth-telling prophet with seemingly nothing to lose.

Then along came Jesus.

Torch of Truth

The work of John set the stage for the coming of Jesus, whose even more pointed accusations of hypocrisy resounded among the religious authorities. John passed the torch of truth to Jesus, who waved it in the faces of all those that refused to see the light.

In that role, Jesus attracted the attention of an entire fleet of religious factions battling for dominance in culture and faith. Each of these groups sent representatives to test him according to their specific vision of law and faith. These so-called experts hoped to burn Jesus by goading him into theological mistakes to discredit him. Instead, Jesus revealed their errors in judgment. Through these interventions, he made the burning point that love, not religious law, was the true focus of the kingdom of God.

Here we find Jesus waving that torch for all its worth:

34 But when the Pharisees heard that Jesus had silenced the Sadducees, they gathered themselves together. 35 One of them, a lawyer, asked Him a question, testing Him, 36 "Teacher, which is the great commandment in the Law?" 37And He said to him," 'YOU SHALL LOVE THE LORD YOUR GOD WITH ALL YOUR HEART, AND WITH

ALL YOUR SOUL, AND WITH ALL YOUR MIND.' 38 "This is the great and foremost commandment. 39 "The second is like it, 'YOU SHALL LOVE YOUR NEIGHBOR AS YOURSELF.' 40 "On these two commandments depend the whole Law and the Prophets."--Matthew 15: 34-40

Jesus understood that the religious legalists he was confronting knew scripture quite well.[4] He wasn't trying to educate the priests and scribes about its contents. He was trying to help them understand its more significant meaning.

Through these confrontations, Jesus shed light on the natural foundations of faith. He knew that he was engaged in a marathon of theological debate, not a sprint. On that journey, he was forced (and quite able) to explain that while the law is essential and plays a role in the kingdom of God, it is not the end goal. His point was that something far more significant is within reach of those willing to surpass the supposed righteousness of the Pharisees, Sadducees, and all the other "sees" to come.

Jesus provided a powerful example for us to follow. Our job is to insist on authentic meaning from scripture rather than relying on merely authoritative or legalistic brands of truth. We cannot afford to purchase the selfishly motivated theology that scriptural legalists sell. Nor should we confine ourselves to what religious tradition tells us to believe. That only leaves us in a transactional relationship with God, with religious authorities acting as the brokers.

Jesus told the world, "I am the truth, the way, and the light,"[5] to give people direction. He meant to guide them away from the rocks of legalism and the stumbling blocks of tradition. In so many words, he was trying to say: "Beware those seeking to falsely take you under their authority.." That lesson was communicated much earlier in the Bible as well. It all begins with the Serpent in the Garden of Eden.

CHAPTER 7

The Serpent's Legacy

One of our priorities as Christians should be to educate ourselves about how false religious authority originates and gains traction because that is where so much dishonesty in this world begins. An essential clue to this pattern appears in the opening chapters of the Book of Genesis when a crafty Serpent attempts to convince two trusting human beings they can "be like God, knowing good and evil."

In that exchange, the roots of religious legalism stand out:

Genesis 3

> 3 Now, the Serpent was more cunning than any beast of the field which the Lord God had made. And he said to the woman, "Has God indeed said, 'You shall not eat of every tree of the garden'?"
>
> 2 And the woman said to the Serpent, "We may eat the fruit of the trees of the garden; 3 but of the fruit of the tree which is in the midst of the garden, God has said, 'You shall not eat it, nor shall you touch it, lest you die.'"
>
> 4 Then the Serpent said to the woman, "You will not surely die. 5 For God knows that in the day you eat of it your eyes will be opened, and you will be like God, knowing good and evil."

The true meaning of the Serpent in Genesis has been the subject of religious debate for centuries. Consider this assessment of the Serpent's role as related on the website bibleinterp.com:[1]

"Recently James Charlesworth has written a massive book entitled The Good and Evil Serpent[15] in which he argues that in the ancient Near East and the classical world the Serpent was mostly viewed positively, not negatively, and he claims this is also true of the Bible, including the Serpent of Genesis 3.[16] However, while his ancient Near Eastern and classical material are fascinating, I would point out that most references in the Bible indicate that the Serpent was viewed negatively,[17] and this is certainly the case in Genesis 3.

Charlesworth claims that the Serpent does not tempt Eve (it merely asks her a question!), it tells the truth (unlike God), is described as wise (not crafty), and is not a symbol of evil. However, if all this is true, it becomes difficult to understand why the Serpent should be so thoroughly cursed towards the end of the story to become the lowliest of creatures (Gen 3:14-15).

Again, the fact that Eve declares "the serpent beguiled me" (Gen 3:13) – an assertion accepted by God (Gen 3:14) – indicates that "crafty" rather than "wise" is the better translation of the Hebrew word 'arum used here to describe the Serpent in Gen 3:1.[18] It is difficult to accept that there is no element of temptation in the Serpent's questioning of Eve. Moreover, it is clear that the Serpent does not speak the whole truth, since while the eyes of Adam and Eve are indeed opened to know good and evil as a result of eating the forbidden fruit, as the Serpent had predicted, it fails to inform them that they will also be expelled from the Garden of Eden as a result of their disobedience, thereby denying them access to the tree of life and ensuring their eventual death, even if they do not die immediately (the latter seemingly a consequence of the divine compassion[19])."

This description covers essential ground, revealing many questions about the Serpent's role in theological history. Yet, it stops short of ascertaining the actual role that the Serpent ultimately plays.

The 'honest-to-goodness' factor enters the story at this point. Let's state it plainly: the Serpent's legacy is that sin is not always the result of people not trying hard enough to follow the commands of God. Sin also results from obedience to corrupt and selfish brands of religious authority. That fallibility leads people into sin and situations far more dangerous than they realize. The Serpent represents the first instance of religious legalism in scripture, but theologians and church leaders have long sought to avoid that fact because it implicates religion as a possible source of falsehood in the eyes of God. That legacy of denial remains the most perilous influence of religion in the world.

Consciousness and Conscience

As we know, the Serpent's legalistic ploy works well to gain control over Adam and Eve. It does so by exploiting one of the commonest weaknesses in all humanity, that of consciousness, defined as "the state of being awake and aware of one's surroundings."

Adam and Eve were not particularly conscious of their surroundings. Their lack of experience limits their worldview, leaving them unaware of the potential consequences of breaking trust with God. That is why they accepted the Serpent's word at face value and followed what appeared to be wise and worldly advice. As a result, the pair finds themselves trying to solve a problem they never knew they had. That is the legacy of legalism in Judeo-Christian tradition. It creates problems of its own making, then claims it is on the only rescuing force available.

The Serpent's legalistic ploy is the first test of human consciousness found in scripture. The outcome is what traditionalists call Original Sin. Religious legalism confuses people about the priorities of God to gain control over their conscience and souls. The Serpent introduced the concept of legalism, but organized religion turned it into tradition. Sadly, that is a theme repeatedly played out for millennia in the Judeo-Christian tradition. The real lesson in this scenario is that God does not like people who lead others astray. That is why the Serpent is ultimately cursed.

Conscience and Christ

The second test conducted by the Serpent is that of conscience, defined as "(the) inner feeling or voice, viewed as acting as a guide to the rightness or wrongness of one's behavior."

The wheels of conscience start to turn as Adam and Eve consider the words of the Serpent, who tricks the couple by getting them to second-guess their conscience. The Serpent assumes the role of a trustworthy authority in a tale that teaches us where our natural enemies frequently lie. Our snakey friend tricks the couple by first quoting God's words, followed by a half-truth disguised as a promise, "You surely will not die." That is the difficult test of consciousness and conscience: It is often those claiming to speak on behalf of God of whom we need to be most cautious.

What the Serpent also signifies is the danger of being lured into seeking salvation on selfish premises. The eagerness of Adam and Eve to "be like God" naively dispenses with the pragmatic aspects of their reality in pursuit of some supposedly higher notion of good. Had they been practical and aware of their circumstance, they would not have jumped at the chance to grab at something outside their mortal reach. That was an act of instant gratification and selfishness.

If we're supposed to learn anything from their example, it's that God values trust more than selfish or aggressive acts of acquisitive piety. To put it plainly, we should never go claiming salvation for ourselves, especially to the point where we dismiss our responsibility in this world. That is salvation greed,[2] a trait that Adam and Eve exhibit and one that remains one of the greatest sins of all.

Purposeful deceit

These are all difficult and complex challenges for people trying to follow the ways of the Lord. The Bible tells us to love our enemies no matter where we find them. How does this principle apply when people we're supposed to be able to trust seek to control or deceive us purposely? Should we submit to that temptation? Turn the other cheek? We should not. And fortunately, Jesus provided direction during his ministry on how to handle such difficult situations.

While his manner of challenging religious and political beliefs earned him many enemies, it also provided opportunities to set standards for us to follow. Jesus' experience in dealing with different types of religious authorities gives us timeless insights about who we might face as well.

Chief among his detractors were the **Pharisees**, the sect of Judaism focused on strict adherence to traditions of the Jewish religion. Next came the **scribes and lawyers**, the men who made it their job to interpret biblical law for the people. Jesus also earned distrust from the **Sadducees**, the political conservatives and wealthy aristocrats who clung to history for answers. The **zealots** were militants hoping Jesus would turn his movement into a political revolution. The **Romans** were politically concerned that Jesus claimed to be a king.

Studying these categories of ideological opponents makes it easy to find their parallels in the modern world. It is darkly comic that these groups are essentially the same brands of legalists and zealots seeking to control the world today. They're just as convinced that "defending the faith" is their holy job even when the corrupt principles guiding their brand of religion are so easy to identify. It's always been about power and control. Nothing has really changed in the last two thousand years.

For example, in 2021, the Rev. Franklin Graham spoke to the website Axios his defense of ex-President Donald Trump.[3] The story began, "Graham stood by Trump through repeated scandals." It goes on to quote Graham, who complained when people asked him why. "Well, Frank, how can you defend him when he's lived such a sordid life?" I never said he was the best example of the Christian faith. He defends the faith. And I appreciate that very much."

Graham proves he's willing to dismiss every brand of sin if it means gaining access to power. His approach to ministry is the exact opposite of Jesus, who listened to his conscience and embraced humility in response to the legalistic authorities coveting control of religion, law, politics, tradition, and pursuit of wealth. Jesus also accurately identified the corrupt nature of the brutal Roman government with whom the religious authorities collaborated to bring about his death. Yet here we are today, still fighting the same battles religious zealots and legalistic power brokers. Fortunately, we can learn how to further resist these temptations by studying how Jesus faced one of the biggest tests of his life: meeting Satan in the Wilderness.

CHAPTER 8
Jesus in the Wilderness

When the time came for Jesus to begin his earthly ministry, he journeyed to the wilderness.[1] The Bible relates an encounter with Satan that serves as a transition point in scripture. Jesus travels from everyday human existence to a transcendent calling in service to God. But, first, he must face a severe test of consciousness and conscience.

The encounter between Satan and Jesus recorded in the Book of Luke is not a literal record of their conversation. No one was present to write down their words. Instead, scripture employs creative license to record their conversation. The discussion takes the form of a play in which two actors play roles on a big stage. Every exchange proves instructional on many levels.

> 3 The devil told him, "Since you are the Son of God, tell this stone to become a loaf of bread."
>
> 4 Jesus answered him, "It is written,' One must not live on bread alone, but on every word of God.'"
>
> 5 The devil also took him to a high place and showed him all the kingdoms of the world in an instant. 6 He told Jesus, "I will give you all this authority, along with their glory, because it has been given to me, and I give it to anyone I please. 7 So if you will worship me, all this will be yours."
>
> 8 But Jesus answered him, "It is written, 'You must worship the Lord your God and serve only him.'"
>
> Luke 4:3

Satan's goals are clear enough. He wants Jesus to worship him in place of God and tries to get his desired subject to buy into short-term benefits over long-term glory. That is the same strategy employed by the Serpent with Adam and Eve. The similarity is not accidental. It shows us that evil often tries to gain control of our souls using legalistic language and tempting promises of power and glory.

Satan tries to control Jesus through two of the most profound human weaknesses: need and ego. First, Satan appeals to need by urging Jesus to perform tricks to satisfy his bodily appetites, especially hunger. Then, when that doesn't work, Satan tries to overwhelm Jesus with flattery by offering him majestic power and authority. Of course, that doesn't work either.

Jesus resists all of Satan's promises because he recognizes that Satan's words come from a false brand of authority. He senses the temptations in Satan's literal promises and legalistic language, yet he does not behave proudly in his response. Instead, he employs humility, patience, and discernment to navigate around all that Satan has to offer. Ultimately, he responds to the devil's temptations with a calm reply: "You must worship the Lord your God and serve only him."

Notice the profound difference between how Jesus responded to Satan and how Eve and Adam reacted to half-truths uttered by the Serpent. The couple trusted the false authority of the Serpent because it repeated the Word of God to gain their trust. By contrast, Jesus immediately recognized that brand of deception and responded with answers demonstrating a complete grasp on the consequences of obedience to evil.

Our model in facing temptation

Jesus Christ is a compelling model in the art of resisting temptation. He shows us how to stand up to false authority even when it seems to come from one that claims to speak for God. Granted, we can never live up to the standard of perfection set by Jesus, but that does not mean we should numbly succumb to religious authority whenever it tries to control us. Instead, we should stand up to it! Call falseness to account! If we happen to falter in that regard, God forgives those who show repentance and seek to make amends.

In this context, Jesus' life has a dual meaning for us. First, he provided a profound example of standing up to false religious authority that might otherwise lead us away from God. Second, his willingness to stand up to that evil unto death proves the significance of that commitment. It as not just to atone for our sins that Jesus died. He also died to demonstrate absolute resistance to worldly forces trying to manipulate and control us by using God (or an Emperor) as an excuse. The act of standing up in meek yet strong defiance of institutionally false religious authority should not be ignored. Knowing that people were also victims of corrupt and selfish political authority, he showed compassion to other accused of criminal acts as they hung suffering and dying on the crosses next to him.

Of course, getting people to revise their vision of Jesus and the meaning of his ministry is difficult work. There are many fixed ideas about what Jesus means to the world. Some choose to center on his role as the foundation for Christianity, while others view him in far more egalitarian terms. That's why we should examine how people view the legacy of Jesus as a whole.

Testimony

I once took a photo of a postcard picture of Jesus that I found lying on a table at a restaurant. The face of Jesus in the photo looked quite European in its features, a classic presentation in which Jesus looks like a white man with rock-star attractive looks and a cowl over his head.

I posted the photo on Facebook with a purposely ironic text that read: "This guy is wearing a #hoodie, hangs out with women of ill repute, is a leader of a Gang of Twelve he calls the #disciples and attacks religious authority almost every chance he gets. If you haven't seen his likeness, it's because he probably never looked like this in the face. The #artist got it all wrong for some reason #jesus does #Christianity need an #Intervention, and that's the subject of my new book."

In response, a recent acquaintance that I'd met during a trip to visit relatives in Texas posted the most beautiful summation of what the post conveyed:

"Thank you for sharing this. I grew up in the church and was a part of every denomination from United Pentecostal to the Church of Christ to the Southern Baptist. For 32 years. It wasn't until I went through the most difficult time of my life when I was completely abandoned by my "Christian" friends that I realized that Jesus and authentic Christianity are the antitheses of organized religion. I came to be of the mindset that if Jesus had chosen to come to earth today, most people would not recognize or accept him. The reason is that he would not be on the front pew of a church, wearing the perfect outfit and enjoying a beautiful performance by a church choir. No. He would be at AA meetings. He would be hanging out in the worst places in town, with prostitutes, drug addicts, at homeless shelters and free food kitchens...with those who truly need him, those who need grace and love the most.

"That's why I can't go back to church. As James 1:26-27 says, "Pure religion and undefiled before God and the Father is this, To visit the fatherless and widows in their affliction, and to keep himself unspotted from the world." Jesus also said all the commandments were met if we love the Lord with all of our hearts and love our neighbor as ourselves. It all boils down to something beautifully simple: just love your fellow man. Treat everyone with respect and just accept people as they are. Who are we to judge anyway? If everyone would think like this, there would be so little conflict in our world. Ok, off my pulpit...again, thank you for sharing this!"

I found her testimony so succinct and honest that it made me think all over again about the origins of organized religion and why it so quickly gets "off-target" from the mission of Jesus Christ. The problem is simple to identify. People tend to embrace (or manufacture) the Jesus or God that suits their purposes. That doesn't always lead to an honest accounting of who Jesus was, or what he came to do. To help us sort through these issues, we turn again to scripture for guidance with a message Jesus delivered in verses we call The Lord's Prayer. Rather than repeating these words of this prayer in rote fashion, let's look beyond a surface translation to gain an honest-to-goodness understanding of what the Lord's Prayer calls us to do.

CHAPTER 9
The Lord's Prayer

The Lord's Prayer[1] is the template shared by Jesus to instruct disciples on praying to God. It offers guidance on how to guard against temptations such as power, greed, and lust. It directs us in how to resist evils stemming from the false religious authority and instructs us to care for creation and bring about the Kingdom of God here on earth. All these directives help guide us from the grip of corrupt tradition.

The Lord's Prayer begins with a call for reverence for the Lord while linking the higher authority of God to our obligations here on earth.

Our Father, who art in heaven, hallowed be thy name. Thy kingdom come, thy will be done, on earth as it is in heaven…

This passage sums up the practical aims of faith. It is our responsibility to bring about the Kingdom of God here to earth by embracing the grace of God and extending it here on earth. That's what it means to say in the phrase "Thy will be done, on earth as it is in heaven." It is not our job to sit here and fret about earning salvation or gaining entrance to heaven. Our calling is doing good in God's name here on earth. In fact, the Lord's Prayer works just as well if it were to state, in plainer terms

Our Father in heaven, hallowed be your name. Your goodness come, your will be done, on earth as it is in heaven…

Connecting the "Kingdom of God" to the concept of goodness is extraordinarily helpful in guiding us on how to live. By contrast, abiding in apologetics that promote ancient, discriminatory laws does not promote goodness in this world. That's why the prayer moves on to the realities of material and practical existence:

Give us this day our daily bread…

This phrase is highly symbolic. It refers both to spiritual nourishment in devotion to God and the food we need for health. Both are the "bread" of life. Bread in this case also symbolizes love, especially the love of God that knows no boundaries.

The Lord's Prayer quickly turns around to warn us that human greed and covetousness is always at work in this world. We must learn to ask forgiveness from those we offend and extend that grace to others as well.

And forgive us our trespasses (or sins), as we forgive those who trespass (or sin) against us...

This call to forgiveness is a challenging instruction for many believers to follow. People that abuse our trust with lies or other harmful actions cause us to feel anger. It is common to react with rage at being betrayed. Yet untamed anger leads to acts of retribution and revenge. That is why asking and giving forgiveness is vital to do. It sustains our relationships in this world and opens channels of forgiveness from God.

The Lord's Prayer also warns us how difficult it can be to avoid temptations that lead us away from God. But the warning here is cryptic because it seems to suggest that God is the one that might lead us astray:

"And lead us not into temptation, but deliver us from evil..."

What a strange phrase to include the Lord's Prayer! Why would the Lord be the one that would "lead us into temptation?"

This phrase confirms everything we've learned so far about the most dangerous sources of temptation in this world. The Lord's Prayer recognizes that evil often imitates goodness to earn the trust of people. We know this because the Serpent commits the first act leading to sin and temptation in the Bible, craftily repeating the Word of God to convince Adam and Eve they can "be like God, knowing good and evil."

The Serpent's legalistic use of God's Word exploits their lack of consciousness and twists their conscience into following the Serpent's desires.

We find the same pattern at work in the way that Satan once tested the faith of Job by taking control of his life with the approval of God! At one point in the Book of Job, God engages in direct and friendly conversations with Satan:

> The LORD said to Satan, "Very well, then, everything he has is in your hands, but on the man, himself do not lay a finger." (Job 1:12)

Scripture also says:

> The LORD said to Satan, "Very well, then, he is in your hands; but you must spare his life." So Satan went out from the presence of the LORD and afflicted Job with painful sores from the soles of his feet to the top of his head. (Job 2:6-7)

What a disturbing, almost abhorrent exchange! Why would God work so closely with Satan to turn a devout believer over to suffer wounds and losses at the hands of the devil himself? Most disturbing is the notion that it was all done on what amounts to a bet! That God works hand-in-hand with the devil is an interesting feature of scripture.

The lesson here is that doing spiritual business with God is never easy. The idea that God allowed Satan to inflict pain and loss on Job to test his resolve is quite unsettling. But dealing with God is not much easier in a direct fashion. Imagine, for example, being Abram and being asked to sacrifice his son Isaac. That certainly sounds like a test invented by Satan, does it not? The honest-to-goodness truth is that God tests everyone's resolve in this world, even Jesus.

Job is ultimately delivered from evil after he suffers the loss of all that he values in this world, his health, wealth, and friendships. But, who among us wants to take that route to salvation? That's why we pray that God does not put us through such trials.

The Lord's Prayer is, therefore, quite correct about the nature of temptation. God has indeed led people into temptation and might well be doing it as we speak. No one ever said it was easy to negotiate with God nor sustain the Kingdom of God in this world. We face tests at every turn.

And yet, to avoid this problem, the top levels of religious authority, including the pope, are now fidding with the Lord's Prayer to make it seem less like God is messing with humanity for the fun of it. Pope Francis has called for a translation of a phrase about temptation in the Lord's Prayer to be changed.

The BBC reported, "The current wording that says "lead us not into temptation" is not a good translation because God does not lead humans to sin, he says. His suggestion is to use "do not let us fall into temptation" instead, he told Italian TV on Wednesday night." Meanwhile, other denominations now translate that passage as "Save us from the time of trial."

Finally, we arrive at the last phrase of the Lord's Prayer, a passage added by some denominations to give the message more balance and the feeling of a conclusion

"For thine is the kingdom, the power, and the glory forever and ever.

This phrase urges us to show respect for the impact of God in our lives. In layman's terms, it equates to "Let's give credit where credit is due." To summarize, the Lord's Prayer says it is our job to bring about the will of God in this world through acts of love and service to others.

The Lord's Prayer and the Bible encourage us to look at life from a big picture perspective, which is a healthy thing. We are encouraged to feel gratitude for life in the here and now. God wants us to extend and appreciate that gratitude so that others can experience the love of God and Christ here on earth. When we immerse ourselves in the Kingdom of God, living out The Word in all its symbolic breadth and purpose, our passage into the spirit is a natural and organic process. One might say that we evolve into the spirit through our relationship with God. In the meantime, it is our job to release Christianity from the grip of those that would abuse it. We release other souls in that process.

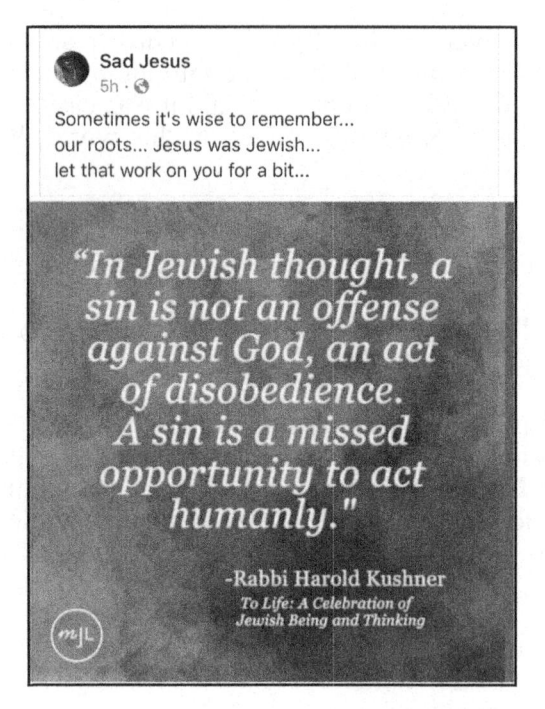

> **Sad Jesus**
> 5h
>
> Sometimes it's wise to remember...
> our roots... Jesus was Jewish...
> let that work on you for a bit...
>
> *"In Jewish thought, a sin is not an offense against God, an act of disobedience. A sin is a missed opportunity to act humanly."*
>
> -Rabbi Harold Kushner
> *To Life: A Celebration of Jewish Being and Thinking*

CHAPTER 10
Releasing Tradition's Grip

To rescue Christianity from the grip of legalistic authority, we must begin with an approach to scripture that frees us to experience God in every moment and every way. That process starts by recognizing that every word in scripture has symbolic value. To examine this fact, we begin by sharing in this famously revelatory passage from the book of John:

> 1 In the beginning was the Word, and the Word was with God, and the Word was God. 2 He was with God in the beginning. 3 Through him all things were made; without him nothing was made that has been made. 4 In him was life, and that life was the light of all mankind. 5 The light shines in the darkness, and the darkness has not overcome[a] it.

John 1: 1-5

In this passage, we learn that The Word is the central unifying symbol for God, Christ, and the Holy Spirit. Yet John 1 states that nature is incorporated in this divine nature, because in creation "All things were made" and remain as one in The Word. Of course, God is not literally a word. Nor is God a collection of words. Words are the device by which we understand the truth that resides in God. We access that truth through The Word, a diverse breadth of scripture communicated in forms that include prose, poetry, and storytelling.

These forms of literature provide many points of access for people seeking evidence of God's influence in this world. Our calling as Christians is to explore the Bible with a heart open to all these channels. It is not our job to wield these words and stories as weapons to control other people in the world. That approach is an act of exclusion and serves as a stumbling block to the truth. That is why breaking legalism's grip on scripture is the first act of true Christian conscience that we must all engage. To do this, we must develop perspective on what the characters found in the Bible signify, and how scripture works to convey truths about God.

Understanding archetypes

In scripture we encounter people from thousands of years ago whose heroics and failures teach us about the challenges of life. These biblical characters are called archetypes,[1] defined as "a recurrent symbol or motif in literature, art, or mythology." The Bible presents scriptural archetypes beginning with Adam and Eve through a long line of prophets and characters all the way to Jesus. Many early Bible archetypes assume hierarchal proportions in a similar fashion to art depicting important people in larger-than-life dimensions and dramatized to express their eternal significance. Through archetypes, we learn positive moral traits such as humility or patience. We also find negative traits such as jealousy, hatred, or greed. People rewarded for their faithfulness and punished for their infidelities and lies. Scripture is all about teaching us values and does so in exceedingly symbolic fashion from beginning to end.

Parables as proof

To prove this relationship between symbolism and truth, we turn to the ways that Jesus taught about human life. He regularly invented stories and characters to portray good and bad behavior. Some of these were difficult lessons for people to understand or accept. For example, the parable of the 10 Talents[2] depicts a hard and demanding master judging his servants for their actions in managing his estate. The lesson is that each of us has a role to play in appreciating the Kingdom of God. To ignore that calling is an insult to God. There may even be punishment involved.

The famous story of the Good Samaritan[3] depicts the care offered by a passing stranger to a man beaten by thieves and left for dead. The Samaritan's actions contrast to the self-proclaimed righteous men who slink past to avoid helping the supposedly unclean victim. The parable's meaning is clear: the Kingdom of God is defined by caring for others, not by following the rules. The parables of Jesus are often painful lessons to those still clinging to the idea that their selfish priorities trump the idea of service and care in this world.

For all these harsh lessons, scripture also presents many moments of symbolic tenderness to demonstrate the true Kingdom of God. For example, the Bible depicts Jesus bending down to wash his disciples' feet the night he was betrayed.[4] His act of humility and servitude holds enormous significance. Jesus is telling us how to live and love each other.

These stories enhance our ability to draw deeper meaning from The Word, which is symbolic to its core. By contrast, literalism and legalism lead us away from truth by limiting our scriptural understanding and hewing to the "traditions of men," focused around a desire for control and power over others. That narrow worldview is common in biblical fundamentalism, a latter-day version of the religious legalism of old. But increasingly, the world is getting fed up with age-old prejudices.

The Pope speaks up for the richness of scripture

In a November 19, 2019, article on the Jesuit review,[5] Pope Francis takes religious fundamentalism and its legalistic roots to task. "We must beware of fundamentalist groups; each (religion) has their own. In Argentina, there are some fundamentalist corners there," he said. "Fundamentalism is a plague, and all religions have some fundamentalist first cousin," he said.

The Pope proposed that interreligious dialogue is one of the ways that contemporary Christians need to engage with other cultures. The solution, Francis suggests, is for Christianity to conduct a self-examination, a reality check, as it were."To see the dangers of fundamentalism, Christians must also reflect on their own history," he said, "including the Thirty Years' War, which began in 1618 as a conflict between Catholic and Protestant states, and the St. Bartholomew's Day massacre of 1572, which saw the targeted assassinations of Huguenots by Catholic mobs in France. "A bit of history should frighten us," the Pope said. "Whoever doesn't feel frightened from within should ask themselves why."

As Pope Francis rightly points out, the Judeo-Christian tradition has a long history of legalistic instincts. It's not as if these instincts have magically melted away through the advent of liberal principles such as democracy and science. If anything, fundamentalist religion has responded to a changing world by inventing all-new ways to deny the influence of modernism. Mostly this involved turning to age-old religious tradition as a "defense" of God. In a September 2021 treatise about the core tenest of faith, Pope Francis wrote, "Beware of the rigidity they propose to you: be careful. Because behind every inflexibility there is something bad, which is not the Spirit of God."

Francis goes on to note that people trying to make sense of scripture in a modern context often have troubles. He is concerned that too many people are put off by the anachronisms of scripture. "Many, even among practicing Christians, say openly that they are not able to read it, not because of illiteracy, but because they are unprepared for the biblical language, its modes of expression and its ancient cultural traditions," he said. "As a result, the biblical text becomes indecipherable, as if it were written in an unknown alphabet and an esoteric tongue."

The pope said that "the richness of Scripture is neglected or minimized by many because they were not afforded a solid grounding in this area,"not even from their families, who often seem unable "to introduce their children to the word of the Lord in all its beauty and spiritual power." In that directive, the pope is sounding a call to approach the bible with something more than a literalistic method.

But it won't be easy to create that type of positive change. As Pope Francis observes, fundamentalist teachings still have enormous influence in the religious world. There are factions within the Catholic Church that resent and oppose his more liberal call to understanding. But that's been the story of religion since its beginning. There are always doctrinal conflicts. Some of these spill into the secular world, causing even more confusion and societal damage.

One of the most famous conflicts of all is the clash between fundamentalist religion and science.This debate has gone on for centuries, and now finds its expression in belief systems such as creationism, the "science of denial" based on a literal interpretation of the Book of Genesis in the Bible. Creationists contend that a literal Genesis debunks the massive body of evidence for science and its workable theories such as gravity, evolution, and plate tectonics. Creationists are inclined to depict their worldview as an easier path to truth. More often it leads to difficulties when people try to superimpose religious beliefs on material facts staring them right in the face.

Bony's Miniature's 28 minutes ago
its unbelievable lol how could he get a degree?

👍 👎   REPLY

Christopher Cudworth 0 seconds ago
@Bony's Miniature's I looked that up. Like most creationists, he got the degree(s) and then had a reverse epiphany in which personal religious beliefs overwhelmed the education. This is consistent across the board in the many creation "scientists" whose backgrounds I researched. They confess it upfront, as if it's no problem to junk material science for the fantastical world of unsupported assumptions built on top of literalistic interpretations of scripture. This denial of knowledge is rife within 35-40% of Americans, which is why you find so many positive comments about these slickly produced by factually inaccurate videos. These supposed experts speculate wildly about what "must have happened." Or, if they did into a subject such as the geology of the Grand Canyon, they focus on the most minute characteristics that might support their theorems about how a grand flood gouged out the canyon. They never seem to bother to look at the Big Picture, such as why the canyon edges when viewed from space are neat and crisp and the surrounding landscape is as smooth as a baby's bottom.The fossil record is the same thing: they look for any sign of a "broken" pattern and say, "Look, the flood did this!" I met a geologist/creationist once who worked in the fossil fuels industry who told me, "I don't care how old the rocks are. I just need to understand the patterns." I call creationism the "Science of Denial." That's all it really is. There is no scientifically useful information that ever emerged from either creationism or intelligent design theory. None of their conjectures contributes to medicine, for example, in any way. Their primary objectives are denying the theory of evolution and its operative scientific relationships, which is everything ever done outside the literal biblical interpretation. Creationism is a lie, in other words, and its proponents preach it as truth because the belief system upon which it rests is a House of Cards in being based of a biblically literal Genesis. That's bad theology and bad science combined. Yet here we are, in the year 2021, forced to argue with numbnut converts trying to convince the world that the "kinds" of animals on the ark traveled from the Middle East across oceans to continents and habitats all over the world where they almost instantly diversified into millions of species through what they grudgingly call "micro-evolution." The entire premise is a horrific farce. And every person commenting on here that says "Great job" to these "scientists" that abandoned truth for the bad theology of biblical literalism (defending a God that does not need defending through human tradition) is a self-deceiving believer too scared, lazy, or uneducated to find out the truth for themselves. As Mark Twain once wrote: "In religion and politics, most people's opinions are gotten secondhand, and unexamined." And look how the religion of denial has now bled into the politics of denial. It all fits together.

My commentary from a discussion
about creationism on Quora

CHAPTER 11
Creationism and the Science of Denial

The belief system known as creationism is one of the most damaging ways that biblical literalism and legalism conspire to undermine common sense and knowledge of great value to humanity.

One of the originators of creationist propaganda is Henry Morris, founder of the Institute for Creation Research (ICR).[1] The organization expresses its mission with a combination of alacrity and hubris: "After almost 50 years of ministry, ICR remains a leader in scientific research within the context of biblical creation. The Institute for Creation Research is unique among scientific research organizations. Our research is conducted within a biblical worldview since ICR is committed to the absolute authority of the inerrant Word of God. The real facts of science will always agree with biblical revelation because the God who made the world of God inspired the Word of God."

The Institute for Creation Research uses a familiar tautology to make that case that it produces the "real facts of science." The presumptive statement that it was "God who made the world" is meant to trump any notion that it could have come about any other way. That is not science the ICR is practicing, but religion. Its creed is a religiously legalistic attempt to control the creation narrative and exert authority over others. In that respect, Morris and the phalanx of determined creationists that follow his example are no different than the religious authorities that Jesus confronted during his lifetime. They care only about forcing people to believe as they do, gain power for their purposes, and possibly enrich themselves in the process.

Hamming it up

The king of latter-day Creationism is Ken Ham,[2] the Australian expatriate whose hatred for the theory of evolution knows no bounds. Instead, Ham and his entire organization are consumed by the cause of biblical literalism and its pursuant legalism. Here is how the Answers In Genesis[3] (AiG) website describes its mission:

"Answers in Genesis is an apologetics ministry, dedicated to helping Christians defend their faith and proclaim the gospel of Jesus Christ effectively. We focus on providing answers to questions about the Bible—particularly the book of Genesis—regarding key issues such as creation, evolution, science, and the age of the earth."

The Answers In Genesis empire now includes two massive monuments to creationist ideology. The first is the Ark Encounter,[3] a supposed replica of the boat used by Noah to rescue all kinds of animals during a worldwide flood. The other is the Creation Museum,[5] an amusement park-style facility featuring literal Bible tales and dioramas in which human beings cavort with dinosaurs.

Collectively, these operations represent a temple to the creationist ego of its founder. All of it centers around the fundamental understanding of scripture as a literal historical and scientific document presented in the "show and tell" model of an elementary school classroom so that no one who encounters its claims will be intellectually challenged. That is precisely what Ken Ham sells, a boatload of willing ignorance.

Indoctrination nation

As Ham is readily admits, the "big issue" for creationists is claiming authority over the narrative of natural history. To accomplish this aim, creationists like Ham spend considerable amounts of time and money spinning the nature of facts to argue about the facts of nature. AiG is bald-faced about these indoctrination tactics, as their website proves:

"AiG teaches that "facts" don't speak for themselves: they must be interpreted. That is, there aren't separate sets of "evidences" for evolution and creation—we all deal with the same evidence (we all live on the same earth, have the same fossils, observe the same animals, etc.). The difference lies in how we interpret what we study. The Bible—the "history book of the universe"—provides a reliable, eyewitness account of the beginning of all things and can be trusted to tell the truth in all areas it touches on. Therefore, we are able to use it to help us make sense of this present world. When properly understood, the "evidence" confirms the biblical account."

AIG commits an amusing if unintentional gaffe in its proclamation of authority with its statement: "The difference lies in how we interpret what we study." In this context, the word "lies" is intended to mean the position in which something resides. More accurately, the Answers in Genesis subliminally admits that it habitually lies about the subjects it studies. That is the premise we are here to examine. Are Answers In Genesis creationists committed truth-tellers as they claim? Or are they habitual and creative liars that ignore factual evidence to arrive at the ideas they choose to believe?

Evidence to the contrary

The AiG organization aggressively advances presumptive statements to defend its authority, stated like this: "The Bible—the "history book of the universe"—provides a reliable, eyewitness account of the beginning of all things and can be trusted to tell the truth in all areas it touches on."

Whose eyewitness account? According to scripture itself, there were no human beings around to witness the earliest processes of creation. Additionally, while theologians love to claim that God is the ultimate authority on every subject, no credible branch of science accepts personal testimony of any kind as the final word on any matter. The scientific method requires experimentation, repetition, and corroboration to arrive at credible theories and workable forms of science. Creationism dismissively dumps those standards in favor of its pet claim, "God said it. I believe it. And that's that." When creationists try to turn the Bible into a scientific textbook, it leaves massive gaps in natural history. And where scripture falls short, creationists just make things up, as we'll see.

Ham-handed followers

The Answers In Genesis and Institute For Creation Research realm attracts many pseudo-scientific sycophants, most of whom abandoned their science training to adopt creationist viewpoints. Among those with degrees in science from accredited universities, one ICR panelist Dr. Gary Parker[6] admits to never being convinced that science is real in the first place. He describes his conversion experience to creationism in this way:

"Since I first heard of evolution in science class, I just assumed (like most people) that evolution was a scientific concept, and I taught the arguments used to support evolution during my first few years as a college biology professor. Then a chemistry professor (Dr. Charles Signorino) challenged my fervent faith in evolution using both evidences from the scientific study of nature (God's world) and the Biblical record of God's acts in history (God's Word). For three years I tried to defend the arguments for evolution I knew so well, but I kept finding the scientifically testable study of God's world made it harder to believe "molecules-to-man" evolution and easier to accept the Biblical record of earth history: God's perfect world (Creation), ruined by man's sin (Corruption), destroyed by Noah's Flood (Catastrophe), restored to new life in Jesus (Christ)."

Parker here admits to never fully grasping the focus or the facts provided in his academic training. In so doing, he represents many such 'reformed" scientists tossing their hats into the creationist camp. He tepidly states that he "taught the arguments" of evolution yet found these weren't satisfying to him. Finally, he stumbles into an outright religious confession as he states: "... I kept finding the scientifically testable study of God's world made it HARDER TO BELIEVE the "molécules-to-man" evolution and easier to accept the Biblical record of earth history."

Parker reveals why (and how) creationists choose to embrace the simplistic worldview of biblical literalism over genuine science. It is all about taking the "easier path" toward what it claims to be true. Sadly, that is one of the main reasons why creationist worldview remains so popular, especially in the United States of America. It purports to provide easy answers to life's complexity.

Creationism rules

Year after year, surveys conducted by Gallup[6] and other polling organizations show that nearly 40% of the American populace[7] embraces the biblically literal creation account. Unfortunately, that means nearly half the American population denies science in favor of a simplistic narrative of how living things were created.

According to a LiveScience article back in 2011,[8] 13% of high school biology teachers favored teaching creationism of some sort in public schools. However, a more recent report conducted by outreach. biomedcentral.com[9] suggests the number of teachers favoring creationism has subsided in subsequent years. "Notably, the percentage of teachers who endorse the creationist option (in this question) has fallen, from 16% in the 2007 sample to just 10.5% in 2019. This change is largely due to generational replacement, as only 7% of the more recent teachers express this view."

Figures like these indicate an increasing skepticism toward creationism as a distrust of fundamentalist religion grows. That trend is alarming to organizations such as Answers In Genesis, where Ken Ham and his phalanx of sycophants obsess about who believes in its teaching, who is going to church, and why young people in particular no longer buy the biblically literal narrative. This has been their primary obsession over the last decade.

In a 2011 AIG website article[10] titled "The Real Deal," written by Ken Ham and Britt Beemer (re-featured in 2015) the two arch-right leaders engaged in massive handwringing while concluding with a glaring admission of the real reasons why people sense falseness in the creationist message,

"We addressed the absolutely essential need to defend the Christian faith/Word of God in order to restore relevancy to Group 1, the young adults who have left the church, never come on holidays, and never plan on returning. But that leaves the other half, Group 2: those who come at Christmas and/or Easter and who plan on returning after they have children. Compared to Group 1, this group has a much higher level of belief in the Bible. Three-quarters of them believe that they are saved, and the vast majority of them report relatively high levels of belief in biblical accuracy, authority, and history. The obvious point here is that over half of the people who have left the Church are still solid believers in Jesus Christ. What they object to, however, is hypocrisy, legalism, and self-righteousness. The Bible is relevant to them, but the Church is not."

Ham and Beemer are either too oblivious or stiff-necked to realize that it is their organization, not mainstream religion or science, that represents the height of hypocrisy, legalism, and self-righteousness. Again, the 'irony of the obvious' is lost on the zealously devout. Creationism as a belief system rests on a massive bed of scriptural contradictions, twisted evidence, raw speculation, and at times, outright lies. All are necessary to cover up the massive gaps in creationist timelines and falsified information about the material world. Yet Ham and his clan press on with their corrupt brand or religion. The biblical characters of the Serpent and Satan have nothing on these latter-day 'brood of vipers' trying to control the religious narrative when it comes to the legalistic manipulation of God's Word.

Patent aims

The central concern of creationism is leveraging the authority of theology to maintain dominion over science. Yet that's what makes them so bad at both disciplines. Creationists prize the literal Genesis creation narrative because it supports the belief that God is in direct control of natural law and can break it at will. This theological point is necessary to make the pursuant claim that Jesus could be bodily raised from the dead in defiance of natural law. A literal Genesis creation narrative and the resurrection of Jesus and his predicted return at the end of the world are the Alpha and Omega bookends of Christian apologetics. Without them, the entire literalistic belief system falls apart. That's a brittle worldview indeed .

We've put our finger on the sole purpose of creationism as a worldview. The goal is upholding the Bible as factually inerrant to support the premise that a literal resurrection awaits people seeking eternal salvation. Personal salvation is the end game.

Cherry-picking miracles

This worldview seems simple enough, but it is rife with contradictions and conflicting perceptions of reality. As we've examined, biblical literalists like to believe that God easily breaks the laws of nature, creating Adam from dust and delivering Jesus from the dead. Yet somehow God can't manage to make life emerge from inorganic matter through natural means? It is theologically and intellectually dishonest to claim that one type of miracle is possible while off-handedly denying another.

To cover their tracks in the intellectual dishonesty department, creationists busy themselves making up stories to cover gaps between the biblically literal narrative and material reality. The pressure to produce these lies is so consuming it leaves no breathing space to honestly consider the actual miracles of material reality. That's the real shame. Men like Ken Ham and Henry Morris and others invest enormous resources trying to numb people to the miracles of science—for which there is plenty of evidence—while preaching about miracles in the Bible that even many biblical scholars find hard to support.

Chemistry is life

Creationists and biblical apologists seem to radically fear the idea that we live in a random universe capable of generating life through basic chemistry. Others can't stand the idea that we're made of the same genetic stuff as mice, bats, insects, or apes. That prejudice seems ridiculous considering the literal Genesis supposition that God formed Adam from dust. We're faced with an interesting question: Is it more insulting that human beings share genetic information with every other living thing on earth or that we're somehow made from a literal handful of dirt?

Truth be told, the mineral composition of human beings is pretty dirty. As reported on news-medical.net,[11] "The human body is approximately 99% comprised of just six elements: Oxygen, hydrogen, nitrogen, carbon, calcium, and phosphorus. Another five elements make up about 0.85% of the remaining mass: sulfur, potassium, sodium, chlorine, and magnesium. All of these 11 elements are essential elements."

In other words, we're not made from anything special. It's both distrubing and amusing how biblical apologists and creationists love to avoid the "dirty" secrets of the Bible while accusing secular science of being too "down and dirty" for their precious tastes.

The cloistered worldview of creationism is rather sad when you study it closely. It all comes down to a selfish desire to feel unique. Should we really be that insecure about our place in the universe? For a religion that claims to focus on selflessness and sacrifice, the focus of scriptural apologetics thinks and acts in just the opposite manner.

Not-so-Intelligent Design

The other hypocritical branch of Christian apologetic thinking is the creationist spin-off called Intelligent Design Theory (ID). The ID realm is even more speciously inventive in its attempts to conflate religion with science in favor of a God-driven world. While creationists occupy themselves elaborating on biblical tales to justify their literalistic worldview, ID theorists busy themselves making up scientific-sounding terms such as 'irreducible complexity' to claim that certain organisms and their body parts are too intricate to have developed without the help of a cosmic designer. Much like creationism, "intelligent design theory" is nothing more than an elaborate attempt to deny material science any right to describe the origins and development of life. In many respects, ID Theory is even more petulant than creationism.

The website Reason to Believe[12] featured a piece written by Fazale Rana in which the author introduces a convoluted theory as to why Intelligent Design Theory provides sufficient grounds to qualify as a type of science. He begins… "I think that science has the wherewithal to provide sufficient clues that allow us to infer the Designer's identity. To appreciate why I would adopt this position, I need to first explain why intelligent design has a place in science." His real point arrives at the inevitable conclusion, "There are many such evidences, but I believe that this short list provides us with sufficient insight about the Designer's qualities that we could reasonably conclude that the Intelligent Designer is most likely the God of the Bible."

Here's the real problem with so-called Intelligent Design. We know from the fossil record and earth science that 99% of the living things that ever existed are now extinct. If the so-called Designer is such a hotshot, why such sloppy regard for their work? There are also plenty of extant life forms, including human beings, that carry vestigial organs and bones around inside their body. These evolutionary "leftovers" hip and limb bones buried deep in the flesh of whales, remnants of their land-dwelling ancestry. It all demonstrates that no organism is created perfect. In fact, it is often imperfections and genetic variation that lead to new life forms, and new designs. Or else we need a Stupid Design Theory to describe all the mistakes made by the designer.

Instead, Intelligent Design Theory asks us to ignore evolutionary evidence in favor of a control-freak god playing the role of a fussy watchmaker. The seemingly "easier path" of creationist and ID theory doctrine actually blinds people to the realities of the world by imposing shallow religious beliefs on a wonderfully complex universe. But as we'll see, the so-called "easier path" always leads to difficulties.

> "A church that doesn't provoke any crisis, a gospel that doesn't unsettle, a Word of God that doesn't get under anyone's skin, what kind of gospel is that? Preachers who avoid every thorny matter so as not to be harassed do not light up the world."
>
> Archbishop Oscar Romero
> Assassinated March 24 1980
> #aninconvenientfaith

Sad Jesus
4d · 🌎
"Church" isn't supposed t... See more

CHAPTER TWELVE

Why the easier path leads to difficulties

Conflicted aims

As we've seen, the "easier path" favored by creationists and intelligent design theory leans heavily on concocted tales and invented terminology to define its version of the truth. The problem with these approaches is that they share a long history of misleading people about material facts and reality based on the dogmatic claims of religion.

For example, the Catholic Church once stubbornly embraced the claim that everything in the universe revolved around the Earth.[1] That model served its authoritarian grip on theology and secular cosmology. The commitment to this falsehood was so pervasive the Church persecuted all those who dared challenge the received worldview.

It took centuries for the Church to finally admit that it had the concept of our solar system wrong. A 1992 New York Times story[2] relates, "More than 350 years after the Roman Catholic Church condemned Galileo, Pope John Paul II is poised to rectify one of the Church's most infamous wrongs -- the persecution of the Italian astronomer and physicist for proving the Earth moves around the Sun. With a formal statement at the Pontifical Academy of Sciences on Saturday, Vatican officials said the Pope would formally close a 13-year investigation into the Church's condemnation of Galileo in 1633. The condemnation, which forced the astronomer and physicist to recant his discoveries, led to Galileo's house arrest for eight years before his death in 1642 at the age of 77."

The story continues: "The dispute between the Church and Galileo has long stood as one of history's great emblems of conflict between reason and dogma, science and faith. The Vatican's formal acknowledgment of an error, moreover, is a rarity in an institution built over centuries on the belief that the Church is the final arbiter in matters of faith."

Despite the shift in official church position after 350 years, some grudging Catholics still choose to believe the Church was never in error. The website CatholicAnswers.com[3] published an apologetic titled "The Galileo Controversy," stating: "The Anti-Catholics often cite the Galileo case as an example of the Church refusing to abandon outdated or incorrect teaching and clinging to a "tradition." They fail to realize that the judges who presided over Galileo's case were not the only people who held a geocentric view of the universe. It was the received view among scientists at the time."

What the author neglects to mention in his opinion is that the Church enforced the "received view" so decisively that no one dared challenge the official doctrine. The church actively suppressed the truth, just as creationists seek to deny science now. The willingness of Galileo and other scientists to challenge church doctrine is what made them courageous and unique. Like Jesus, they risked their lives to tell the truth. Sadly, their legacy of truth-telling from the scientific view continues to be buried under layers of denial to this day. That is a severe problem for modern society at every level of engagement. When people fail to grasp or accept material reality, it sets them up to accept other falsehoods as normal facts.

Denial as a way of life

The Catholic Church is far from alone in its habit of denying reality to support its worldview. Even in the modern age, the Flat Earth Society[4] combines biblically literal scripture, conspiracy theories, and outright speculation to justify their belief that the Earth is flat as a pancake. Despite incontrovertible evidence that the Earth is spherical, the number of people supporting Flat Earth Theory is rising. A survey by You.gov[5] examined this trend: "While an overwhelming majority of Americans (84%) believe that the Earth is round, at least 5% of the public (Author's note: 15M people) say they used to believe that but now have their doubts. Moreover, flat earthers find traction in their beliefs among a younger generation of Americans. Young millennials, ages 18 to 24, are likelier than any other age group to say they believe the Earth is flat (4%)."

LiveScience.com also examined the subject in an article titled Flat Earth, What Fuels the Internet's Strangest Conspiracy Theory?[6] It discovered that Flat Earth Theory is gaining popularity among people eager to define reality for themselves. "You need security and control, and you don't have it," one researcher said, "so you try to compensate for it." But, of course, that describes creationism as well.

That raises the question of how many other people choose to deny reality to protect their belief system. The answer is that it is exceedingly common, especially among religious believers convinced they are defending themselves and God from the intrusions of a secular world. This brand of denial is dangerous because it forces people to contradict common sense knowledge in favor of age-old, long-disproven traditions. These over-simplified bricks of anachronistic beliefs form stumbling blocks to a broader understanding of our material circumstances in this universe.

One of the most giant stumbling blocks in the Bible is the tale of Noah and the Great Flood. Intended as a moral fable about the wickedness of humanity and its propensity to ignore morality in favor of selfish behavior, biblical literalists instead turn the Flood narrative into a literal description to explain all geology, biological diversity, and global distribution of life on Earth. That's only where the dishonesty begins.

The flood narrative

The tale of Noah and the Great Flood[7] begins with a cryptic explanation of why humanity and every other living thing deserves to be wiped from the face of the Earth:[8]

> 5 The Lord saw how great the wickedness of the human race had become on the Earth and that every inclination of the thoughts of the human heart was only evil all the time.
>
> 6 The Lord regretted that he had made human beings on the Earth, and his heart was deeply troubled.
>
> 7 So the Lord said, "I will wipe from the face of the earth the human race I have created—and with them the animals, the birds and the creatures that move along the ground—for I regret that I have made them."
>
> 8 But Noah found favor in the eyes of the Lord.

In this passage, the Bible shows God in a state of deep regret over the state of humanity and all of creation. Typically, it is the human penchant for pride, lust, greed, covetousness, and disregard for life that drives God to commit genocide. Why God decides that all the Earth's animals need to get wiped out in the process is a mystery. Still, God chooses Noah and his family as a new foundation for humanity, and spares a selection of animals to preserve stock for the future.

Let's pause for a moment to consider the scriptural meaning of Noah and his family. Noah and his family are archetypal examples of people "saved by grace."[9] They represent a chance to start over in life and also as a sign that salvation awaits those who show trust in God. To some degree, God extends forgiveness to humanity in the process. It all folds into the notion that God is ultimately merciful and loving. If we are grateful in spirit and mind, it is supposed to be grace that enters our hearts. But here's a word of advice from scripture: it's best not to test the Lord your God. Most get far more than they've bargained for.

Before the Flood, Noah tries his best to extend that grace to the world, but he is mocked, so he continues building an ark to protect representatives of God's creation from the destruction from coming. Yet, even as he suffers ridicule from people doubting the urgency or sincerity of his mission, he sticks to his plan. In that respect, Noah foreshadows the coming of Jesus Christ.

God spares members of Noah's family to breed among themselves and act as stewards for the stock of domestic and wild animals aboard the Ark. The number of animals recruited into the Ark is highly symbolic. The biblical account is contradictory about whether Noah took two of each kind of animal or seven, but in any case, the animals symbolize God's care for the rest of living things as well.[10]

> Take with you seven pairs of every kind of clean animal, a male and its mate, and one pair of every kind of unclean animal, a male and its mate, --Genesis 7:2

The number seven often symbolizes completeness in the Bible. The more common depiction is that animals boarded the ark "two by two," a version popular in children's books and convenient to the claim that only male and female genders exist in the natural world.

Critter apologetics

As to the total number of other animals taken on board the Ark, devoted creationist Dr. Nathaniel T. Jeanson from Answers In Genesis openly speculates on that subject in an article titled *The Origin of Species After the Flood*.

Jeanson's article openly steals its title from Charles Darwin's 1859 book *On the Origin of Species*. That is a creationist's notion of how to appear scientific. Steal what you can to appear credible and deny the rest. Jeanson's freehanded take on the origin of speices also openly borrows scientific terminology such as "genetics" to feign credibility. He states: "Modern science is giving us even more windows into this enigma of antiquity. The more we learn about the origin of species, the more hints we gain into Noah's vistas. The stamp of the Flood reverberates down to the present day—in the form of genetics."

From there, Jeanson wades into a rambling explanation of how animal diversity came into being—and how few animals were required to achieve that outcome:

"Using the family criterion in combination with the "breath of life" criterion, the total number of kinds on board the Ark was low. Today, the number of living mammal, amphibian, reptile, and bird families (including the aquatic ones) is just over 500."[11]

"If we include fossils, the number increases. In relative terms, the increase is significant, but in terms of absolute numbers, the new total represents a small fraction of the diversity of life on the planet. Among mammals, amphibians, reptiles, and birds, the mammals have the most diverse fossil record. Only about 30% of all mammal families that ever existed are alive today.[7] Assuming a similar percentage for amphibians, reptiles, and birds, we can estimate how many total families in these groups of creatures ever existed. If 510 families exist in these groups today, and if this represents just 30% of all that ever lived, then a total of 1,700 mammalian, amphibian, reptilian, and avian families[8] once existed on Earth. This number—1,700—represents an upper estimate of the total number of kinds that Noah took on board the Ark.[13] Even if Noah also took terrestrial invertebrates, like flies, ticks, and fleas, these creatures are so small that they would have added little to the total cargo space. So this small gaggle of creatures survived on the Ark for about one year and then exited—at a particular point in the ancient past."

Jeanson continues, in an aggressively simplified manner: "If we limit our discussion to the vertebrates (e.g., creatures possessing a backbone), Noah would have taken on board mammals, amphibians, reptiles, and birds. Again, only the terrestrial or aerial creatures would have made the boat. The aquatic members of these groups of creatures could have survived the Flood outside the Ark."

The focus of the article and its supporting "research" is completely speculative and largely defensive in tone because Jeanson senses the major flaws in his creationist claims. For starters, he recognizes that millions of the world's species could never fit aboard the Ark. To rationalize his claims, Jeanson engages in reductionist math to speculate how few "original kinds" were necessary to act as fodder for life's diversity."

Jeanson's specious arguments really fall apart when he attempts to leapfrog entire life groups. His claim that "aquatic members of these groups could have survived the Flood outside the Ark" assumes that all fresh, brackish, and saltwater species could ably survive in the same waters during a yearlong, worldwide flood. That contention alone is absurd. The supposed level of catastrophic devastation, estimated by some creationists to be so forceful it tossed continents around like corks, defies his claims that marine life could easily have survived such a flood.

To illustrate that point, here is how yet another creationist describes conditions during the worldwide Flood: "The Bible, which aside from being 100% accurate on every subject to which it speaks, tells us that the worldwide cataclysmic Flood in the days of Noah caused the continents to move into the places we find them today. We propose that what we see today is the result of the worldwide cataclysmic Flood as recorded in the Bible in Genesis chapters 6-9, and although the continents are still drifting, the rate of drift averages approximately 5 cm per year worldwide."

There is no verse in Genesis 6-9 describing continents floating across the face of the Earth during the worldwide Flood. That is a creationist fiction that equates to an elementary student cutting and pasting a map together to explain the complexities of continental movement. These grasping attempts at defending the creationist narrative resemble the desperate tactics of a witness caught in a lie during a court proceeding. Stealing information to create an alibi while dumping facts that conflict with reality is an admission that your story has gaping holes in it from the start. Lying like that is better known as perjury, "the intentional act of swearing a false oath or falsifying an affirmation to tell the truth." Creationism is nothing more than theological perjury. It is also guilty of bad theology by forcing the Bible to defend stories that it never contained in the first place. If it seems unkind to mock creationist beliefs, it is in response to the blatant dishonesty at work in their contentions.

About those dinosaurs

The creationist explanation for the disappearance of dinosaurs is also comically ridiculous. The AIG website[14] takes this crack at it: "Dinosaurs were created by God on day six of creation, approximately 6,000 years ago. Dinosaurs were originally vegetarian. During the global Flood, many were buried and fossilized, but two of each kind survived on Noah's Ark. Dinosaurs eventually died out due to human activity, climate changes, or other factors."

This supposed alibi for the disappearance of dinosaurs is followed by an even more outlandish and childish take on the science of paleontology: "Evolutionists claim dinosaurs lived millions of years ago. But it is important to realize that when they dig up a dinosaur bone, it does not have a label attached showing its date. The Bible states that God made the land animals, including dinosaurs, on day six (Genesis 1:24–25), so they date from around 6,000 years ago."

Creationism and its sister ideology intelligent design theory are not science in any honest sense of the word. Instead, they are bad theology pretending to have scientific value. We'll now examine why that practice is so damaging to the concept of truth and harmful to the world at large.

CHAPTER 13
Lessons in bad theology

It is essential to understand the nature and source of bad theology to help us comprehend the damages it causes. In a 2012 post titled "What makes bad theology?" Christian writer Victor Scott addresses the issue in his blog Jeremiah's Vow[1]:

"Bad theology lets us off the hook for our actions and puts us in more favorable circumstances. We all come out feeling better about ourselves, even if the truth of the matter is something else. Bad theology is bad precisely because it puts us in the position of having to defend God from his own Word. God does not need defending."

Scott identifies why Christian apologetic thinking typically bungles the real meaning of scripture by trying to defend the Word of God from a literalistic perspective. A biblically literal narrative promises a shortcut to truth while eclipsing any hope of seeing the bigger picture. That's bad theology. As a result, that bad theology engenders a worldview with an inherently stiff-necked mix of denial and judgment at its core. By nature, it is also jealous about its authority, especially in competition with any outlook appearing to contradict its inherently limited worldview. That's the reason why apologetics is required at all: it requires defending because its foundations are so inflexibly formed.

When that brand of bad theology gets turned into laws and rituals, the outcome is equally rigid, judgmental, and typically legalistic. History has proven too many times that the bad theology of legalism leads to willful ignorance too easily translated into cultural and religious oppression. Almost without exception, the cause of bad theology is anachronism,[2] defined as "a thing belonging or appropriate to a period other than that in which it exists, especially a thing that is conspicuously old-fashioned."

The guiltiest party when it comes to embracing anachronism is biblical literalism with religious legalists in tow. Both brands of anachronism cling to old and outdated scripture out of love for tradition. This is exactly what Jesus maligned in the religious authorities of his day. Despite clear scriptural evidence that Jesus despised these habits, Christian apologetics cling to scripture relics with obsessive fervor, sometimes not even knowing why they believe them anymore. It is their religious security blanket. They are theological hoarders, people that refuse to clean house because there is too much sentimental attachment to the objects they covet.

Cleaning house

The Bible passages that most qualify as anachronistic are scriptures projecting patriarchal and prejudicial attitudes on women, minorities, and gay people. The Bible also blames mental illness and other afflictions on "demons." But the world has rightly moved on from the ugly and ill-informed nature of these age-old prejudices. Modern culture dispenses with age-old prejudices by granting respect and full citizenship to womean, refusing to embrace racial discrimination and acknowledgging that being gay is an integral part of the human condition.

Yet age-old beliefs die hard. Religious tradition has a hard time letting go of these scriptural antiques out of fear that relinquishing one aspect of the Bible leads to loss of ownership over the authority of all scripture. Christian apologists cannot stand that idea. They would rather cling to their version of the truth than admit that the world can and does change. Overcoming these attitudes requires us to confront the anachronisms leading to bad theology. The "trinity of bad theology" caused by anachronism impacts the world in three ways:

Anachronism drives disrespect for human and civil rights by demanding blind adherence to ancient customs and traditions.

Anachronism defies science while offering a vastly incomplete description of natural history based on a narrative necessarily brief because it was originally an oral tradition about creation.

Anachronism dismisses taking care of the Earth as an unnecessary burden on the human race under the selfishly interpreted badge of "dominion" and a belief that Jesus will come along with a "big fix."

This "trinity of bad theology" is directly responsible for the bulk of culture wars in America and worldwide. Moreover, it has a long history of generating tribal, religious, and political conflicts, racial prejudice, and environmental degradation around the world.

In love with slogans

Bad theology seeks to escape moral accountability by spouting relativistic slogans such as "Love the sinner, hate the sin." Sayings such as these defend a deeply conflicted worldview by claiming to represent the love of God while justifying the persecution and oppression of others. This type of moral confusion is produced in people trying to reconcile the anachronism inherent in scripture with Christ's call to compassion for all human beings. The idea that nothing in the Bible could be wrong causes a deep level of conflict within those who cherish the idea of biblical infallibility and inerrancy. More objective minds have always known this is not the case.

Blocking bad theology

Given religion's disturbing habit of corrupting the truth and grabbing the reins of political power for selfish purposes, the Founding Fathers[3] specifically banned a state religion from taking over the American republic. That is precisely why they wrote the First Amendment into the Bill of Rights with its clear statement that Congress shall not establish any state religion. They ardently wanted to protect the nation from bad theology. Unfortunately, zealous Christian believers to this day interpret "religious liberty" as the right to install their beliefs at ever level of the law. That's better known as theocracy.

The common claim in support of theocacy is that America originated as a "Christian nation" based on Christian law and values. However, that claim was never valid because the Founders clearly understood the risks of letting religion take over. The reason? Theocracy has a lousy track record with human rights because its authoritarian instincts directly contrast with the principles of democracy.

Age-old problems

In the modern era, we're faced with media-savvy institutions and organizations run by Bible-thumping apologetics and creationists seeking to "defend God" with age-old interpretations of scripture that deny human rights and block civil progress in culture, scientific, and political arenas. The result is a legacy of continuing oppression and persecution of anyone the legalistic church chooses to brand a sinner. The same instincts seek to isolate people as "the other" according to ancient judgments, many of which Jesus never even mentioned. That is another example of the irony rife within religious conservatives eager to impose their "traditions" on culture today.

Religion too often gets its way on these matters by claiming scripture as an absolute and unchanging source of truth. Yet, scripture does provide some interesting examples of how God regards those who claim a high and mighty position of authority in this world.

Mostly, it shows how foolish people can be when they decide to play God and impose the traditions of men upon the world.

CHAPTER 14
Playing God. Imposing Tradition.

The Tower of Babel lesson

One of the most famous examples in scripture of people growing too sure of themselves and wanting to play God is the tale of the Tower of Babel. BibleStudyTools.org[1] describes the role of pride and arrogance in fueling the situation:

> "The population was growing, and they all spoke one language. The people decided to build a tall, proud symbol of how great they had made their nation. The Babylonians wanted a tower that would "reach to the heavens" so that they could be like God and that they would not need Him. They began to construct a great ziggurat."

Scripture shares that God found offense in these attitudes:

> "Let us make a name," the people tell themselves. «6 And the LORD said, Behold, the people is one, and they have all one language; and this they begin to do: and now nothing will be restrained from them, which they have imagined to do." — Genesis 11

The people constructing the Tower of Babel and Adam and Eve in the Garden of Eden share similarly naïve objectives. Both overreach in their attempts to "be like God." The outcomes are profound. Adam and Eve are booted out of the Garden of Eden and the people building the Tower of Babel have their language confused and are scattered by God to the winds. These examples prove that it is aggressive naivete and human arrogance that typically earn the wrath of God, but it gets particularly ugly when people take the authority of God into their own hands and become abusive by way of their own traditions. The most potent lesson of abusive human nature is found in the story of Sodom and Gomorrah.

Of Sodom and Gomorrah

The scriptural tale of Sodom and Gomorrah presents two cities that God finds lacking in virtue. Their corrupt culture and abusive traditions disgust the Lord, who vows to wipe them off the earth.

First, we view these problems from afar as the scene opens with God speaking well of Abraham:

> 18 Abraham will surely become a great and powerful nation, and all nations on earth will be blessed through him.
>
> 19 For I have chosen him, so that he will direct his children and his household after him to keep the way of the Lord by doing what is right and just, so that the Lord will bring about for Abraham what he has promised him."
>
> 20 Then the Lord said, "The outcry against Sodom and Gomorrah is so great and their sin so grievous 21 that I will go down and see if what they have done is as bad as the outcry that has reached me. If not, I will know."

It is interesting that this passage begins with a statement characterizing Abraham as a "great and powerful nation." This sentence proves that Abraham is an archetype for the values God wants to see in an entire population of people. Leading up to the story of Sodom and Gomorrah, this portrait of Abraham intentionally contrasts the values God also likes to see in cities, nations, and the entire world. The message is clear: be faithful like Abraham, and you may prosper.

Rather than go himself, God sends a pair of emissaries to check out the situation in Sodom and Gomorrah. Abraham stays behind because he senses the seriousness of God's anger. He seems panicked that the Lord is about to do something rash and tries to convince God to be patient before killing off all the residents in the two cities. It's a unique conversation that takes place with Abraham speaking directly to God.

> 22 The men turned away and went toward Sodom, but Abraham remained standing before the Lord. 23 Then Abraham approached him and said: "Will you sweep away the righteous with the wicked? 24 What if there are fifty righteous people in the city? Will you really sweep it away and not spare[c] the place for the sake of the fifty righteous people in it? 25 Far be it from you to do such a thing—to kill the righteous with the wicked, treating the righteous and the wicked alike. Far be it from you! Will not the Judge of all the earth do right?"

The negotiations between God and Abraham continue until they produce an agreement between them that if even one righteous person is revealed, God will spare the people there. Unfortunately, it doesn't turn out that way.

Turn of events

God's emissaries enter the city and the greeting they receive does not go well. They nearly fall prey to a brutal local custom allowing townspeople to abuse strangers found in the city after dark. Knowing the risk these visitors face if they are not protected, a man named Lot takes them into his own house. That only directs their anger toward Lot.

> 4 Before they had gone to bed, all the men from every part of the city of Sodom—both young and old—surrounded the house. 5 They called to Lot, "Where are the men who came to you tonight? Bring them out to us so that we can have sex with them." 6 Lot went outside to meet them and shut the door behind him 7 and said, "No, my friends. Don't do this wicked thing. 8 Look, I have two daughters who have never slept with a man. Let me bring them out to you, and you can do what you like with them. But don't do anything to these men, for they have come under the protection of my roof." 9 "Get out of our way," they replied. "This fellow came here as a foreigner, and now he wants to play the judge! We'll treat you worse than them." They kept bringing pressure on Lot and moved forward to break down the door.

The townspeople sought to enforce their authority according to the local custom of gang-raping anyone outsiders for sport. Their appetite for violence is clearly indiscriminate, as indicated by the fact that Lot offers up his two virgin daughters in place of his guests. There is a parallel story in Judges 19, where a man gives up his concubine in similar circumstances. She is raped to death by the crowd.

We learn from this conversation that Lot is an emigrant to the city. The locals try to use that status as leverage, threatening him with even worse treatment if he doesn't oblige their plans. All this coarse and brutal negotiation makes clear that the sins of Sodom and Gomorrah were never about "having sex" with anyone at all. Rape of any kind is not sex. It is an act of aggressive violence. Only a willfully ignorant reader of scripture refuses to recognize that truth.

Rape as a tool of power

The attackers outside Lot's door had rape[2] on their minds because it is a way of expressing power over others. Their intentions resemble the prison bulls in the movie Shawshank Redemption,[3] in which a set of cruel inmates repeatedly attacks the main character Andy Defresne (played by Tim Robbins) because it was a "tradition" to engage in such treatment of hapless or weaker prisoners.

Andy's prison friend Red describes these rapes not as an expression of sexual desire but as something else entirely: "The Bull Queers cannot be classified as homosexual or gay, Red says. "You have to be human for that to apply...".

The same holds true for the men outside Lot's door. Their intentions are inhumane. When it comes to gang rape, it is often the most aggressive and abusive individuals that lead the way while others follow along. In Sodom and Gomorrah, the entire town embraced the idea that raping strangers was a legitimate way to express dominance over people caught in vulnerable circumstances.

In no way does that tradition indicate that homosexuality was the sin of Sodom and Gomorrah. The cities earned God's anger through abuse of authority and the brand of vigilante law that emerged from it. In fact, scripture tells us that the sins of Sodom and Gomorrah had nothing to do with an act of sex between two men.

> Ezekiel 16: 49-50 "Now this was the sin of your sister Sodom: She and her daughters were arrogant, overfed and unconcerned; they did not help the poor and needy. They were haughty and did detestable things before me. Therefore, I did away with them as you have seen."
>
> -- New International Version

The biblical tale of Sodom and Gomorrah warns us that the abuse of authority is serious business in God's mind. The Bible depicts a God angry with people invested in the mistreatment of strangers and possessed of dismissive, selfish attitudes. Those are the sins that a natural disaster buries under sulphur and ash.

Aftermath

In their flight from the city, Lot's daughters lose their mother when she is turned into a pillar of salt for disobeying God's orders not to look back at the destruction in their wake. This hardly seems fair or just, but the God of the Old Testament is not known as the most merciful deity. That's likely why Abraham was panicked at the outset of the story. As a man attuned to the capricious vigor of both God and nature, Abraham sensed pending disaster to come.

The story follows Lot and his daughters[4] into the hills, where they are forced to live in exile. In the aftermath of abuse and great destruction all around them, they seem to suffer a form of post-traumatic stress disorder.[5] Left in the care of their angst-filled father who quite willingly offered them up to be raped by a violent crowd, the two young women fear their lives are ruined.

Fearing for their destiny and loss of hope for a family of their own, the daughters conspire to get their father drunk and rape him. They commit this act of incest in hopes of getting pregnant so that they can bear children of their own. This proves how cycles of abuse get passed through families.

The tale of Lot and his daughters is story shared by Christian, Jewish, and Muslim traditions. For these reasons, there are differing theories about why Lot's daughters behaved as they did. Christianity has primarily excused Lot by depicting his decision to protect the guests in his home as a moral action. His choice is also excused under the patriarchal belief that a man's daughters were a father's property. From a modern perspective, this seems absurd, and Lot's actions are rightly considered abhorrent. Yet Christianity for millennia claimed that the sin of Sodom and Gomorrah was homosexuality.

That's a clearly selective and corrupt take on the story, but it serves a purpose. Ignoring Lot's despicable attitude toward his daughters directs attention from the abusive nature of patriarchal rule over society. Religious tradition refuses to hold Lot accountable because it is easier to falsely conflate gang rape with a "gay lifestyle" than to confess the abusive nature of patriarchal traditions that favor dominance and control over women and society as a whole. Patriarchy is all about establishing dominance and exploiting weakness to confirm the position of Alpha males and their view of property and propriety.

That's why the patriarchal side of Christianity depicts the primary sin of Sodom and Gomorrah as homosexuality. In large part it is this "sodomy" lie, along with other bits of anachronistic scripture, that led to persecution of gay people for more than two millennia. The apologetic wing of Christianity ignores calls to abandon the toxic myth of homophobia because patriarchal tradition covets the idea that masculine, heterosexual men deserve to be in control.

This take ignores the fact that Lot was not likely a moral man from the outset. His choice to live in proximity with sin yet claim innocence is taken to task in a Jewish view[6] of the subject:

"According to the Midrash (Tanhuma, Vayera 12), Lot, from the outset, decided to dwell in Sodom because he wanted to engage in the licentious behavior of its inhabitants. His negative behavior comes to the fore when the townspeople mill about his door, demanding that he hand over the angels, and he instead offers his daughters to the mob. The Rabbis observe that a man usually allows himself to be killed in order to save his wife and children, while Lot was willing to allow the townspeople to abuse his daughters. In response to this, the Holy One, blessed be He, says to Lot: By your life, the improper act that you intended to be done to your daughters will indeed be committed, but to you."

This insight reveals takes toxic masculinity and age-old patriarchal attitudes to task.

Promise Keepers

Over the last few decades, efforts to protect the role of male dominance have taken on sneaky disguises in the Christian community. One of those efforts rallies men together in a program called Promise Keepers.[7] The organization boldly claims, "We're building on the past to define the future." Talk about an obvious attempt at enforcing patriarchy and celebrating the power of anachronism! To make sure the message is pounded home, the group typically holds big rallies featuring high profile personalities cheering about male pride, praying for power, and pushing marital control in big assemblies at sports stadiums. The group preaches 'respect for women' in its patriarchal way, but always in a context where men lead and women are expected to follow. Groups such as PK only prove that the ownership factor within patriarchal tradition remains a high priority.

Pussy grabbers and sexual harassers

Given the devotion to dominant male leadership in the Christian culture of America, it is no surprise that the evangelical community embraces toxically impenitent control freaks and women abusers such as Donald Trump. As he positioned himself as a candidate for President of the United States, far-right conservatives worked overtime to dismiss Trump's sexist behavior and confessions, including statements such as these made in a taped interview with Billy Bush:[8]

> **Trump:** You know, I'm automatically attracted to beautiful — I just start kissing them. It's like a magnet. Just kiss. I don't even wait. And when you're a star, they let you do it. You can do anything.
>
> **Bush**: Whatever you want.
>
> **Trump**: Grab 'em by the pussy. You can do anything.

Despite this abusive confessional, the patriarchy rallied around Trump, who during a televised debate with Hillary Clinton at his side, characterized his ugly statements as mere "locker room talk."

Likewise, Trump's then-favorite media outlet was a high-stakes locker room, because Fox News leadership and top male talent were also proven to be sexual abusers. Lawsuits brought by women within the organization exposed President and CEO Roger Ailes[9] as a persistent sexual harasser. The same held true for Mr. No Spin Zone, Bill O'Reilly,[10] who was sued for his chronic sexual habits of sexual harassment too.

Somehow groups like Promise Keepers and other so-called "Christian" organizations remain largely silent when events among their ideological peers unfold. More often, the perpetrators issue a barely apologetic statement with a promise that they'll get treatment for their "addiction," or else they use some other excuse to beg forgiveness for their horrific behavior. Within a few monthsor a year or two, they're typically back in action and welcomed back[11] with open arms by conservatives that admire power more than principle. Figures on the political left, such as Bill Clinton[12] (a professed Christian) and Anthony Weiner,[13] have engaged in their share of toxic behavior as well. They don't deserve a pass any more than figures on the Christian Right.

The point here is that none of these people is being held accountable by the religion that claims to hold the keys to morality. Instead, the repressively anachronistic wing of the Christian religion turns it head to avoid responsibility for its own shameful history of patriarchal dominion and its present-day expression in repressive cultural conflicts. Frankly, Christianity has such a long history of treasuring authority and pursuing favors from powerful (often abusive) people that it barely has any credibility left to speak about matters of morality.

Jesus despised that brand of religion. He would absolutely freak to learn about the Catholic clergy scandal in which priest actively committed pedophilia while being protected by the church.[14] Thousands of Catholic priests were shuttled from parish to parish to hide their abusive deeds and guard the reputation of the church. That corrupt tradition represents hypocrisy so rich that the church has rightly become the butt of cynical jokes about the problem.[15]

But the Catholic church is not alone in its hypocrisy. Every year, congregation leaders[16] large and small get caught in acts of adultery and sex scandals. Most eventually admit their sins, then beg mercy, ask forgiveness, and use their supposed contrition as an excuse to start life all over again. Disgraced televangelists such as Jim Bakker tried to shut their accusers up, but typically the truth does come out. The Bakker sex scandal is explained on History.com,[17] "On December 6, 1980, Bakker and Hahn had a sexual encounter in a Florida hotel room. Although they each told different stories of what had happened, Bakker eventually paid Hahn over $350,000 to remain silent. When the arrangement became public, the scandal helped to bring down the entire PTL ministry."

Jessica Hahn went on to sell her story to Playboy and posed for nude photos. She may have seemed like the winner in that deal, yet much like the daughters of Lot, too many women wind up living in confusing over the emotional and physical scars they've received as victims of abuse from supposedly trustworthy people. Bakker is now back hawking End Times prophecy and selling useless prepper junk to his naive followers.

Pro-life farce

There are few public movements that are bigger examples of hypocrisy than the so-called "Pro-Life"[18] wing of Christianity. Threatening women over the issue of abortion while ignoring the fact that every woman seeking an abortion was first impregnated by a man is the ultimate form of patriarchal hypocrisy. Some of those men are rapists. Others are domestic abusers. Some are seducers. Still others are sexual dilettantes or rabid deniers of their responsibility in the sex act. In all those cases, it is women that are forced to make tough decisions over their pregnancy while men largely escape unharmed or unhindered by what they've done. Some are just couples that accidentally got pregnant through consensual sex. Pro-Lifers lump all these situations together under the banner of banning all abortions. This is one more example of the "irony of the obvious" in which supposed Christians, rather than working to fix the actual cause of unwanted pregnancies, choose instead to punish the victims (women) of corrupt behavior while claiming the side of righteousness.

It's no surprise how many repressive, patriarchal men fight for the Pro-Life movement. Their instincts persist in claiming ownership over women's bodies under all circumstances. Some even claim that women should be forced to bear the children caused by rape. But until the Christian religion and its political accomplices actively engage in preventing men from causing unintentional pregnancies, it is the "Pro-Life" movement that remains a patriarchally hypocritical farce. As for the women engaged on that front, it does no good to terrorize other women through self-righteous threats or "after-the-fact" condemnations. It doesn't make a damned bit of sense to ban abortions if ignorance and male dominion causes unwanted pregnancies. The Pro-Life movement acts righteous while ignoring the source of the problem and all the viable prevention measures available today. If Jesus were to return and weigh in on the issue of abortion, he would also tell the entire Pro-Life movement, "If you have to rely on the law to carry out God's will, you have already failed."

Hooray for Planned Parenthood

The secular world offers far more honest and practical means to prevent unwanted pregnancies and abortions. It all begins with sex education,[20] which conservative Christianity has long resisted. Yet that is the single most effective and direct means to teach people how to avoid unwanted pregnancies. It is healthy to understand the realities of sex and the possible consequence of sexual interaction. Sex education is one of the most moral brands of information available. Teaching pregnancy prevention in the process, and following that up with effective means of birth control is the best way to prevent unwanted pregnancies and reduce the number of abortions. The ideal world is one in which abortions won't be necessary except in cases where the life or health of a mother or child is at risk. As liberals have long advocated, the goal is the make abortions increasingly unnecessary, and rare.

By contrast, the supposedly Christian approach of relying on so-called "abstinence education" protects no one because it amounts to little more than religious wishful thinking. Perhaps it is time to actually take the issue of sexual education and its relationship to abortion more seriously. That would require collabortion between healthcare providers, insurance companies, and groups such as Planned Parenthood[21] to install programs and policies that actually help women prevent unwanted pregnancies rather playing the repressive game of treating women as chattel to be controlled or punished by the church and its political allies.

Repression is the cause

It is important that we better understand the forces behind the so-called "pro-life" movement. Repression is the driving force behind the desire to control others, especially on issues such as abortion, a principal flashpoint between religious beliefs and secular law. Repression is, however, a conflicted state of existence because its instincts tend to be singular and all-consuming rather than discerning or considerate. In matters of sexual behavior, the repressive instinct is to emphasize the taboo claims of literalistic scripture in seeking to block all sexual activity except for the procreative act within the confirnes of marriage between a man and a woman. But even that attitude has patriarchal roots and dates back to the period when women, including wives, were considered the property of their husbands or fathers.

That is no longer the case in advanced civilizations. Women are no longer the property of men. Freed from that type of bondage, women are free to make choices about when to have sex and what to do with their own bodies. For the last fifty years in the United States of America has protected the right to legally terminate a pregnancy. Yet that right is now under threat from a Supreme Court whose newest members promised under oath protect established law. They essentially lied to get installed as Supreme Court judges, and are now behaving as judicial activists who overturned abortion rights in America. They are hypocrites in robes, just like the legalistic authorities whom Jesus castigated for their false righteousness thousands of years ago.

Same-sex relationships and gender fluidity

The challenge of honestly acknowledging human sexuality gets even more difficult when religious people try to deny same-sex attraction and gender fluidity. Repression of these realities also stems from the fearful need to control and define the world according to anachronistic and often patriarchal religious beliefs. That's why being gay is branded sinful or impure. It doesn't line up with so-called "traditional" gender roles, passing along the male seed in biblical fashion, and pumping out children at will. Resisting those traditinal roles is what makes repressive people extremely uncomfortable, and often angry.

Rather than just playing a defensive game with repression, some people go on the offensive by persecuting gay people. The reasons for this brand of repression are revealed in a study conducted by Taylor-Francis Online. "Although most religions emphasize that people should respect others, most religions tend to categorize homosexuality as something "unnatural" or "impure" (Yip, 2005).Due to trends of secularization, the influence of religion on individuals' daily lives is argued to have become less prominent, but the general attitude toward homosexuality remains negative in many countries (Adamczyk, 2017; McGee, 2016a, 2016b)."

Religion, especially scripturally literal religion, bears heavy blame for vicious characterizations of gay people as unnatural or sinful. Even some of the most respected figures in Christian history come from repressive roots, and never completely relinquished those instincts.

Ardent repression

Some of our most treasured sections of Sscripture still bear marks of ardent repression. Recall that St. Paul had dark beginning to his religious activism. His work as Saul included persecuting and even killing Christians for their faith. After his conversion experience, he turned his instincts toward defining and controlling the beliefs of others. In chameleonic style, he adapted his controlling nature to write theological to cities and cultures across the Middle East. [21] In social media terms, Paul was guilty of "oversharing" his beliefs across a spectrum of groups and contexts. He was quite desperate to get people to see things his way. What a field day he might have had with access to a program like Facebook or Twitter!

Along the way he was consumed by the problem of controlling some aspect of his own nature along the way. Paul confessed to having a "thorn in his flesh." Was it some physical affliction difficult that vexed him, or was it lust that caused him consternation?

We don't know what thorn in the flesh haunted him, but his prior behavior in persecuting Christians indicates a vicious repressive streak that he could barely control in himself even after his conversion experience.

Let's be honest about his gifts. Despite these struggles, Paul was a genius in many respects. His beautifully written letters contain great insights and wisdom. His observations on the nature of love in 1 Corinthians represent some of the wisest and most wonderful words ever written on the subject. Let's consider them here:

> "Brothers and sisters: Strive eagerly for the greatest spiritual gifts. But I shall show you a still more excellent way. If I speak in human and angelic tongues but do not have love, I am a resounding gong or a clashing cymbal. And if I have the gift of prophecy and comprehend all mysteries and all knowledge; if I have all faith so as to move mountains, but do not have love, I am nothing. If I give away everything I own, and if I hand my body over so that I may boast but do not have love, I gain nothing. Love is patient, love is kind. It is not jealous, is not pompous, it is not inflated, it is not rude, it does not seek its own interests, it is not quick-tempered, it does not brood over injury, it does not rejoice over wrongdoing but rejoices with the truth. It bears all things, believes all things, hopes all things, endures all things. Love never fails."

But here's the kicker: Nothing in that wonderful passage says love exists only between a man and a woman. All those traits of love can be expressed between people of any natural gender, including transgender people,[22] whose sexual orientation is more fluid than Paul, even with his gift of understanding, could hope to comprehend during the age in which he lived. Paul's genuine genius was finding commonality among all people, and we should happily apply those standards to every human being on earth in the modern age. His missive about love demonstrates that love is boundless, not bound together with the twine of willful ignorance, hate, and discrimination. It is sad and unfortunate that so many legalistic Christians refuse to recognize that the power of love is open to all, and that God embraces all people in it.

From apologetics to apologies

The longstanding repressive instincts of the Christian religion have clearly caused more harm than good for millions of people over the ages. There needs to be an apology to all those persecuted or harmed by Christian doctrine used in manipulative or savage forms of repression. There is no reason why contemporary human beings should be expected to live according to the ignorance of old, abusive traditions conceived through ancient repressive filters. It is inexcusable that stiff-necked believers continue their efforts to force the world to live in a past that no longer exists so that they can cling to claims of absolute wisdom, authority, and control over others. They are doing nothing more than playing God and imposing tradition on the rest of us. Jesus didn't tolerate it in the religious authorities of his day. Neither should we tolerate it in religious authorities in our day and age. We need to free ourselves from the grip of this brand of repression. Our intervention on these matters should examine all potential sources of bad theology and the repressively addictive behavior that comes from it. We need to be especially wary of guilt emanating from feelings repression wrought by corrupt and wrongful religious traditions. Only then can we fix the shortcomings inherent in the Christian religion and achieve an honest-to-goodness Kingdom of God on earth.

CHAPTER 15

From repression to oppression

The harsh insanities of Scripture

The Bible often uses hyperbole to make points about morality. There is always danger in taking the legalistic hyperbole in Scripture too literally. When Jesus says we should pluck out an eye than succumb to lust, that's not a literal instruction. Instead, it conveys the seriousness with which we are supposed to regard certain types of sin, especially when it comes to our most destructive drives. We're supposed to put those urges in perspective and avoid acting on them, not dig out an eyeball the first time we experience a moment of lust.

The point here is that the emotional scars of succumbing to lust and causing relationship pain and loss are just as real as physical ones. The "eye" that we're supposed to pluck out is an uncontrolled desire that can lead to adultery and other abuses of trust. That's what Paul was likely talking about with his "thorn in the flesh." Put simply, Scripture tries to protect us from our worst instincts. However, that does not mean walking around in a state of repressive grief or inflicting self-pain to prove some religious point. Jesus never advocated that.

Clean and unclean reality

The world has effectively agreed that many of the repressive laws[1] contained in Scripture are no longer applicable in civil society. For example, we no longer treat women as "unclean" during their monthly menstrual cycle or shun them unfit for social contact. Yet that's what the Bible advocates. That brand of repression would only hold if we stuck to a literal, anachronistic interpretation of the Bible. There are many such examples in the Old Testament, and plenty in the New Testament as well.

Repression leads to Oppression

The formula of scriptural anachronism is clear: repression leads to oppression. As outlined on goodtherapy.org:[2] "Oppression occurs whenever one person exercises authority or power in an unfair, abusive, cruel, or needlessly controlling way. For example, a parent who locks a child in the closet could be said to be oppressing that child. Slavery, the refusal to allow women to inherit and own property, the denial of equal rights to people with disabilities, and the involuntary commitment of people who deviate from social norms are all examples of oppression."

Chocolat truth

Repression and oppression may control certain personality traits for a while, but they often lead to spectacular collapse when people succumb to the conflicting pressures of discipline and pleasure building in their own mind. The movie Chocolat[3] captures the dynamics of repression and oppression playing out in a small European town. The plot centers around the fearful convictions of the town Mayor, who considers the townspeople an unruly domestic stock: "Sheep are not the docile, pleasant creatures of the pastoral idyll," he contends. "Any countryman will tell you that. They are sly, occasionally vicious, pathologically stupid. The lenient shepherd may find his flock unruly, defiant. I cannot afford to be lenient."

This attitude of repressive religious fervor permeates the entire community. A woman named Josephine describes the oppressive atmosphere that requires her to submit to abusive husband named Serge: "You don't misbehave here. It's just not done, did you know that? If you don't go to confession, if you don't... dig your flowerbeds, or if you don't pretend, if you don't pretend... that you want nothing more in your life than to serve your husband three meals a day, and give him children, and vacuum under his ass, then... then you're... then you're crazy."

Later in the story, the arduously religious town mayor succumbs to temptation and gorges himself into a stupor eating sweets after breaking into the local chocolate shop to destroy a tempting window display assembled by the charmingly mysterious character played by Juliette Binoche. The disappearance of the Mayor on Easter Sunday leaves the young priest in town without a sermon topic because the mayor typically dictates it to him. Instead, the young priest speaks from his heart. "I think we can't go around measuring our goodness by what we don't do - by what we deny ourselves, what we resist and who we exclude. I think we've got to measure goodness by what we embrace, what we create, and who we include."

That is one of the most nobly Christian things anyone could say. The honest-to-goodness truth is that repression and oppression are not the the foundational values of the Christian faith. They only produce conflict, especially as repression and oppresson spread through the world of politics, law, and constitutional justice as people pruse ways to make the law conform to their beliefs. Typically, these folks seek out like-minded individuals to confirm their choices, often on the shallowest of premises. As Mark Twain once wrote, "In religion and politics, most people's opinions are gotten secondhand, and unexamined."[3]

Latter-day tribalism

Like-minded groups gravitate to language that affirms their fears or desires. Social media exacerbates this problem. When those channels are manipulated by outside forces seeking to influence elections or foment unrest, the effects upon society are devastating. The domestic terrorist attack on the United States Capitol was a direct result of persistent misinformation campaigns leveraging the tribal instincts of people claiming disenfranchisement at the hands of the government. The people committing acts of domestic terror tried to claim it was an act of protecting liberty and freedom. In reality, it was an act of oppression based on false claims of election fraud. President Trump began his plan by seeking to repress fully counted votes on election night,[4] claiming early in the evening that the results showing him in the lead, and ws therefore the winner. Those claims were false, because a massive number of mail-in and absentee ballots remained to be counted. Those totals determined the actual victor was President Joe Biden by millions of votes..

Turning from a repression tactic to actual oppression of the election outcome, Trump plotted to overturn the election by any means available. He filed lawsuits claiming the election was fraudulent.[5] 99% were thrown out of the courts for lack of evidence. Then vote recounts were demanded, and these turned up no significant fraud either. Trump took to outright lying to foment rage among his supporters. The lie was big enough to capture the collective imagination of Trump's supporters and proved sufficient to create an appetite to overthrow the government. That is how the lie of oppression works. Find a narrative that appeals to the persecution of complex of people dissatisfied with their lot and aim that rage at the target of one's ire. It is a classically fascist tactic, and one that often welcomes religious or corporate company.

The politics of religio-fascism have now expanded to passing bills designed to suppress (oppress) voting rights at every level of government.[6] Trump and the Republicans, with support from religious conservatives and evangelicals, have gaslighted the American populace leveraging the Big Lie about a stolen election while accusing Democrats of being the oppressive force in US politics. This tactic is all too familiar. For the last 2000 years the religio-fascist wing of Christianity gaslighted Jews as the enemy, an aggressive tactic to distract the world from its own oppressive instincts and actions.

Left-wing trajectory

In this quick review of oppressive campaigns present and past, we find have identified bold commonalities among the most conservative branches of politics and religion. Each shares instincts for control, repression and oppression to gain power. There are similar forces on the political left. It can be argued that liberalism has its controlling instincts as well. But while liberal penchants for control are also well documented, these efforts have long sided with the cause of social justice, an approach far more in line with the legacy of Jesus. This tradition is particularly truth in relation to policies upholding civil rights and economic justice. This required a massive shift on the part of Democrat party in America. During the 1930s, Democrats were run by a faction of largely Southern, bigoted zealots[7]. The Democrat party evolved into a political movement led by President Franklin Roosevelt that ultimately pulled American out of the Depression, installed social programs such as Social Security and Medicare, and guided the nation to victory against the axis powers of Nazi Germany and the militaristic empire in Japan. The nation then invested in education for veterans of that war with the GI Bill,[8] leading to a period of growth and prosperity in the 1950s and beyond

The country then moved to the middle with the election of a Republican President Dwight D. Eisenhower, who built the nation's interstate highway system and supported social programs for the large part. Against the grain of many conservatives in the midst of the Korean War, the former General Eisenhower warned against the consuming power of the military-industrial complex. He said, "In the councils of government, we must guard against the acquisition of unwarranted influence, whether sought or unsought, by the military-industrial complex. The potential for the disastrous rise of misplaced power exists, and will persist."[10] In this day and age, those words sound like the proclamation of a devout leftist.

Of course, we now know that his advice was tragically ignored. Both political parties dragged the country into the Vietnam War, an enterprise that cost the nation billions of dollars and thousands of lives. We still didn't learn our lesson. More recently, the USA spent $7T in unbudgeted war expeditures in Iraq and Afghanistan,. The latter invasion lasted a full twenty years. The entire decision to invade Iraq and stay in Afghanistan was foun and accomplished little as the Taliban waited us out and took the country back over within a few weeks of our departure. That folly in the Middle East was the product of a conservative ideology naively imagining that the United States could reform the region around democratic principals.

The disconcerting backstory of America's meddlesome Middle East adventures cynically drew upon the evangelical Christian community's barely disguised hope that such conflagrations close to Israel would lead to the onset of Armageddon and possibly bring about the end of the world according to literalistic scriptural prophecies. That is the ideological hope of Zionism,[11] and as a devout evangelical himself, President Georg W. Bush was largely on board with that brand of thinking. Or at least he did not appear to object to it. His partner in crime, Vice President Dick Cheney, seemed not to care about all the religious stuff. His motives were more about control of oil supplies and profiting his corporate interests including Halliburton and the many contractors serving as mercenaries in the Iraq and Afghanistan theaters. From a biblical perspective, Dick Cheney was cut much more in the mold of the Roman oppressors in ancient Israel willing to collaborate with religious zealots if it ultimately suited his interest in power and complicity. In that regard, Cheney was quite happy to accept any kind of Christian malarkey if it supported his goal of access to profits and supply from Middle Eastern oil markets.

For all their claims of doctrinal integrity, we need only look at the resistance Jesus showed toward the religious and political conservatives of his day to understand whose side he would choose on when it social policies today. The fact that the United States of America invaded Iraq based on governmental lies about Iraq as a threat, then wantonly killed hundreds of thousands of Iraqis during an ill-conceived invastion with zero plans for an exit strategy was bad enough. Then the US military also took political prisoners whom they tortured in the same murderous cells used by Saddam Hussein to threaten and control his citizens. All this was done while Right-wing American interests, including conservative Christians, railed about the threat represented by fundamentalist Islam. The irony could not be any richer, of course. When its actions are fully exposed, American fundamentalism is just as murderous as its counterpart in Islam.

The pattern here is quite familiar. The fearful tactics used by Christians to persecute Islam are esentially the same militantly legalistic motives used to persecute Jews for two thousand years. This is the dishonestly corrupt nature of legalistic Christianity. It is hypocritical in both its denial of Jesus' true legacy and in its claims of innocence in the eyes of God. And it all stems from treating scripture as an infallible source of truth. To bring Christianity and America back to their true and honest origins, we need to fully understand the driving forces behind the methods of legalistic religious and political conservatives. This is easy enough to identify. They both share a belief in treating the foundational texts of their belief systems as perfect and inerrant. Upon thse beliefs, they claim the right to control society...with approval from God.

CHAPTER 16
In originalism we cannot trust

Christian legalists that embrace biblical literalism find great company with political legalists embracing constitutional originalism.[1] Both sets of textual purists believe their documents to be immutable, unchanging sources of truth and conscience. Constitutional originalism is defined as the belief that "all statements in the constitution must be interpreted based on the original understanding of the authors or the people at the time it was ratified."[2]

The thought pattern behind Constitutional originalism directly parallels the tradition of biblical literalism. Much like biblical literalists, constitutional originalists embrace anachronism as the heart of their belief system. The laws of the past are revered as the sole foundation for the future. Yet what we consistently get from these two traditions, especially in combination, is a society divided by cultural conflict, economic injustice, and environmental abuse. We need to understand why this is the case.

Here is one of the basic problems. Constitutional originalism is a conflicted belief system by its mere definition. Back when the Constitution was written, slavery was still an institution, women could not vote, and guns could only shoot perhaps a round a minute. Times were different, and the "original" meaning of those constitutional laws have no place in modern society. Constitutional originalism is a specious farce because it is a contradiction of terms. The constitution was never meant to be a document "fixed in time." The many amendments to the United States Constitution are proof of that. The Founding Fathers knew they did not get everything right the first time on many issues. Neither would they be offended by the fact that the progressive factions of society—of which they were a part in their day—continue pressing for positive changes in civil rights and liberties. These are in keeping with the philosophy of the Constitution and the collective belief that "all are created equal."

Our work on the Constitution is never complete, and never will be. We've abolished slavery, granted minorities and women the right to vote, and expanded civil rights across a number of fronts, but religious and political conservatives keep trying to drag the nation backward. These factions favor discriminatory policies that limit human rights yet granted personhood to corporations through the Citizens United case.

Judicial activism

Not all actions taken to amend the constitution have turned out well. Nor do they respect the supposedly sacrosanct philosophy of constitutional textualism or originalism. Consider the fact that political conservatives chose to discard the Second Amendment call for a "well-regulated militia" to grant essentially unrestricted gun rights to individuals. There are now more guns in America than people, of which more than 20 million fall into the category of military-grade "assault weapons" designed to tear the human body apart. So much for the verity of constitutional originalism and a "well-regulated militia." It's all a lie now.

The Founding Fathers would likely look at judgments such as these and ask, "What the hell are you thinking?" Corporations are people? Individuals can run around the streets of America brandishing military-grade weapons at will? Where is your common sense, people?

To deconstruct originalism, it is important to take a comparative look at the actions the nation has taken to improve the rights originally granted in the Constitution versus decisions causing harm in society. Then we can better understand the gravitas of potential decisions yet to come.

The First Amendment

The First Amendment clarified the scope of civil liberties in America. It includes the Establishment Clause in a phrase that "prohibits Congress from making any law respecting an establishment of religion." That provision more broadly states that Congress shall establish no law "impeding the free exercise of religion, abridging the freedom of speech, infringing on the freedom of the press, interfering with the right to peaceably assemble or prohibiting the right to petition the government."

The First Amendment to the United States Constitution specifically confronted the traditions of repression and oppression that plagued societies throughout history. The "Establishment Clause"[2] provides for the Separation of Church and State. That specific ban on installing a state religion was critical to achieving the entire list of rights that followed. That provision that is vital in protecting people from being forced to participate in a religion or its beliefs in any way. The reason for that specificity is that all religions bear aspects of tribalism leading to discrimination against others.

Despite this explicit declaration against theocratic rule, many Christians still like to claim that America is a "Christian nation"[3] on the grounds that their faith was the dominant belief system at the time the country was established. The website Americans United for a Separation of Church and State[4] contains a clear smackdown of this notion. "The U.S. Constitution is a wholly secular document. It contains no mention of Christianity or Jesus Christ. The Constitution refers to religion only twice in the First Amendment, which bars laws "respecting an establishment of religion or prohibiting the free exercise thereof," and in Article VI, which prohibits "religious tests" for public office. Both provisions are evidence that the country was not founded as officially Christian."

On these grounds, one would think that constitutional originalists would be the people challenging persistent claims that America is a Christian nation. Instead, we often find an alliance between biblical literalists and constitutional originalists whose mutual attraction to literal textualism makes them "blood relatives" in a rhetorical and active sense. Nowhere is that 'blood relationship' more evident than the constitutionalist originalists' interpretation of the Second Amendment.

The Second Amendment

Just as biblical legalists love to emphasize certain aspects of scripture while ignoring others, constitutional originalists love to cherry pick the parts of the Constitution they favor while dismissing those deemed inconvenient to their selfish interests. That is certainly the case with the Second Amendment, whose first phrase reads, "A well-regulated militia, being necessary for the security of a free state…"

Here's the honest-to-goodness take on this phrase. Initially, the purpose for permitting citizens to own guns was to arm the populace in the event of war with a foreign nation. At that time, state militias would be called upon to help protect national interests. By strict definition of the term, militias are no longer the method by which the nation provides a defense or conducts wars. That fighting system was replaced by a federal military whose Commander-in-Chief is the President of the United States. Yet even without the citizen-based need for a "well-regulated militia," the first phase of the Second Amendment should not be tossed aside. It remains essential for the "security of a free state" to govern the manner in which guns are purchased, owned, used, and distributed among the populace. In recent years, the purpose of a "well-regulated militia has shifted to concerns over the level of military-level firepower available to individual citizens and the damage they can inflict upon society within seconds of opening fire in public spaces.The frequency of deadly mass shootings means that call for a "well-regulated militia, being necessary for the security of a free state…" is now more important than ever, but for new reasons.

Our nation is also struggling to manage the balance between the total number of guns owned by Americans and the enforcement of law in the United States. Even the police are under siege due to an essentially unregulated proliferation of deadly weapons in the United States where guns now outnumber people. Police are forced to react with deadly force in order to protect their own lives. As a result, the popular meme Blue Lives Matter means nothing if the United States refuses to control an essentially unregulated militia able to outgun law enforcement at will.

Organizations such as the NRA thumb their noses at gun regulation even as mass shootings persist. We've witnessed schoolchildren being gunned down in classrooms,[4] worshipers shot in cold blood inside their church, temples and mosques, [5] and conconcertgoers mowed down by a gunman firing down on them from a tall building.[6] Each of these shooters had their "reasons" to kill, and easily got their hands on powerful grade weapons to carry out their mission. The gunman at Sandy Hook killed twenty-nine elementary schools kids in under four minutes.[7] None of these incidents speaks to a well-regulated militia. What they do illustrate is the utter insanity of constitutional originalism as a belief system. No other developed country in the world suffers the rates of gun violence and suicide found in the United States. All because constitutional originalism has allowed to run amok by conservative courts and whorish politicians taking campaign contributions from gun lobbyists.

The notion of what even constitutes a well-regulated "militia" has undergone radical interpretations since the Second Amendment was written more than two hundred years ago. A teenager named Kyle Rittenhouse acted as if he was part of a militia fighting civil unrest in Kenosha, Wisconsin during the Black Lives Matter protests aimed at raising awareness about racist police practices. Rittenhouse showed up in the city carrying an AR-15 style rifle and was either ignore or encouraged by local police to play at being a soldier on duty. But when Rittenhouse was chased down the street by people seeking to disarm him, he panicked and shot two people dead and injured another. In the wake of these acts of vigilante stupidity, he claimed 'self-defense' and faced little penalty for his murderous ways. Nothing about his actions exemplifies the defintion of a "well-regulated militia," yet Rittenhouse suffered little legal consequence and actually received financial support from radical right-wing gun proponents eager to defend him from any sort of prosecution for his gun-toting ways. Between the mass shootings and other gun crimes, the threats toward our government from right-wing militias, and the January 6, 2020 insurrection in which democracy almost fell to radicals showing defiance toward our own constitution, we must face the fact that the United States of America is facing a war from within, and the sick part of the formula is that so many Christians side with the radicalism responsible for these threats against the republic.

War on America

The effects of this war on America are real. American citizens die every day due to variouse kinds of gun violence. The BradyUnited.org website[8] reports that, on average, there are 316 gunshot victims per day in the United States. One hundred six people are shot and killed. 39 are murdered, 69 die from gun suicide. 90 are shot unintentionally and survive. Every day, 22 children and teens (1-17) are shot in America.

On an annual basis, more than 115,000 people per year get hurt by gunshots. 14,000+ are murdered. More than 24,000 die by gun suicide. In addition, 547 women are killed by their husband or male dating partner. Nearly 39,000 people die each year from gun violence, and in 2020, that number topped 41,000. The number one cause of death for children in America is now gun violence.

Nothing about these gun statistics suggests that the United States of America is paying attention to the "security of a free state" as defined by the Second Amendment. One notable statistic is that more people in the United States of America have died from gun violence on their own soil than all the military personnel killed in foreign wars.[9]

Despite these facts and the long spate of mass murders occuring almost daily in American society, gun proponents refuse to accept that the 'right to bear arms' is too vague an interpretation of the Second Amendment, especially in a county where the estimated 363 million firearms now outnumbers the human population by almost 30 million guns. With that kind of availability, it is inevitable that some irresponsible will get their hands on weapons, and mayhem ensues.

Yet ardent gun proponents claim that even more guns are necessary to reduce the impact of gun-related crimes. That vigilante mindset is captured in the colloquial phrase, "The only thing to stop a bad buy with a gun is a good guy with a gun." That means we're supposed to revert to a Wild West system in which vigilantes carrying weapons are the public's primary defense against being shot in public. But even 300+ police and SWAT team members on the scene at the Uvalde school shooting in 2022 refused to engage with a single mass shooter killing children and teachers at will. The gun lobby is gaslighting Americans by preaching the "good guy with a gun" narrative. It doesn't work, and it never will. The only way to preven mass shootings with military-grade assault rifles is to ban these weapons for public ownership.

Likewise, the only way to protect the public from rampant gun violence is to redefine the concept of a "well-regulated militia" and amend the language in modern terms. Otherwise, we're all vulnerable to the distorted and perverse notion that vigilante law is the only dependable form of public safety in the United States of America.

Illegal guns

Admittedly, many of the weapons used to commit shootings and crimes exist outside the "trackable" world of technology and data. These undocumented weapons are the real "illegal aliens" living in America. These are trafficked and sold on the streets and through other illegal channels. This overflow supply of weapons renders existing gun control laws useless in the face of the flood of guns covering America. A Chicago Tribune story[10] in September, 2021 documented that a handgun stolen from a gun shop in Wisconsin has been used to commit more than 27 murders in the city.

But what if most guns actually were "well-regulated?" We have GPS units in our phones and vehicles, and a great percentage of us are personally tracked wherever we go in our daily business. Insurance companies are even allowed to install safe-driving sensors in our vehicles. So when it comes to guns, we should install GPS tracking units in every gun sold in America. A signal should be given when the weapon is engaged or fired outside a gun range. That data alone can be a deterrent for rampant gun use. The penalty for removing a gun-tracking device should include enormous financial fines and a minimum jail term significant enough to deter tampering under any situation.

Law-abiding gun owners should welcome measures this kind. They do not infringe on the right to bear arms. They merely emphasize the responsibility involved. The Constitutional call for a "well-regulated militia" clearly states that the government has a right to know exactly who owns guns and how they are used. That is quite precisely what a 'well-regulated militia' means these days.

If Concealed Carry laws really matter, then it is more important than ever to track individual weapons and their use. Surely the technology exists to track every shot fired from a gun, which would help police in crime scenes and reconstructing the events of a murder or gun accident? We'd always know who shot first, and even from what range they fired their weapons. As for Open Carry, the only people that require that to protect their person are the terminally fearful and unaware, If they can't recognize danger using common sense, they need social and civic education, not weaponry to exist safely in society.

The influence of technology impacts all of our lives. We engage with it from the Internet to the number of hamburgers or tacos we buy with our debit cards. It's far past time to apply regulatory technology in every gun owned in Americans. Even military bases don't allow personnel to pack weapons on their person while on base. Only when those personnel go on active duty are the guns distributed. What does that say about the existence of a 'well-regulated militia' in the United States of America There is no reason why our nation should expect the streets we live on to be more dangerous than a military zone in some far-flung part of the world.

Pro-life, or just pro-gun?

These statistics raise the question of why there is not more of a Christian outcry when so many lives get taken by gun violence every year? Unfortunately, the answer is buried beneath conservative political alliances and moneyed interests that refuse to be challenged on the issue. Add in the complicity of a Supreme Court dominated by constitutional originalists, and the goal of accomplishing a "well-regulated militia" doed seem far off. But it is the complicity of conservative Christians on rampant gun ownership that is most confounding. Despite the horrific toll of gun violence in America, some people still attempt to justify their belief in guns from a supposedly Christian perspective. Such is the case with Larry Pratt,[11] the executive director emeritus of Gun Owners of America.

In a 2018 Daily Beast[12] story, Pratt shared his perspective on why Christians have the right to own guns. The article asks: "So which is it? Does he (Jesus) want the disciples to defend themselves with swords (guns, for the modern Christian) or not? Larry Pratt, the executive director emeritus of Gun Owners of America believes he does. According to Pratt, the Second Amendment's statement that "the right of the people to keep and bear Arms, shall not be infringed" is literal and sanctioned by God. "The Founders considered that self-defense and the ownership and carrying of guns is a God-given right," Pratt tells The Daily Beast. "And there is a basic principle regarding the protection of life found in the Book of Proverbs [25:26]: "Like a muddied spring or a polluted well are the righteous who give way to the wicked."'

It is clear that Pratt is willing to dispense with any real pretense of morality to justify gun ownership. His statements demonstrate how biblical literalism and constitutional originalism are will to stretch the verity of any Proverb to suit their purpose. These bits of twisted theology only confuse issues of conscience, especially when they converge in equally selfish and corrupt aims.

Rogue militias and the Serpent of death

Even more disruptive to the "security of a free state" is the growing faction of anti-government, unregulated militias actively threatening to overthrow the United States government.[13] These groups claim to fight what they perceive as governmental tyranny, specifically over the right to bear arms. The threat posed by these groups is not idle. For example, members of several high-profile militias participated in the January 6, 2021, insurrection attack on the United States Capitol building.[14] This seditious activity demonstrates the perverse effect of selective thinking on the part of constitutional originalists that celebrate the "right to bear arms" over the call for a "well-regulated militia." The truth is that the Second Amendment has been turned around and aimed at the government and the people it was originally designed to protect.

Constitutional originalists claiming sacrosanct status for the "right to bear arms" depend on the half-truth of ignoring the first half of the amendment to preach the second. That is a deception designed to bully Americans into accepting radially reduced notions of public safety. But the outcomes of those calculations mean death for thousands of people each year. The current interpretation of the Second Amendment is a crime against humanity.

Because here's how it works. Constitutional originalists and their partners in crime, the "textualists,"[15] have turned the Second Amendment into a self-fulfilling prophecy by claiming an ever-greater need to own guns for self-defense. Now there are so many guns in America that people need guns to protect themselves from other people with guns. That dangerous tautology is the cause behind thousands of deaths and mass shootings that now occur with depressing frequency. To make matters worse in moral terms, the close alliance between constitutional originalists and biblical literalists is the devil's bargain producing all these injuries, suicides, and deaths from gun's violence. In biblical terms, America has listened to the hissing voice of the Serpent promising greater knowledge of good and evil if more Americans take up guns as a sign of God's Providence. "You will not surely die," the Serpent whispers again. And the half-truth of legalistic religion lives on. It is far past time for Americans to engage in a reality check on the issue of guns alone. Gun addiction and the violence it produces is an epidemic.

Times change

Guns are far from the only issue on which Christian legalists and constitutional originalists conspire for selfish purposes. But Christians on the right side of history have always fought back against the legalistic cabal of calculating religion.

To demonstrate the value of these efforts, we'll review the gains made in civil rights as proof there is hope in this game of politics and religion, even though it often swings like a pendulum. As documented on History.com,[16] both the abolitionist movement and Prohibition were in part driven by religious belief, "In the 1820s and '30s, a wave of religious revivalism swept the United States, leading to increased calls for temperance, as well as other "perfectionist" movements such as the abolitionist movement to end slavery."

The disparate outcomes between these two social movements show the difficulty in applying strictly Christian beliefs to civil law. As we'll see, while slavery is a violation of human rights under any moral law, and was eventually banned in America, there were many Christian voices on the Confederate side quoting the Bible as evidence that slavery was justified under the direction of God. The same brand of confusion and conflict occurred over the issue of "temperance," the effort to ban alcohol use in the United States. Confusiong over religious beliefs drove both of these conflict, which is why the Founding Fathers blocked Establishment of a state religion through the First Amendment. It's plain to see that as a collective, Christians often have no better grasp of morality than any other group.

So let's dig into the subject of slavery to help us understand the conflicted state of mind created by Christianity and the corresponding impact of bad theology in the American experiment. When abolitionists began to question the merits of slavery in relation to human equality, it was bad Christian theology that served to justify the institution of slavery in America.

Justifying slavery through Christianity

The website historyengine.richmond.edu[15] describes it this way: "Slave owners had many justifications for why holding people in bondage was acceptable. From the idea that African Americans were a lesser race who needed taking care of by white patriarchs to the economic justification, slave owners were always trying to find new ways to dispute those who disagreed with their choice to hold others in captivity. Charleston slaveholders were no exception in attempting to find justifications to mask their guilt. Often, religion came into play, on both the slavery and anti-slavery sides of the debate. In 1835, at the end of two long articles about religion and slavery in the Charleston Mercury, it was said that both the Old and New Testament give permission to hold others as slaves. In the Old Testament, God and the Patriarchs approve. As for the New Testament, Jesus and the Apostles show that slavery is permissible. Therefore, slavery, to those who wrote the article, was not an anti-Christian institution. It was just the opposite. Furthermore, they added, it is impious to say slavery is anti-Christian because such a conclusion contradicted God."

Abolitionists fought back with their take on scripture. Author Rebecca Graf outlines their methods in her Medium column titled "Abolitionists Use Scripture to Support Their Cause."[16] She wrote:

"Abolitionists turned to the Bible just as quickly as those who defended slavery. The chancellor of Protestant University, William Wilson, stated that slavery was "at war with the image of God in which man was created" as it treats other humans as less than human as God created him and lowering the person to property. God made man in His image. He shaped Adam and his descendants and gave them a soul from His own breath. While supporters trumpeted that God ordained slavery, Wilson shot back, "It is at war with the written law of God....Shame on those lips which, in the name of Christianity and its Holy Ministry, have ever, for any consideration, attempted to vindicate or palliate slavery from the Book of God!"

The faction of moral folks calling themselves abolitionists persisted in their attempts to get slavery banned in the United States. Ultimately it took the Civil War to accomplish that task. As a result, the 13th Amendment ultimately read, "Neither slavery nor involuntary servitude, except as a punishment for crime whereof the party shall have been duly convicted, shall exist within the United States, or any place subject to their jurisdiction." Even that Amendment did not complete the task of granting full rights of United States citizenship to black Americans. It took another Amendment to the Constitution to accomplish the next step. As noted on history.com

"After the Civil War, the 15th Amendment, ratified in 1870, prohibited states from denying a male citizen the right to vote based on "race, color or previous condition of servitude." Nevertheless, in the ensuing decades, various discriminatory practices were used to prevent African Americans, particularly those in the South, from exercising their right to vote."

For all the back and forth it took to end slavery in the United States, the sum total of lives lost during the Civil War go on the ledger sheet of bad theology and its Confederate allies, whose biblically literal interpretation of scripture and its outright racist notions of white superiority as a "Chosen People of God" were responsible for their wrongheaded justification of human slavery. Sadly, even after the Civil War, rampant forms of bigotry continued across the nation. These were driven by the same brands of corrupt 'biblical' beliefs about white privilege and the right to rule supreme over all other people.

Jim Crow and the KKK

Following the Civil War, much of the nation continued down a prejudicial path through the enactment of Jim Crow laws,[17] mainly across the South, where racial segregation ruled supreme. Unfortunately, even these remnants of slavery and the discriminatory evils of segregation were not harsh enough for some white supremacists. The persecution of African Americans rose to violent fury under the guidance of the Ku Klux Klan,[18] the racist organization claiming Christian roots[19] while advocating white supremacy under claims of being the Chosen People of God. Thousands of black United States citizens were tortured and lynched by white mobs seeking vengeance for whatever reason they could concoct to persecute black Americans.

Bad Christian theology justified the violence. Looking back at the roots of the KKK, a Washington Post story titled "A White Preacher Used the Bible to Revive the Klu Klux Klan"[20] explains how some white Americans used the Bible to justify prejudice and hate. "Klan members believe "the Bible is the family history of the white race," according to the report. "They believe that white Christians are morally and spiritually superior to other races."

The article also noted: "With the help of a public relations team, headed by Edward Clarke and Elizabeth Tyler, the Klan's rosters exploded. "The popularity came from the combination of religion and nationalism it promoted, both of which appealed to white Protestant Americans who feared that immigration and changing social mores would overthrow their social dominance," wrote Baker.

The same themes are resounding in America to this day. The question remains whether America has the will to fully challenge white supremacists. The nation is frequently slow to recognize the potency of these forces, and the need to act against them.

Hope and tragedy

For most of the first half of the 20th century through World War II and into the 1950s, much of black America lived with the scourge of institutionalized racism.[21] Yet black voices began to penetrate this insanity, leading to civil rights protests that were eventually joined by white Americans determined to demand liberty for all. Nevertheless, it took nearly two hundred years for America to move from the era in which some of the Founding Fathers owned slaves to the point where an American president signed full civil rights into law.

As described on History.com,[22] "The Civil Rights Act of 1964, which ended segregation in public places and banned employment discrimination on the basis of race, color, religion, sex or national origin, is considered one of the crowning legislative achievements of the civil rights movement. First proposed by President John F. Kennedy, it survived strong opposition from southern members of Congress and was then signed into law by Kennedy's successor, Lyndon B. Johnson. In subsequent years, Congress expanded the act and passed additional civil rights legislation such as the Voting Rights Act of 1965."

Yet the forces of racism still sought to inflict more pain. The 1968 assassination of Christian minister Dr. Martin Luther King[23] signaled that factions of America still harbored hate for black civil rights leaders. Perhaps it was too much to expect that America was ready to accept that a man with Dr. King's Christian insight was African-American. He identified the imperfections in us all with insights rich in honest theology:

> "We must develop and maintain the capacity to forgive. He who is devoid of the power to forgive is devoid of the power to love. There is some good in the worst of us and some evil in the best of us. When we discover this, we are less prone to hate our enemies.
>
> -Martin Luther King Jr

King also indicted the fearful need to feel superior to others: "I refuse to accept the view that mankind is so tragically bound to the starless midnight of racism and war that the bright daybreak of peace and brotherhood can never become a reality... I believe that unarmed truth and unconditional love will have the final word."

-Martin Luther King Jr.

These inspiring words reached into the hearts of many. Yet during the period in which Dr. King's murder took place, President Richard M. Nixon was quick to accuse black culture of the militancy and civil unrest that arose in the wake of King's demise. In fearful response, Nixon moved to arm the nation's law enforcement personnel with military-grade arsenals. A 2018 article in The Guardian[29] chronicled the vengeance behind its response. "In the wake of the riots suburban gun purchases skyrocketed, and Nixon, through the Law Enforcement Assistance Administration, funneled money to police departments to buy exotic anti-riot weaponry: body armor, tear gas, even surplus tanks. As a result, by the early 1970s, an anti-riot urban infrastructure was in place, one that psychologically, bureaucratically, and even physically severed the ghetto from the rest of the city, and the city in turn from the suburbs."

This initial move to militarize the police in response to racial discord contributed to the perpetual problem of racism within police ranks that persists to this day. The video of a white police officer kneeling on the neck of a helpless George Floyd until he died of asphyxiation on May 25, 2020 led to a high-profile Black Lives Matter protests that escalated into property destruction and violence as anti-fascist (Antifa) demonstrators took demonstrations to a dangerous level. Yet one can't view their actions out of context, because the violence was committed in response to violence. Some might even view these actions as a defense response to the institutional racism and government tyranny launched by Nixon way back in the 1970s.

Missing in action is any Christian conservative call for the value of all lives. Instead, the Blue Lives Matter 'movement' drew the Back The Blue claim that it was police who are the real victims of societal violence. That is certainly true, but that requires a reality check as well. The principal reason police lives are at risk in America is gun proliferation. Officers in blue face the prospect of being shot in the line of duty every day. That's because there are so many guns in America

The corrupt strategy of attacking minorities or people of color and then blaming them for offering resistance has a long history in America. That was the main tactic used to enforce a belief system known as Manifest Destiny, the claim that America was destined by Providence to be a Promised Land for white settlers as Chosen People of God.

> **Andrea Junker**
> @Strandjunker
>
> I've said it once, and I'll say it a thousand times: There are three branches of government. Your church is not one of them.

CHAPTER 17

Echoes of manifest destiny

It was bad Christian that helped drive the nation to the Civil War over the issue of slavery. That same belief in white supremacy also fueled the worldview of Manifest Destiny, an all-encompassing belief system that led to the theft of land and life from Native Americans across the North American continent.

A story on History.com[1] describes it this way: "Manifest Destiny, a phrase coined in 1845, is the idea that the United States is destined—by God, its advocates believed—to expand its dominion and spread democracy and capitalism across the entire North American continent. The philosophy drove 19th-century U.S. territorial expansion and was used to justify the forced removal of Native Americans and other groups from their homes."

The effects of that onslaught were devastating. In what amounted to the American brand of genocide, millions of indigenous people succumbed to attacks wrought through invasion of territory, wars and disease. Native American leader Chief Pontiac spoke the painful truth about how Manifest Destiny contributed to this carnage. "They came with a Bible and their religion, stole our land, crushed our spirit... and now tell us we should be thankful to the 'Lord' for being saved."[2]

The ways of inhumanity

The level of lies and deception used to trick Native Americans out of their tribal lands and impose the doctrine of Manifest Destiny requires volumes to document, but we can summarize here. Between treaties[3] made and broken, aggressive military campaigns, and the slaughter of bison by the millions, white Americans invaded and devastated the West, all while claiming God was on their side.

The destruction of nature across the continent also steamrolled as business interests quickly exploited resources from the Mississippi River west to the Pacific Coast. The Gold Rush drove yet another massive land grab, providing a shiny excuse to invade Indian lands with the full backing of the U.S. government. As noted on GreenBiz.org,[4] "During the U.S. gold rush, U.S. hydraulic mining operations in California completely denuded forested landscapes, altered the course of rivers, increased sedimentation that clogged riverbeds and lakes and released enormous amounts of mercury onto the landscape. California wildcat miners used an estimated 10 million pounds of mercury from the 1860s through the early 1900s. Most of it was released to the environment as tailings and mercury vapor."

The environmental costs of each wave of new expansion and exploitation were huge. Right on the heels of the bison slaughter, market hunters shot billions of Passenger Pigeons until the species went extinct, hunted out of existence by the early 1900s.[5]

Prairie plant and animal communities that once dominated the American Midwest and West were also wiped out within a generation. Millions of prairie acres were plowed under within fifty years, exposing soils that took ten thousand years to form in the wake of the Ice Age. By the time the 1900s arrived, just 1/10th of one percent of the original prairie remained in states such as Illinois.[6] The destruction of the prairie simultaneously eradicated billions of insects and birds, mammals and reptiles, elk and bear, fish, and the amphibians dependent on prairie ecosystems for survival. The prairie went from abundant wilderness and extensive wetland ecosystems to a homogenous landscape crushed under the thumb of human dominion, replaced by farm fields and barbed wire fences. Now, one hundred years later, the agriculture industry is anxiously wringing its hands over the soil loss it largely caused.[7]

People once raved that prairie soils were the best farmland on earth, a sign that Providence had smiled upon them. Yet those soils suffered a fate of biblical proportions as aggressive tilling exposed every inch of loose ground. Within a single human generation, the driving forces of wind and rain erosion stripped away what nature took so long to build. Soils that once stood six or eight feet deep washed downstream to the Gulf of Mexico. This is the modern agricultural lament, that U.S. farmers have exhausted the most valuable soil resource on earth. So much for the notion that human dominion over the earth has automatically providential benefits.

A February 2021 story on NRP.org[8] titled "New Evidence Shows Fertile Soil Gone from Midwestern Farms" bluntly states what many people have surmised. "Farming has destroyed a lot of the rich soil of America's Midwestern prairie. A team of scientists just came up with a staggering new estimate of just how much has disappeared. The most fertile topsoil is entirely gone from a third of all the land devoted to growing crops across the upper Midwest, the scientists say." The story observes that a simple flyover of the Midwest shows that the dark topsoil best suited to growing crops, known as A-horizon soil, is now gone, lost to wind and soil erosion. The effects are most visible on rolling hills where pale soil sits open like a bald spot on the head of a middle-aged man."

The article notes, "Farmers already know that these eroded hilltops are less productive, and many of them are looking for solutions. "We're essentially trying to make up for many years of fairly thoughtless practices," she says.

The Cowboy legend

The wholesale conversion of rangeland to cattle and sheep ranches prospered around the legend of independent cowboys driving cattle and whistling their way into history. Unfortunately, that legend has had extensive costs as unrestricted grazing by cattle and sheep stripped native plants and grasses down to the nub. Over a century, this disturbance of the natural land dynamic allowed invasive species to take over much of the arid lands west of the 100th Meridian. The process occurred from human intrusion, according to GlobalRangelands.com:[9] "Humans have both intentionally and accidentally introduced many non-native plants and animals to Western rangelands. Some of them have produced benefits for humans while remaining under management control. Others have escaped and "gone wild" with unintended negative consequences. While we can debate the degree to which any particular exotic plant or organism has a right to exist on Western rangelands, one thing is for certain. Some of these plants and animals are spreading like wildfires and have become serious threats to the environment, human health, and economic well-being."

The article elaborates on the nature of the problem: "Invasive species are plants, animals, or insects that have evolved elsewhere and have been purposely or accidentally moved to a new location. Some have invaded habitats by themselves. However, human exploration, colonization, and commercial trade have dramatically increased the diversity, scale, and impact of the invasions. Introduced species often find no natural enemies in their new habitat and therefore spread quickly and easily."

The devastation taking place out West is however being fixed through collaboration between organizations like the Audubon Society and ranchers willing to work together in a market-based solution called conservation ranching. But there's a long way to go in working with ranchers claiming the right to graze cattle free of charge on federal lands. They do so at the expense of the American taxpayer, so their perception of independence is not accurate. The alternative is grain-fed beef and other forms of meat, and these forms of food production have an enormous cost, especially when it comes to water rights.

Water rights

The issue of western water rights is especially divisive. According to the USDA.gov website,[10] "Agriculture is a major user of ground and surface water in the United States, accounting for approximately 80 percent of the Nation's consumptive water use and over 90 percent in the many Western States." One of the harsh facts driving that figure is that more than 80%[11] of the freshwater used in America goes toward growing crops to support meat production.

The organization mercyforanimals.org[12] adds to that operative by sharing sobering statistics about the amount of water used in raising animal products: "According to data from the Pacific Instituteand National Geographic, a single egg takes 53 gallons of water to produce, a pound of chicken 468 gallons, a gallon of cow's milk 880 gallons, and a pound of beef 1,800 gallons."

Even as agriculture scarfs up billions of gallons of fresh water, its carbon footprint is believed to contribute significantly to global warming and climate change. One of the consequences of climate change is a marked increase in flooding, which further damages soils in critical areas near rivers and streams. Persistent flooding leads to grounds starved for oxygen. That leads to crop die-offs, planting delays, and soil leaching as flood runoff sucks out minerals and microbial allies that contribute to soil productivity.

Meanwhile, climate change is expected to generate increasingly arid conditions in formerly temperate zones. America has previously seen the consequences of that dynamic in the era known as the Dust Bowl.

The Dust Bowl

In one of the greatest environmental deceptions in world history, the United States government promised Great Plains settlers in the early 1900s that "rain would follow the plow." The belief was that somehow nature would bend to human will, a vestigial remnant of the notion of divine providence at work. The result was a devastating period known as The Dust Bowl.[13] As described on the Foundation for Economic Education website,[14] it was terrible policy that contributed to America's already troubled status. "In the 1930s, in addition to dealing with the Great Depression that had much of the industrialized world in its grip, Americans, particularly in the Plains States, were also coping with the Great Dust Bowl, considered the greatest single human-caused environmental catastrophe in the country's history. Though the Depression still looms larger in the American mind, the Dust Bowl was no less traumatic or devastating for those who lived through it, and, like the economic crisis, it transformed American society as thousands of people lost their farms, their way of life, and, in some cases, even their lives."

The ruse was essentially an extension of the concept behind Manifest Destiny and the belief that God somehow willed ownership of the

American landscape to white European settlers, a hubris that made people think that nothing could go wrong. Government propaganda led to homesteaders carving up the soils of the Great Plains to plant crops. The strategy succeeded briefly, but collapsed when arid western soils ill-suited to raw tillage turned to fine dust.

The level of devastation that took place during the Dust Bowl seemed beyond belief when it was happening. Those engulfed in the waste and fury felt like victims of biblical destruction. Indeed, the website Our Rabbi Jesus[15] and its author Lois Tverberg describes it this way, "For several years, massive dust storms blackened the sky for days at a time. They called them "black blizzards" because at times (they) were so blinding that you couldn't see even a few feet in front of you. In addition, livestock died from dust inhalation, and farm buildings were buried in several feet of dirt."

The story continues, "Exodus commentaries point out that this is likely what the plague of darkness was when Egypt experienced three days of darkness that could be touched. (Exodus 10:21-22). Dust is "touchable" darkness. The Middle East occasionally experiences dust storms like Oklahoma in the '30s. I've experienced the more mild hamsim more than once in Israel, when a hot east wind from off the Sahara fills the sky with dust, turning it brownish-grey."

The Bible shares many such instances in which God either seems to have abandoned the world or actively participated in its devastation. Scripture gives God is given credit for these devastating events in history, but it is just as likely that the Egyptian plagues of frogs or locusts, even a river turned the color of blood—are the product of natural systems pushed to extremes by climatic or other conditions, including human activities. The nine plagues that afflicted Egypt were likely caused by overuse of the environment, resulting in ecosystem disturbances. Scripture leverages these ancient natural disasters to claim God's work in action, but the source of these events is really not the issue. In all circumstances, people need learn to change their ways or bad things happen. .

Perhaps God and nature are trying to teach the world a lesson these days? There are certainly enough moral reasons why God might choose to punish the United States of America. Its many sins include the slave trade, the genocide of Native Americans, and the outright and ongoing rape of the land for short-term interests. Each of these abuses of humanity and the environment constitute outcomes of essentially biblical scale. With tales and traditions like those at the heart of the nation's formation, perhaps we ought to consider the idea that God is displeased with the incivilities imposed on the world by the United States of America? According to scripture, no one is immune from God's ultimate judgment. No person. No nation. Not even God's favored servants are spared the rod when God makes decisions. For example, when King David asked to build a temple to honor God, he was denied.

"But God said to me, "You are not to build a house for my Name, because you are a warrior and have shed blood.› (1 Chronicles 3)

In other words, God told David, "You have too much blood on your hands." The same might be said of a "Christian nation" where the supposed "servants of God" enslaved, tortured, and killed millions of people. That sobering comparison raises the question of whether some contrition and a reality check is due in the current era? Could climate change be the long-prophesied apocalyptic punishment for a world gone out of control? It is time, as John the Baptist once called out from the wilderness, for a call to honest-to-goodness repentance.

CHAPTER 18

Cause and effect

To answer the question of whether God is using nature to punish the world, we need to take a realistic look at the events we call natural disasters or "acts of God." Earth history is filled with incidents such as volcanic eruptions, floods, droughts, tornadoes, hurricanes, earthquakes, and even asteroid strikes that drove massive extinctions. These natural cataclysms shaped the world and its diverse life forms. Some choose to call these events an "Act of God" because their scale and impact are so sudden or massive that we feel moved to describe them in supernatural terms. Yet not all cataclysmic events have natural causes. We live now in the anthropogenic age,[1] the first period in history when human beings have the proven capacity to produce major effects on the planet.

Anthropogenic change

The world is witnessing an increasing number of natural disasters whose cause and severity are directly traceable to human activities. Our impacts on the environment are well documented. Increased frequency and intensity of storms and droughts, floods and heatwaves, tornadoes, hurricanes, and sea levels on the rise. All these climatic effects were accurately projected years ago by scientists studying the possible impacts of climate change. These predictions are based on data, not biblical prophecies. Science warned us that Earth's overall capacity to repair and replenish itself in the face of human onslaught is being exhausted. That means we must take responsibility for them, not blame God for our stupidity.

Given the wide range of deleterious human activity on the planet, one could logically argue that humanity is a plague all its own. The world's human population currently stands at more than 7 billion people. The United Nations[2] projects that the human population will reach 9.8 billion people by 2050 and 11.2 billion by 2100.[3] Therefore, we need to ask a serious question: at what point does the human toll on the planet reach a tipping point? Will God allow humans to wipe themselves off the face of the Earth? Or worse yet, is God mad enough and is nature disturbed enough by humanity to wipe us all out? In biblical terms, might God say, "Screw the Rainbow Promise. These stiff-necked, selfish people have no respect for creation. Let's let creation engage in some payback…"

The Earth groans

There are many ways that the Earth's capacity to sustain life and replenish itself is being severely tested in the early part of the new millennium. Fish stocks around the world are suffering steady depletion. Coral reefs that act as fish breeding grounds are dying due to ocean warming. Plastic waste and microplastics clog the ocean, killing fish and cetaceans that ingest it. Nuclear radiation emanating from Japan's damaged Fukushima power plant spreads across the Pacific. Drought-driven fires in Australia and North America burn millions of acres. Fires set in Brazil's Amazon jungles to clear rainforest for agriculture rob the world of oxygen-producing trees and plants. The planet is groaning under the burden of sustaining human consumption and greed and still we find religious zealots claiming "only God could do that."

These are all the outcomes of human influence over the environment. In combination, they threaten the existence of life itself. That is an insult to what we call God's creation. Yet, some people still insist that humanity is incapable of affecting creation at that scale.[4] That claim is made on the grounds of dominionism,[5] the religious belief that humanity owns the right to use the earth as it pleases. The sick truth is that a host of willing allies is eager to exploit and profit from that belief and leverage the supposed authority that comes with that opinion.

The alliance of lousy theology and selfish ideology

Despite clear signs that human beings are at painful odds with creation and God, there exists an alliance of religious, political, and commercial interests that persistently denies any suggestion that human activities cause environmental problems on a global scale. "It's simply not possible for human beings to affect creation that way," the so-called logic goes. "Only God could do that."

One of the loudest and most persistent of these voices was the king of denial on shallow premises, the late Rush Limbaugh.[6] His blog in August 2019, written before he died of lung cancer following years of smoking (irony?) exemplified the brand of cloying ignorance he wielded as a weapon against concepts he disdained on ideological grounds. Limbaugh stated: "The climate has been up and down how many ways with ice ages, where North America used to be overrun by ice? The only debate is whether advanced capitalist lifestyles cause these problems? That's what these people want us to adopt, and that's bull. The idea that is expanding the life span, increasing the standard of living, this is what's destroying the climate? It's a crock. But nobody denies the climate's constantly in flux, and nobody should deny there's nothing we can do about it."

"We can't make it hotter; we can't make it colder. Do you know at PBS they think that I am dangerous because I said that? They did a whole segment on how stupid and dumb Rush Limbaugh is and how dangerous it is that somebody like me is on the radio saying we can't control the temperature. Can somebody give me an example where we have done that? Can you tell me of a day where it was oppressively hot and people were dying and we were able to cool it down outside, the weather? There's not a soul. Never happened."

Any climatology student can explain where Limbaugh's logic is massively flawed. The belligerantly stubborn talk-show host speciously conflated weather with overall climatic conditions. The National Center for Environmental Information[7] explains the difference."Whereas weather refers to short-term changes in the atmosphere, climate describes what the weather is like over a long period of time in a specific area. Different regions can have different climates. To describe the climate of a place, we might say what the temperatures are like during different seasons, how windy it usually is, or how much rain or snow typically falls.

The article continues: "When scientists talk about climate, they're often looking at averages of precipitation, temperature, humidity, sunshine, wind, and other measures of weather that occur over a long period in a particular place. In some instances, they might look at these averages over 30 years. And, we refer to these three-decade averages of weather observations as Climate Normals."

When NPR challenged Limbaugh's lack of knowledge about the difference between weather and climate, their goal was to help people understand the broader perspectives of science versus the narrow judgments of opinion.

Unfortunately, Rush Limbaugh is (or was) not alone in his shallow assessment of climate risks. His conservative counterparts in government are just as naïve in their understanding of climate change. As reported on CNN.com,[8] "Sen. James Inhofe, R-Oklahoma, who strongly denies that climate change exists, brought a large snowball on the Senate floor Thursday as a real-life example that the globe is not warming." He stated: "In case we have forgotten because we keep hearing that 2014 has been the warmest year on record," said Inhofe, who is the chairman of the Environment and Public Works Committee, while holding the lumpy snowball in his hand. "I asked the chair, do you know what this is? It's a snowball just from outside here. So it's very, very cold out. Very unseasonable."

Shallow reasoning

Shallow examples such as these serve the cynical political purpose of mocking complex scientific topics by using falsely simplified models to make science seem like "the enemy." The strategy is to portray climate scientists as tricky people trying to deceive the public.

That approach to casting doubt on climate change has enormous appeal to people whose doubts about climate science stem from their version of religious truth. Thankfully, not all religious people buy the conservative schtick. As reported in a Pew Research study "Religion and Views On Climate and Energy,"views about climate change vary by religious affiliation and level of religious observance. Hispanic Catholics (77%), like Hispanics overall (70%), are particularly likely to say the Earth is warming due to human activity. Most religiously unaffiliated (64%) and 56% of black Protestants say climate change is mostly due to human activity. By comparison, fewer white mainline Protestants (41%) view climate change primarily due to human activity. White evangelical Protestants are least likely to hold this view; 28% among this group say the Earth is warming primarily due to human activity, 33% say the Earth's warming is mostly due to natural patterns, and 37% say there is no solid evidence that climate change is occurring."

As the survey indicates, not all Christians or evangelicals are climate change deniers, but the tendency to deny climate change is most pronounced among white Christian evangelicals. As you may recall from facts cited in earlier chapters, that number represents nearly 40% of the American population. That same percentage also embraces creationism as the foundation for their natural history worldview. The connection between science denial and climate change skepticism is likely tied to fundamentalist religion.

The evidence is out there. In an article originally published in Newsweek magazine,[8] writer Kashmira Gander considers the issue of why some evangelicals choose to deny the reality of climate change: "Some evangelicals argue that global warming is of little concern when the end times are approaching. Indeed, it could even be proof of it. Bible verses are also pointed to as evidence humans are required to subdue Earth, that God is in control, and global warming is part of His plan. Others see it as a liberal hoax, and a means to push folks away from religion towards the government."

The article quotes academic researcher Robin Veldman, whose book *The Gospel of Climate Skepticism: Why Evangelical Christians Oppose Action on Climate Change*[9] explores how religion affects views on climate change. Veldman observed: "Part of being a part of the evangelical community is showing that you keep good theologically conservative company, and environmentalism is associated with being liberal. In America, theological liberalism and political liberalism are kind of viewed as the same thing. So it does raise questions if you become interested in the environment."

Conservative ideology is akin to bumper bowling, a rigged game designed to give people a feeling of success and inclusion with as little talent, effort, or critical thinking as possible. The other reason political and religious conservatives hang together on the issue of climate change is the tribal instinct to band together as a group. And yet, as with every tribe in history, conflict within the group is almost inevitable. That is certainly true on the political side of cause and effect.

The website Argus[9] chronicled the debate within the Republican party on climate change as some of its key members sought to find a middle ground on the subject. But the middle ground has not been a popular topic in recent years, especially as the politics of division took hold in America:"More rank-and-file Republicans say they want to find solutions to cutting greenhouse gases and adapting to the effects of warming temperatures. But Trump's skepticism of climate science is becoming an obstacle to unifying on "energy innovation" climate message they think will be more compelling to voters than Democratic proposals such as the Green New Deal.

"Senator Lindsey Graham (R-South Carolina) said he wanted Trump to closely review the science, admit climate change is real" and come up with solutions. Failure to agree that climate change is a problem will make it harder for Republicans to make their case to voters why innovation from the private sector is the best response to climate change, he said."

"We will win the solutions debate, but the only way you are going to win that debate is to admit you have got a problem," Graham said today during the launch of a new Republican caucus that will promote conservation and resolving environmental problems. Senators Lisa Murkowski (R-Alaska), the chairman of the Energy and Natural Resources Committee, and Cory Gardner (R-Colorado), who sits on the panel, are also members of the caucus.

"Trump has long claimed climate change is a hoax, and his administration worked to dismantle initiatives to reduce emissions. As recently as January, Trump mocked the idea of global warming because there was a cold snap."I believe there's a change in weather, and I think it changes both ways," he said in June.

It was no surprise that Trump basically quoted the words of Rush Limbaugh, whose audiences represent the same typically low-information faction of science-denying religiosity in America. Trump openly catered to white evangelical Christians who, according to several polls[10] formed the bulk of his approval rating while in office. That coincides closely with the percentage of Americans that support a biblically literal interpretation of the Bible. The pattern here is obvious. Science denial is a core belief of legalistic Christianity and politics.

Quite conveniently (and cynically), the brand of religion that denies science also casually dismisses environmental abuse as the inevitable product of living in a "fallen world" thanks to the sin of Adam and Eve. That's a handy worldview to call upon when it comes to seeking moral approval for exploitative ventures. This alliance of bad theology in service to the whims of selfish ideology earns religion a seat at the table of power. That is the quid pro quo of the conservative alliance.

Privatize the profits, socialize the losses, punish the poor

Cynical economic objectives drive the alliance between religious, political, and economic conservatives. The goal is to privatize the profits and socialize the losses[11] wherever possible.

The sick part of that formula is that poor and minority populations often suffer the worst impacts of pollution. On the backend, fixing those environmental problems costs billions of dollars. That shunts the costs of environmental abuse onto the public sector, specifically, American taxpayers. Thanks to the irresponsibly exploitative alliance between religious and political conservatives, Americans are stuck with a system of "reverse socialism"[12] in which society pays the economic penalties for capitalistic criminal abuse of the environment while the so-called economic purists walk free.[13]

That's the hypocritical aspect of "free market" economics preached by the political and religious alliance. Conservatives often decry "socialism" as an economic system, yet their policies all-too-frequently require massive government and social investment to fix what exploitative industries have broken. While some companies have been forced to pay the costs of oil spills, acid rain, groundwater pollution, airborne toxins, and buildup of chemicals in our food chain, the American taxpayer still bears the greater cost of dealing with environmental degradation and the illnesses caused by the industrialization of society.[14] In other words, the free-market capitalists seeking to avoid environmental accountability have long been lying to us about the benefits of unregulated markets and industries. They are adept at calculating the exclusionary math necessary to privatize the profits and socialize the losses. But the truth does catch up to them eventually.

The costs of pollution

The costs to human and environmental health are devastating. In studies on the Clean Air Act alone, the costs of unregulated pollution on human health are massive. As reported on the EPA website,[15] "Using a sophisticated array of computer models, EPA found that by 1990 the differences between the scenarios were so great that, under the so-called "no-control" case, an additional 205,000 Americans would have died prematurely and millions more would have suffered illnesses ranging from mild respiratory symptoms to heart disease, chronic bronchitis, asthma attacks, and other severe respiratory problems. In addition, the lack of Clean Air Act controls on the use of leaded gasoline would have resulted in major increases in child IQ loss and adult hypertension, heart disease, and stroke. Other benefits that could be quantified and expressed in dollar terms included visibility improvements, improved yields of some crops, improved worker attendance and productivity, and reduced household soiling damage. When the human health, human welfare, and environmental effects which could be expressed in dollar terms were added up for the entire 20-year period, the total benefits of Clean Air Act programs were estimated to range from about $6 trillion to about $50 trillion, with a mean estimate of about $22 trillion."

These are hard statistics for polluters to fob off. That's why conservative think tanks such as the Heritage Foundation began employing sophisticated public relations tactics to fight off the growing perception that free market policies were corrupting the environment. Some of these tactics included hiring their own paid scientists to produce competing reports aligned with conservative ideology. These were packaged in a cynical propaganda technique called greenwashing.

Greenwashing

As ecological protection proved increasingly popular with the public, some industries aggressively embraced a tactic known as "greenwashing." Many contracted high-powered public relations firms to conceive and implement disinformation campaigns designed to convince the public their activities were environmentally friendly.[16]

Some of these worked, but the public also began to catch on to false narratives. All this "green" money marketing and PR was designed to brand companies favorably in the eyes of consumers. There is money to be made by impressing environmentally conscious buyers that a product or service respects the earth. But consumers aren't easily fooled, either. The Harvard Business Review story notes that people quickly developed suspicions about what, and how, they were being sold on a "green" level. The HBR noted: "But the water may still be a tad icy. As the market research firm Ipsos Reid reported last year, "Consumers appear to be wary of companies who label their products as being 'green' or environmentally friendly." The study found that seven in ten Americans either "strongly" (12 percent) or "somewhat" (58 percent) agree that "when companies call a product 'green' (meaning better for the environment), it is usually just a marketing tactic."The court of public opinion is indeed a tough place in which to win over consumers. The other place where reputations get made or graded is the actual court system in the United States of America.

By 2008, the Green revolution was transitioning from dishonest to honest tactics with large-scale PR firms pitching "green" stories. The Harvard Business Review[17] reported, "The world of public relations has discovered green with a vengeance, and the big global firms seem locked, loaded, and ready to ratchet up their drum beating. Nearly all the major PR firms have set up practices focusing on sustainability and corporate responsibility, including Edelman, Fleishman-Hillard, GCI Group, GolinHarris, Hill & Knowlton, Manning Selvage & Lee, Porter Novelli, and Weber Shandwick."

"The greening of P.R. reflects a newfound reality: It's now safe, or at least safer, for companies to tell their green stories. Two companies helped break the ice. First was G.E., whose ecomagination campaign launch in 2005 signaled to the world that a big company that hadn't previously been seen as a green leader could come out publicly with a bold plan. and not get viciously attacked."

Environmental justice system

While the world of public relations pushed green marketing and ran with it, a legal industry evolved around environmental justice. The United States government recognizes the problem of environmental crime as a reality. The Environmental Protection Agency website specifies the aims of its Environmental Justice wing, defined as: «the fair treatment and meaningful involvement of all people regardless of race, color, national origin, or income, concerning the development, implementation, and enforcement of environmental laws, regulations, and policies."

All this is necessary due to the direct "cause and effect" relationship between industrial polluters allies eager to cover the sins of exploitation for whatever gains they can achieve; economic, political, or cultural. In the end, it's all about control of the cultural narrative and who gets the call the shots on public policy. That's why political, economic, and industrial allies love to partner with religious authorities claiming human "dominion" over the earth. Leveraging the supposed authority of God enables selfish people to escape responsibility for the ills they produce.

But again, these tactics frequently punish the poor and disadvantaged the most. While highly dramatized, the movie Erin Brockovich starring Julie Roberts sought to illustrate how the high stakes game of environmental justice is played from both sides of the fence. The sad fact is that legalistic religion too often sides with the "bad guys" when it comes to protecting environmental health and human rights.

Taking responsibility

One glance at the introductory texts of the Beatitudes in Matthew 5: 3-11 points out the contradictory logic of allowing environmental destruction to fall on the shoulders of the poor and disadvantaged. It tells us that the powerful will not remain in charge forever, and that making the right choices in terms of how we regard and respect creation as stewards is the godly thing to do:

> 3 "Blessed are the poor in spirit, for theirs is the kingdom of heaven. 4 Blessed are those who mourn, for they will be comforted. 5 Blessed are the meek, for they will inherit the Earth. 6 Blessed are those who hunger and thirst for righteousness, for they will be filled.

The Beatitudes remind us that we are staring straight into the reality of what Christians should do regarding the "haves" and "have nots." Jesus tells us that those who might appear weak, or overly sympathetic, or radically liberal in spirit are indeed the most blessed in the eyes of God. They will win out in the end. That's a warning to all those selfishly grabbing power and wealth in this world, and claiming God is on their side while they do it.

Fixing what's been broken

We do know that it is possible to fix what humanity has broken in this world. In the 1970s, the environmental movement gained traction and even a Republican President in Richard M. Nixon was basically forced by awful circumstances to clean up the environment. America got so polluted the situation demanded action. That led to a series of legislative measures that included the Clean Air and Clean Water Acts, the Endangered Species and the Migratory Bird Treaty Acts. All these laws contributed to protection of the environment. They also worked.

Predictably, political and economic conservatives battled against regulation and decried penalties against polluters, claiming they hurt competition, profits and economic growth. But they were lying. The auto industry did not go broke due to governmental requirements requiring vehicles to use unleaded gas.[17] Nor did it collapse while meeting stricter emission control standards.[18] Government laws drove the development more fuel-efficient cars and trucks and many power plants cleaned up their acts, reducing acid rain that was rendering waterways sterile. [14]

All these regulations contributed to a healthier environment, yet there is more to do. The advent of electric, natural gas, and hydrogen-propelled vehicles holds promise to replace dirtier fuels. Greener forms of energy and improvements in electrical grid storage and stability point to a future where dependence on burning fossil fuels is not so dominant. Improved management of nuclear energy holds promise as well. These efforts require investment and good stewardship, and there are still problems to solve. Progress is rapidly being made. The solar (or photovoltaic) and wind power industries are innovating ways to capture and store electrical power in better batteries. An advanced grid network will deliver better efficiency using current-intelligent fuses to protect equipment. There is no question that improvement of this kind takes time, but falling back on anachronistic power sources such as coal and oil are not the long-term solutions when the world needs to create sustainable, clean energy to fuel progress and reduce the impact of anthropogenic climate change.

Greener world

Fortunately, some businesses and industries have begun to grasp the concept of social responsibility and its economic benefits. Architects now design LEED-certified, energy-efficient buildings to make better use of electricity, HVAC resources and the raw materials used in construction. Other industries use sustainable sourcing to produce greener products. Organic farming continues its growth while golf courses and corporate campuses have cleaned up their act with natural plantings to cut down on mowing and use of pesticides and herbicides. All this proves that positive change really is possible.

Despite all this visible and documented environmental progress, a segment of Christian believers still call environmentalism a "liberal" issue due to its association with science and the theory of evolution, the supposed enemy of scriptural knowledge. This remains a stumbling block to society's advancement.

It is frustrating to realize why so many Christians refuse (or are theologically unable) to connect the dots between the abuse of the environment and human greed. After all, greed is the human characteristic that scripture most frequently blames for harming this world. All signs from the past point to God demanding repentance from humanity for our greed and selfish desires. From the Garden of Eden to Noah, and from Sodom and Gomorrah to the crucifixion of Jesus by a cabal of selfishly motivated religious and political authorities, it is greed that God most despises. Yet evangelical Christians continue to side with environmental greed and waste, hoping that Jesus will come back to fix it all.

James Watt was a devoutly religious zealot that served as US Secretary of the Interior under President Ronald Reagan. He most famously stated, "When the last tree falls, Jesus will come."

Religious beliefs like these keep us mired in the mess created by the bad theology wrought by apologetics and "defending God" on the basis of a literally interpreted Bible. It is time to rescue Christianity from the longstanding grip of traditions dependent on the willing ignorance and anachronism required to think like that. The damage of that approach is clear. It leads to hypocrisy, greed, corruption, truth denial, and cold-hearted rationalization. The time for a reality check is now. Christianity's apologetic community must be held to account for "defending God" according to the "traditions of men." That's what Jesus did in his indictment of the religious authorities of his day.

Our most holy mission is to save the world and all its living things from the political and religious zealots allied with selfish business interests eager to grab wealth and power without responsibility or consequences for their destructive ways. This process begins with an honest-to-goodness call to conduct a fresh new inventory of scripture in keeping with the legacy of Jesus Christ.

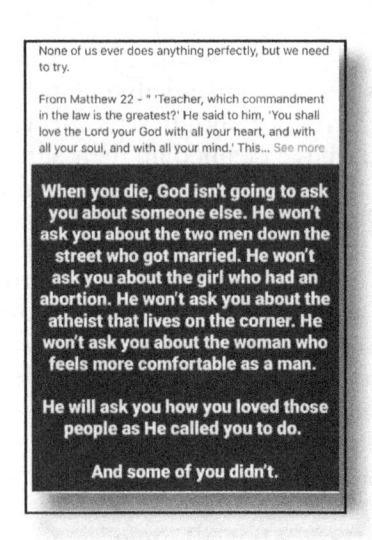

> None of us ever does anything perfectly, but we need to try.
>
> From Matthew 22 - " 'Teacher, which commandment in the law is the greatest?' He said to him, 'You shall love the Lord your God with all your heart, and with all your soul, and with all your mind.' This... See more
>
> **When you die, God isn't going to ask you about someone else. He won't ask you about the two men down the street who got married. He won't ask you about the girl who had an abortion. He won't ask you about the atheist that lives on the corner. He won't ask you about the woman who feels more comfortable as a man.**
>
> **He will ask you how you loved those people as He called you to do.**
>
> **And some of you didn't.**

CHAPTER 19

Scriptural inventory

Not all Christians have fallen into the grip of biblical literalism, legalism, and the intolerant tradition it generates. But we need to identify the roots of where these damaging influences began.

Looking back, we can honestly identify that one of the worst sins of religious tradition was locking down the scriptural canon as the final, immutable, and absolute voice of God. That happened in the third and fourth centuries when Christianity first consolidated with political power. Twenty centuries later, we've seen plenty of evidence of how that combination of religion and politics leads to corruption. We've also learned that back in the beginning of the faith tradition, there were legitimately diverse opinions about the meaning and legacy of Jesus. Lie all institutions concerned more with power than truth, Christianity suppressed these perspectives as either radical or outright heresy. And so the storyof an authoritarian religion began.

It is entirely unlikely that the Holy Bible will be expanded in some way to incorporate these alternate voices. However, that is not our concern here. The main problem is that ever since the books of the Bible were canonized, we've essentially been told that God never spoke through human means again. Has God indeed been silent the last two thousand years, or has God actualy been silenced by religious authorities so protective of their book that they've censored voices God for all practical purposes? Is the Bible the only instrument of communication available to us to understand the will of God? Could we even be missing something important about out how we are supposed to understand the Bible in the first place? If God is indeed everywhere as the Bible suggests, then we should be on a constant lookout for signs of that presence in our daily lives. As Jesus taught us, it is our job to pursue wisdom from all sources available to us.That's the only honest way to approach truth as a whole.

Sadly, it is Christian tradition, especially of the legalistic variety, that has tuned out the voice of God the last two thousand years. It all began with eliminating alternative Christian voices during those early years when the scriptural canon was still being formed. After that, the door to truth was sealed with the phrase "only scripture can be used to test scripture." That leaves the Christian world spinning its wheels in the mud of the Bible's most anachronistic passages. The legalistic branch of Christianity is stuck in a ditch of its own making while blaming the rest of the world for driving it there.

Opening up the Book of Life

By the dictates of legalistic religion, we're not allowed to seek the voice of God through any other portals that scripture. That bans us from looking for evidence of God's work in our everyday experience and slams shut the Book of Life. The irony of this approach is that it denies the teaching methods of Jesus, who used parables based on organic symbolism and daily life to convey the truth about our spiritual and moral lives. Scripture says that Jesus didn't abide by the strictures of religious tradition or confine himself to a limited view of scripture in his day. Neither should we.

Close-minded tradition shuts out a vast array of cultural, literary, and scientific insights that inspire us with awe and wonder about the variety and meaning of life. By contrast, religious traditions founded on biblical literalism and legalism forcibly eclipse the keenly symbolic and material relationship between the Word of God and nature, also known as creation. Cutting nature out of the picture is the greatest mistake of all because it blinds us to the miracle and balance of our planet. Lacking that greater understanding of the frailty of our material circumstances, it is too easy to become lazy and ungrateful. That is an abuse of trust with God.

We've seen how close-minded creationists work to deny the astounding story that science provides about the material processes delivering order and design across the entire spectrum of nature and the universe. Despite what creationists like to claim, we can trace the source and logic of these systems and see how the complexities of nature evolved over time. We can witness these processes at work in everything from the chemical structure of minerals to the interlocking feathers of birds. Evolutionary change is taking place before our eyes as millions of life forms interact in an eternally changing matrix of geology, climate, habitat, and the Earth's unique position in the universe. Denying all that based on a literal take of the Book of Genesis is stiff-necked, and frankly sinful.

Instead, nature provides organic symbols that scripture uses to describe God and the spiritual concepts we depend upon for wisdom and truth. These are far more powerful communications about God than any set of literal words on a page. By opening the Bible to the fresh air of material creation, we breathe life back into scripture and bridge the gap of separation from God. We open the Book of Life.

Human awareness

Human beings are unique in sharing with God an awareness of these processes at work in the universe. That is how humankind is made in God's image. This kinship with God is expressed in feelings of love toward creation and one another. That's what Jesus compels us to do. In that regard we are indeed «specially created." That does not mean we need to isolate ourselves from the rest of creation to appreciate or grow that awareness. Nor do we need to "defend" the Bible from science or any other field of knowledge. That is bad theology.

In this call to shared awareness with God, we can approach the entire breadth of scripture as a living document. It is a tool of understanding, yet it also provides evidence that God's voice exists outside the walls of scripture. That's what Jesus was trying to tell the religious authorities trying to keep God locked up in a temple. He told them to stop treating scripture, or the Temple, as if God were walled-in and isolated from the rest of the world. Unleashed from the constricted views of jealous or defensive apologetics, we can connect to scripture at its organic foundation, engaging with symbols drawn from creation to bridge the gap between our earthly lives and the spiritual goodness we yearn to know.

We can call this approach a Religion From Earth. It is the foundation from which we measure our ability to respect God. Stewardship of creation also shows love and respect for human beings and the other living things that exist in this world. Loving creation is an act of loving others. It does not make a god out of nature. It simply recognizes that the world serves as a foundation for our understanding of God's grace. That metaphorical relationship between creation and God is what positions the Bible as a «living document" rather than a text constrained to a record of events that literally only happened once. That is not how the world works. It is also not how we're supposed to understand it.

The reason this foundational connection between creation and God is so important is that the notion of «God with us" requires an honest-to-goodness context by which to conduct our earthly lives. Recall that the Lord's Prayer calls on us to conduct ourselves in that manner. «Thy Kingdom Come…Thy will be done--on earth as it is in heaven." The Bible clearly states that if we act without care or conscience in this life, salvation remains out of reach.

With these objectives in mind, let us embark on a wonderfully insightful journey together and make the connection between earth and heaven in a Religion From Earth.

CHAPTER 20

Religion From Earth

Meditational lessons in honor of such diverse saints as Francis of Assisi and Chief Pontiac. By Dr. Richard Simon Hanson, Professor of Religion Emeritus, Luther College

Sections

OF EARTH AND OURSELVES
THE DEATH OF THE WILDERNESS
THE EARTH IS THE LORD'S
THE SPEECH OF GOD
OUR PLACE IN CREATION
JESUS AND THE ECOLOGICAL CRISIS
THE COSMIC CHRIST
PROPHETIC JUDGMENT ON OUR WAYS
THE SEED OF THE FUTURE
A WAY OF RETURN: ST. FRANCIS OF ASSISI
THE WAY OF WISE MANAGEMENT: ST. BENEDICT
A WAY OF WORSHIP
SALVATION
OF PURPOSE AND REASON

OF EARTH AND OURSELVES

In the wake of popular books that proclaim the impending destruction of the earth, and in view of the other-worldly concerns of the heartiest strains of Christianity, it might seem improper to suggest such a thing as earth religion for Christians. Indeed, some may even suppose that there is a contradiction in the very terms of the title. Is not Christianity a religion of hope beyond the grave, rather than a concern for earthly existence? Jesus assured the man who condemned him to death that his kingdom was not "of this world," and for nigh unto two millennia many Christians have taken "this world" to mean the earth upon which we make our homes as mortals. Is not the very essence of Christianity a divorce from this planet and a love affair with heaven?

Not all of us who are Christian will accept such a popular notion of what we are supposed to be. There are a number of us who remember that Jesus talked mostly of how to live our lives in the now of earthly existence. We remember that he spoke much of the Kingdom of God, but we also recall that it is always among us and always coming to us; that salvation is something that happens to us in the midst of our existence, not something to which we go at the end. There are a number of us who believe that the earth is our home, that we are not strangers here and that we are called to be responsible disciples in the years that are given to us to live in this strikingly beautiful place.

We believe that the earth is the Lord's and that we are the Lord's and, because of that, that we must live life responsibly within our natural environment. Therefore, we feel a need to defy the preachers of doom and the peddlers of pie in the sky with an assertion of gospel that repeats the message of the goodness of God's creation and the redemption of human existence within it. We know of forgotten words within our tradition that need to be exposed and sounded in our time. Christianity does not have to be a religion of escape, and persons who are concerned about the ecological crisis of our time do not need to turn away from Christianity to act out their concern.

It was some 28 centuries ago that a Jewish prophet named Isaiah went into the sanctuary of the temple on Mount Zion and heard angelic voices singing, iHoly, holy, holy is the Lord of hosts." He might have thought that the song was an approbation of the heavenly realms, but then he heard the voices continue with a statement that does not translate easily into English – *meló kol ha'áretz kevodó*, "the fullness of earth is his glory." What a sensational proclamation! The earth is God's glory, it says, the very earth upon which we live and move and have our being. Not only God's handiwork, not only a reflection of the glory of the Almighty, but the very glory itself! God has clothed himself with the very creation of which we are a part. We and all other creatures who fill the earth are the threads in the robe of God.

This is a basic motif in the biblical tradition. It should be as basic in the religion of all Jews and Christians. In the face of those who deny the validity of earth we must assert this claim boldly and strongly – this and all other biblical messages that show us the indissoluble connection between God and creation.We must end the notion that the earth is doomed and forsaken place and that heaven alone is to be the focus of religious attention.

But even more important than that is a need to assert powerful messages of ecological concern that have been part of our tradition from the beginning, sounded from time to time, neglected more often and now, more needed than ever. It is all there, all that we need to believe to be responsible citizens of our planet earth. It is for us who are aware of it to put it forth for our time, in order that we may reverse the destructive designs of our generation of humans and, at the same time, to hold before the world a way of being religious that harmonizes ourselves and our natural environment.

There is a "this world" that is not in total harmony with the natural kingdom that is God's. It is the ìthis world" of our human societies. Indeed, there are many such worlds. We construct them with our own rules and fancies. We live in them and sometimes we live in them so wholly that we forget how we are to be connected to the greater world of God's glory within which our little worlds exist. Some of them are very little worlds – as little as playground societies and bridge clubs – and others are not quite so little. They are the nations within which we govern ourselves and the sizable industrial corporations by which we process the items we think we need. At their best they are innocent necessities for human existence. At their worst they are defiant enemies of the natural order, greedily devouring earth's resources and rapaciously destroying much that is beautiful and good. There are people whose loyalties are so totally bound into these worlds that they become enemies of the rest of us and of earth itself. In the names of the little worlds to which they are devoted they will destroy even a last living creature of its kind on this planet. They have done it before, and they will do it again. In the interest of what they call self-defense, they build arsenals of destruction which will harm all living creatures on earth if they are ever used.

Jesus counseled his followers against being of "this world." What did he mean? Certainly not the realm of the foxes or the lilies of the field or the birds of the air with whom he felt a strong kinship. Much more likely he meant the world of religious institutions and political structures. It was clearly a world ruled by fear and deception, for he described its ruler as a prince of darkness and father of lies. It is a demonic kind of world in which men live as enemies instead of brothers.

We cannot be so naïve as to think that we can escape being part of the social and political and economic structures by which we give order to our human existence. To shop in the grocery store is to be part of the economic order. To be a person is to be a citizen of one or another country. There is no way to travel outside the borders of one's citizenship without carrying proof of that. How can we possibly avoid being part of this world? The only question worth asking is whether we must give total allegiance to those necessary orders of our communal existence. Orders of priority are possible. We can put citizenship of earth before citizenship of nation. We can serve life in its natural dimensions ahead of our social fears. We can be more loyal to friends than to ideologies. Though we cannot avoid being of these worlds of our human concoction, we can avoid being totally that, and that is a matter of considerable importance. We can devote ourselves first and foremost to Jesus' Kingdom of God, "On earth, as it is in heaven."

It is to this end that I speak of an earth religion for Christians. I believe it is important that we know our connections to the planet of which we are a part as well as to the universe to which it, in turn, belongs. The earth is our source of life. It is also our home. All that it is and all that is in it should be held sacred. Without the earth and all its components we simply would not exist. That is what connects us to our Creator. Nor do we have any dearer identity than that of an earth creature. No matter what my name or my particular cultural tradition, I am ultimately the Adam who is made of the dust of the earth. The only way in which I can be a child of God is to be, as well, a child of the earth.

My story begins there. That is where it shall end. Insofar as identity is sacred, this bond with the earth is sacred as well. Let us return to that identity, if we will. Let us be what we are meant to be: children of one God at home on a planet designed to be our Garden of Eden. Let us respect the glories of our Creator's handiwork – which is only to respect ourselves all the more – and, in doing that, show true homage to our Creator. Let us find satisfaction in being of the dust of the earth as well as the breath of God. Let us return to the source of our being by way of the channels that connect us. To that end, I suggest earth religion for Christians because I am a Christian speaking to fellow Christians. But I also hope that much of what I have to say can mean something to other humans as well.

THE DEATH OF THE WILDERNESS

From before the beginning of the biblical tradition, people told a story of how civilization destroys the wilderness and its creatures. It is the story of Gilgamesh.

Gilgamesh was king in the city of Uruk. As such, he represented civilization. Civilization, we must remind ourselves, is the very business of building cities and living in them. As king of Uruk, Gilgamesh represented all of the grandeur and glory of wealth of that human creation, the city. His greatness was the greatness of human industry, art and commerce.

One day a trapper's son encountered a savage out in his hunting grounds. The savage was strong and covered with hair. He was a companion of the beasts and he aided them in their struggles against the human hunters. Disturbed by this, the trapper and his family reported the appearance of the wild man to Gilgamesh, king of Uruk. Gilgamesh and his people decided that the savage should be captured and taken into the city. Suspecting that his weakness was the weakness of all men, they baited him with a harlot girl. She was stationed at the water hole where he was last seen. There she awaited him and, when he appeared, she mated with him and won him for herself.

At this point the savage was changed. He ceased to be the companion of the gazelles and the other wild beasts. Domesticated by the woman's love, he followed her back to the city and there he encountered Gilgamesh. The two met as rivals. Sensing the strength of the other, they faced off and wrestled each other until Gilgamesh was forced to bend one knee to the pavement. At that point they were satisfied. The contest ended and they declared a bond of eternal friendship. Gilgamesh, the man of the city, and Enkidu, the man of the wilderness, found themselves to be brothers. Gilgamesh amazed Enkidu with the wonders of this marvelous city. Enkidu, in turn, enthralled his counterpart with tales of the forests and the mountains.

Gilgamesh was so enthralled, in fact, that he asked Enkidu to lead him into the wilderness for an adventure. One of the tales that gripped him was the tale of a fierce wild bull that guarded the mountains of the forests of cedar. Gilgamesh felt that he must challenge the creature and thus prove his superiority over the grand and terrible beast. Surely he, the king of the city of Uruk, should be able to defeat the legendary monster. Especially with the help of Enkidu.

Wise old men warned him against the adventure, but Gilgamesh was only further encouraged by their caution. Enkidu tried to dissuade him with ever more dramatic accounts of his ferocity. But the pride of Gilgamesh rose in proportion to the tales. He had to go into the wilderness to meet the great bull and Enkidu had to go with him as a guide.

After arduous adventures en route, the two heroes arrived at the mountainous home of the great bull, whose legendary name was Huwawa. He was fully as fierce as the tales about him had reported him to be. Both heroes had to put forth their fullest and cleverest efforts in order to subdue him, but subdue him they did, and in triumph they bore his gigantic horns back to the city of Uruk as a trophy. But at this point we learn the truth behind the symbolic language. The horns were only a token of the real loot, for at this point in the ancient story we read descriptions of huge piles of fine cedar timber. It was the forest that Gilgamesh was after. His journey to the mountains was for the purpose of finding more lumber for the building projects of his city. He had denuded the mountains in order to cover his palaces with panels of cedar.

As a penalty for this deed, the gods decided to take the life of Enkidu. The savage-turned-civilized-man had betrayed his covenant with the wilderness. He who once protected the beasts from the traps of the human hunters had now joined the plunderers in stripping the forests bare. For that his life was demanded. Against the sobs and protests of Gilgamesh, his friend, Enkidu, took sick and died. With the death of the wilderness went the death of the savage. Gilgamesh had thought that he and his primitive counterpart could coexist as brothers. His thought was but wishful thinking. To civilize the primitive man was to destroy his primitive nature. The man of the wilds was dead and Gilgamesh was left to weep the tears of regret.

The lesson in this ancient epic is a powerful one. When civilization enters, the wilderness goes. There is no way that one can have both. When the savage meets the man of the city, the man of the city prevails. The savage learns the ways of the city and is affected by them. Seldom, if ever, does the city man lean and adopt the ways of the savage.

The historical evidence of the ancient world repeatedly demonstrates the great truth of the epic. As one travels today in the worlds of the ancient civilizations, one sees too much of the grim evidence of how the wilderness has been destroyed by the city. Mountainsides, once green with forest, are now barren heights of windswept rock. Valleys that were at one time the lush gardens of successive civilizations are now salt flats as a result of prolonged irrigation. Soil that once covered the slopes is now part of the coastal plains. Wherever one turns in the ancient Near East or the Mediterranean, one sees the evidence of that peculiar destruction brought on by the man of the city. It is a one-way road of travel and, alas, we still seem determined to go that way.

History has lessons for those who will read it, but who are those who will read? The developers and industrialists of our time will destroy every last inch of wilderness if we give them permission. The Western Hemisphere could benefit well from the lessons of the hemisphere which somehow endured the early civilizations that were a prelude to our brand of progress, but only a minority are wise enough to learn the lesson. Like Gilgamesh of old we seem prone to strip the mountains, and then we can only cry in regret.

There was once a man who turned back for part of the way. That man was the Hebrew patriarch Abraham. He came out of the culture of Ur and then took to the hills to live the life of a nomad. The move is recounted as that in the biblical book of Joshua.

Your fathers lived of old beyond the Euphrates, Terah the father of Abraham and of Nahor, and they served other gods. Then I took your father Abraham from beyond the river and led them through all the land of Canaan and made his offspring many.

(Joshua 24:2-3, RSV)

For reasons that are not totally clear, Abraham turned to a more primitive way. He heard the voice of the High God, it says in the tales of his descendants, and he followed that voice's commands. He wandered with his family and his flocks and he stopped where the grazing was good. He felt himself destined to live in the hills and so it was that the hills of Canaan became the heritage of his children's children.

The way of Abraham came to be known as teshuváh. In the language of his descendants that work means turning and it is one of the most important words in their religious vocabulary. It is the word that is sometimes translated as repentance in the Christian vocabulary. The simpler meaning is more instructive, for it suggests that people can turn in their ways, even turn back to good things that were left behind in our human haste to go forward.Scholars have noticed a certain primitivism in the writings of the biblical prophets. In a time of urbanization they cried out for a return to the ways of the desert. Some have seen it as a flaw in their otherwise progressive thinking, as a kind of anachronism to which idealists are frequently prone. Perhaps it was neither a flaw nor an anachronism. Perhaps it was an important recognition that some of the ways of the past were better than modern ways, and that we should return to them if at all possible. A passage from the words of the so-called Second Isaiah represent the motif.

> Hearken to me, you who pursue deliverance,
>
> you who seek the Lord.
>
> Look to the rock from which you were hewn
>
> and to the quarry from which you were digged.
>
> Look to Abraham your father
>
> and to Sarah who bore you;
>
> for when he was but one I called him
>
> and I blessed him and made him many. (Isaiah 51:1-2, RSV)

Another bit of ancient Hebrew vocabulary is also instructive. It is the pair of words by which the biblical prophets and story-tellers spoke about past and future. In their language, the past is represented by the word for front or forward. What was laid out before them was the past. That was what they could see because it consisted of what had already happened or been done. And their word for the future was the word for what is behind. The future, after all, was what they could not see. We have reversed that, of course. We look into the future and forget the past. The past, we say, should be left behind. It is but a prologue. The future only can matter.

Perhaps there was more wisdom in their way of thinking time than in ours. Or at least as much wisdom. We think of ourselves as moving forward in time and in our thinking is the blind assumption that we always move on to something better. No matter that the evil of the twentieth century has outdone the evil of all centuries preceding it and no matter that the wars of tomorrow shall be infinitely worse than the worst we have seen in our time. We are impelled by a certain blind thought that the future can only be better. The ancient Hebrew was at least wise enough to see that the future is largely unknown and that the past alone is accessible to our view. In their imagination the Hebrews expected disaster as often as salvation in the future. Who knew what tomorrow could bring, for it could bring as much of both ill and good as one could see in the past. And when they looked back, they often saw good to which they knew they should return.

It is this perspective as much as anything else that I mean to offer in these chapters. There is good in the past that we should not have left behind, but it is not found in laws and traditions designed to keep people in line or provide them some sort of guide map for getting into heave. The good that can be retrieved is found in "turning" to ways of the past that not only respect creation, but call us to a humbler approach to our existence. I believe that kind of good that can be kept if we determine not to lose sight of what it means to our souls. As Abraham turned to the desert and found life as a gift from God, so we can execute similar turnings and find ways of salvation that are waiting and beckoning to us.

THE EARTH IS THE LORD'S

It has been said so many times that perhaps it has become a cliche of sorts: the earth is the Lord's. But what do we make of that? No religious statement could be more basic and true, yet its meaning is lost when it is merely repeated in rote fashion. *The earth is the Lord's.* What of its corollary? Perhaps we need to examine what the statement assumes, namely this; that the Lord is, by definition of scripture at least, the earth-maker.

Those who believe in God express faith in the existence of a complete and supreme authority over all who live and move upon earth as well as the rest of our galaxy and all other galaxies, too. It is important to examine this claim because there are notions of God that are somewhat more selfish and narrow. There is the notion, for example, that God is a special God for Christians or for Jews or for certain kinds of Christians or Jews. There is the very popular notion that God has nothing to do with earth and all things material or natural, but that He is purely a God of unseen places. There are notions that God is little and private and lives inside the bosoms of devoted believers. In the face of these and all other notions that take God to be something created for use by one sect or another, we must not allow ourselves to be confined by the selfish aims of others. Either there is a God, or there is not. No one owns the concept.

The fuller religious premise is this: To have been conceived and born and to exist is to be God's. To stay alive is to do so by the grace of air and water and nourishment. That is also God's work, as in "give us this day, our daily bread." These are the religious premises for God's authority over us. For others, the question of God is more academic. Lacking hard evidence to convince them otherwise, God does not exist. Yet one thing remains. We are all still dependent on this thing we call creation for our existence. Regardless of its origins, it how we interact with creation that determines both our material survival. How we regard and treat creation is a reflection of our spiritual nature.

Science proposes that we are a product of an ongoing creative process called evolution. We've already seen that many aspects of scripture acknowledge this fact. Deeper still, we are all formed of the same elements that permeate the universe. That is most basic, organic and fundamental truth of all. That means we need to be able to find ways to communicate effectively about our collective situation, for that is humanity's most important reality check. Coming to terms with our ultimately frail state in this universe—our collective mortality—is the subject around which gather to determine what to do about it.

Our commonality between the religious and non-religious comes down to a sense of wonder. That is one thing we can all share. Yet it is also one of the first things we tend to lose in the growth cycle from childhood to adult. Keeping a sense of wonder about the world is critical in maintaining an appreciation of grace (in the religious sense) and a sense of gratitude (on a secular level) about the unique balance of this planet and place where we live. If we take that commonality to hear, it is the mere existence of this world that engenders a sense of wonder. The earliest scriptures capture this wonder in poetic form:

You have been our abode, O Master,

through all generations.

Before the mountains were born,

before the earth was begun,

from beginning to end you are God.

(Psalm 90:1-2, translation by the author)

The Lord rules: let the earth dance!

Let its many islands rejoice!

Surrounded by clouds and mist,

triumph and justice enthrone him.

Fire proceeds before him,

flames, enshrouding his back.

His lightning illumines the world.

The earth beholds it and writhes.

The mountains are melting like wax before the Lord,

before the Master of earth.

(Psalm 97:1-5, translation by the author)

It is no new claim to assert that God is Creator of heaven and earth. Monotheistic religion holds that single "fact" most dear. Whether or not we accept the full implications of that statement, it is critical to examine its source and significance When people tell the story of creation, they are focused in their beliefs, but it is possible to become so focused on the literal nature of the tale that its fuller meaning gets lost between its recitation and its broader meaning.

When a creation story is told to children, it tends to be accepted as fact. Yet there are parts of the story that conflict with a sense of rationality as the mind grows more mature. Trying to wish away conflict between a literal interpretation of the Genesis creation story and what we now know about the true age of the earth and its geological history does not impress God in any way. Who can believe, and how does it matter, exactly, that the world was made in six days? Part of the difficulty is this, that such believers embrace no other biblical story of creation than the hymnic version of the opening chapter of the opening book of the Bible. What if we started with some of the other biblical accounts of creation, such as the account of the 104th psalm? It serves an equally reverent purpose.

> Bless the Lord, O my soul!
>
> O Lord, my God, you are great.
>
> You are clothed in splendor and glory,
>
> wearing the light as a cloak,
>
> stretching heaven like a tent.
>
> He covers his chambers with water,
>
> using the clouds as his chariot,
>
> walking on the wings of the wind,
>
> making the winds his messengers
>
> and bolts of fire his servants.
>
> He planted the earth on its moorings,
>
> never again to be moved.
>
> Chaos enshrouded like a cloak;
>
> water stood higher than mountains
>
> but at your rebuke they fled.
>
> At the sound of your thunder they ran.
>
> The hills rose, the valleys sank down
>
> to the points which you had decreed.
>
> You set the immovable bounds

which protect the earth from the sea.

He puts the springs in the brooks

and they flow between the hills,

watering the life of the meadows,

quenching the thirst of wild beasts.

Overhead dwell the birds of the air,

warbling among the branches.

As you water the hills from above

you satisfy earth with your produce,

bringing forth grass for the cattle,

vegetation for man to till

to make the earth produce bread.

(Psalm 104:1-14, translation by Dr. Richard Hanson)

In this psalm and other psalms, and in the Book of Job, and in the Book of Habakkuk, there are accounts of creation that understand it to be a continuing process and not just a once-upon-a-time event. There are those things which are of the past—the forming of mountains and seas and all other features of the landscape that precede us in time. But there are endless events of creation that just keep on happening around us – the forming of springs, the falling of rain, the growth of plants, the conception and birth of creatures. We walk in the midst of creation, in the midst of the wonders of the God who creates. We are not left to talk about "when creation happened" or to calculate how far in the past. Creation is what is happening all around us and we are part of it. That scriptural approach happens to align perfectly with what we know of the processes of evolution.

In all the biblical talk about God, one theme remains central: God is always creating and creation is always God's work. It is an active process. And despite our growing knowledge of the material nature of the universe, there will always remain things that we have yet to learn. The book of Isaiah describes the wonders of creation yet also illustrates how our understanding of the earth's position in the universe has changed:

Who has measured the waters in the hollow of his hand

and marked off the heavens with a span,

enclosed the dust of the earth in a measure

and weighed the mountains in scales

and the hills in a balance?

To whom then will you compare me,

that I should be like him,

says the Holy One.

Lift up your eyes on high and see:

who created these?

He who brings out their host by number,

calling them all by name;

> by the greatness of his might

> and because he is strong in power

> not one is missing.

(Isaiah 40:12, 25-26, RSV)

    To say that God is Creator is not to say that we completely understand God. It is only to say that we know God by what we can see. God is more than a verb or a noun. Moses discovered this at the burning bush when the cause of the burning bush was revealed as *ahyeh asher ahyeh* – I make happen what I make happen. Cast into the third person it became the secret name of God which is not even pronounced by later generations of Jews, the name yahweh. Yahweh means he makes happen and the name is a verb rather than a noun.

    And to know God by the deeds of creation is to know that creation testifies to the energy that is God causing it to be. Ancient psalmists knew this and reveled in it. we could well join their reveling and be inspired to faith that is joyous and altogether healthful.

Praise him, sun and moon!

Praise him, all shining stars!

Praise him, O heavens beyond heavens

O waters above all the heavens!

Give praise to the name of the Lord,

for at his command you were made!

(Psalm 148:3-5, translation by the author)

The cycles of morning and evening sing out.

The fields of the wilderness are wet

and the hills are clothed with gladness.

The slopes are covered with flocks

and the valleys are groaning with grain.

They shout, yes, they sing.

(Psalm 65:9, 13-14, translation by the author)

The language of old sought to bring it all home. Earth is the Lord's and earth sings to the Lord! Great is the company of the witnesses and we, too, should be of that company. To honor the Lord is to honor all that the Lord does and that means we must honor all the works and wonders of nature. To do anything less is to show our disrespect for our Creator. Faith demands that we love the earth, not leave it to someone else to abuse. Indeed, our leaving is only a return to earth's bosom.

You send man back to the dust

and say, "Return, O mortal!"

(Psalm 90:3, translation by the author)

You take their breath and they die

and go back to the dust they came from.

Yet you send back the breath and create,

renewing the face of the earth.

(Psalm 90:3, translation by the author)

THE SPEECH OF GOD

When my children were young, I taught each of them a little game that had no name but could have been called Listening to God. The game consisted of a question and answers. The question was asked by myself, the father. The answers were given by God and reported to the child. "What is God saying today?" I would ask, and the answers would include such delightful items as, "God is saying sunshine and right now he says butterfly. Oh, look at the white flowers! God just said flowers!" The answers were rain and wind on the blustery days and clouds when the world was gray. The lesson was simple. I wanted my children to know that all creation is a speech of God.

The idea came to me one day when I was pondering the opening chapter of the Bible. That grand succession of statements – "God said, let there be light... let there be a firmament... let the waters be gathered... is an emphatic way of declaring that creation is a speech of God. God is not speechless. He surrounds us with millions of words. Oh, to be sure, they are not in the speech of human tongues, either Hebrew, Greek or English, for they are in that speech which is all action, so that one need not say of God, "Your actions speak louder than your words." God's words equating to deeds, one only need say, "Your actions speak loudly."

The heavens declare God's glory;

the skies display his handiwork.

Each day pours forth a speech;

each night proclaims some knowledge.

There is no speech, not a word,

but what their voice is heard.

Their sound has gone out in the earth,

their words to the edge of the world.

(Psalm 19:1-5,

translation by the author)

Last winter I tried the game on an older set of children. I was part of a program that treated the dual subjects of ecology and religion, and my students were gathered around me on an island at the edge of the Boundary Waters Canoe Area of Minnesota and Ontario. We were living on the edge of the wilderness in the midst of winter, warming ourselves with woolens and wood-burning stoves, baking fresh bread each day and learning the ways of the forest in winter. I explained the simple rules of the game and gave them 24 hours in which to listen for God's speech of nature around them. The responses to which we all listened the next day were most heartening. I share them in part with you.

"The message is white – dazzling white in the light of sun and softer white in the shadows, but white upon white broken only by the dark, blackish shapes of the trees and the blue of the sky above. And what is this white? It is all colors homogenized into one dazzling blast of light. God speaks color and all colors are God's."

"The message today was silence, the silence of very deep snow and very deep forest. Never before have I felt such silence. Is silence a sound, I ask, the sound most peculiar to the world that is God's? I think of the sounds of the city where I live. They are harsh and obscene and there are so many that I become accustomed to constant levels of sound that mix a hundred sources of sound into one steady buzzing that fills my brain even through the night. Here today I heard silence for the first time in my life. It was uncanny. I have never heard anything like it. God's word to me this day was silence."

"Standing on the lake in the night I am aware of two realities: a light, cold breeze that brushes my cheeks and a skyful of stars overhead. Surely this is a message of glory and simplicity in one – the breeze so simple and the millions of stars so glorious. God speaks two words at once: the tiny, gentle word of the breeze and the colossal chorus of the stars above me. How can anyone not believe?"

"I study the snow. At first sight it is one vast, flat word of whiteness. But then I bend close and, with a jeweler's glass, I look at the crystals of which it is made. I look at dozens of hexagon crystals. No two are alike. There are trillions of them all around me, yet each is a distinct and separate word on its own. This is the world in which I live. It is a world of infinite speech and infinite numbers of distinctly different words in the vocabulary. The snowflakes are only one example of the infinity within each kind and category of reality."

"There is a certain tree that stands in front of our outdoor toilet. At some time it has been struck by lightning and split in half the length of the trunk. When even a slight wind blows, the tree responds by turning and, as it turns, it speaks with creaks and groans that I fancy to be cries of pain. Or is it a testimony to the strength of the tree that it groans and withstands the wind? Someday it shall fall, but for now it stands with defiant strength and speaks to me the strength of all creation. There is strength in that which is wounded and strength in all that is small. God speaks strength in infinite ways as well."

"I ponder the idea of strength and behold two kinds about me. One is the strength of the wind: bold, assertive and positive. The other is the strength of the snow. Seemingly passive, it is tossed by the wind or driven to be impacted against whatever object it is forced to encounter. I study the surface of the snow and I notice that it undulates. One snowflake has gripped another and begun the building of a drift that will stand against the wind. I examine the crystals closely in the drift of snow and I see that they are interlocked in such a way that one could not be extricated from the other. Then I understand the strength of the snow houses we built for shelter. The snow has its own strength and, together with the wind, it performs the creative dance of yin and yang, the opposing forces that work together for harmony in God's creation.

Is it easy to see what a therapeutic adventure it might be to play my little game? Before very long one is filled with a sense of wonder at the dazzling array of messages all about and comforted by the thought that God is very near. With so much speaking about me, how can I ever be lonesome? I am actually surrounded by words of God.

Where can I go to escape?

Where can I hide from your presence?

If I climb to the skies you are there;

if I lie down in Hell, there also.

Could I flee on the wings of the dawn

and camp far beyond the ocean,

even here your presence would follow.

Your strong arm would grasp me.

If I say, "Let the darkness enshroud me!

Let the daylight around me be night!"

I find that the dark cannot daunt you,

that night seems as bright as the day

and darkness like light.

>   (Psalm 19:1-5, translation by the author)

During the Middle Ages there were mystic saints who tried to find God through meditation and concentrated study. Some of them claimed to have come very close, but he closer they approached, the more they felt themselves drawing near to the brink of a great abyss. At the threshold of where God should have been they felt themselves about to encounter an uncanny and unfathomable nothing. They felt undone. They felt profoundly lost.

In reaction to these, another mystic of the sixteenth century, Isaac Luria, discovered a greater truth. In creating our world, said Luria, God undid Himself and dispersed his parts as sparks that are hidden in every phenomenon of nature. In doing this, God made Himself close to every part of creation – as close to us as our breathing, as close to whatever we can meet in our daily walk. I behold a plant and I know it to be containing a spark of God. Therefore, I respond with a hymn of praise or a prayer. I speak to the plant – to the spark within it, that is – and I find myself responding to the great Almighty God who has drawn so close as to address me in this fine, but simple, way.

Another philosopher of the twentieth century, Martin Buber, has developed an important set of insights out of this thought of the nearness of God and the ways in which God addresses us. In his book entitled I and Thou, Buber explained how life can be a response to the God who speaks to us in all the sparks of creative energy that fill our world and the universe.

The Christian word for this is incarnation. We Christians proclaim it as the essence of what was going on in the life of Jesus. This was God drawing close to us, we say. This was God coming to us because we cannot come to Him. There is something special about this, of course, but it does not rule out what is proclaimed in many parts of the Scriptures – that God speaks by doing and that all of creation is that speech. We need only open our senses to ihear" that speech and then life can consist of our answering to that One who speaks in each and every moment of our existence. For why should we not answer if we are being talked to so much?

OUR PLACE IN CREATION

In one of the oldest stories in the world we read this account of the creation of mankind.

Then the Lord God formed man of dust from the ground and breathed into his nostrils the breath of life; and man became a living being.

(Genesis 2:7, RSV)

What is our place? It is a place between the dust of the earth and the spirit of God. ("Spirit" is, after all, only the Latin word for breath. In the language of the Bible the terms "spirit," "breath" and "wind" are all one and the same.) It is with those whom the Hebrew forefathers called nephesh hayyah – "living being" or "creature." Nephesh hayyah is the category that includes all creatures that breathe in order to live. Of such are we.

Back in the days when certain Greek philosophers cut the style for sophisticated thinking, many people got the notion that man does not belong on earth, that he is a creature of the skies who fell one day from his heavenly status and got himself stuck with a body. The higher life, to them, was to think one's way out of the body and its passions and fasten the mind to heavenly realms. Earth was considered a prison from which we need to be saved or released and salvation was to go to heaven and leave the earth behind.

This kind of thinking, which is known as Gnosticism, had a great impact on the early Christians. So great an impact, in fact, that millions of Christians still tend to think that way. They believe themselves to be strangers on earth and regard the earth as a wicked place the one should be glad to leave. Or when they catch themselves loving it they feel obliged to act guilty for that love.

Needless to say, such thinking does not fit realistically well with a more honest biblical point of view. In the books of the Bible we are reminded again and again that we belong on this planet and that we are part of its family of creatures. Even when we are bidden to praise the Lord it is in company with the rest of creation. They and we are fellow members of one giant chorus.

Give praise to the Lord from the earth,

O monsters and all powers of chaos!

-- lightning and storm, snow and clouds,

hot desert wind which blows at his word,

mountains and all high hills,

fruit-bearing trees and cedars,

wild creature and very large beast,

reptile and bird on the wing,

kinds of the earth and all peoples,

princes and all of earth's leaders,

healthy young men and maidens,

old men and children!

And with the rest of creation,

we also share the fate of returning to dust when we die.

You send man back to the dust

and say, "Return, O mortal!"

(Psalm 90:3, translation by the author)

Do not put your trust in leaders,

in a man, who can give you no help.

When he dies he returns to the ground

and on that day his plans must be ended.

(Psalm 146:3-4, translation by the author)

For the fate of the sons of men and the fate of beasts is the same; as one dies, so dies the other. They all have the same breath and man has no advantage over the beasts… All go to one place; all are from the dust and all turn to dust again. Who knows whether the spirit of man goes upward and the spirit of the beast goes down to the earth?

(Ecclesiastes 3:19-21, RSV)

...and the dust returns to earth as it was, and the spirit returns to God who gave it.

> (Ecclesiastes 12:7, RSV)

We have a special rank in the order of creatures, of course. It is we who have what we brand dominion over the rest. Though it is not emphasized nearly so much as our mortal creaturehood, there are two or three biblical chapters which proclaim it.

So God created man in his own image, in the image of God he created him; male and female he created them. And God blessed them, and God said to them, "Be fruitful and multiply, and fill the earth and subdue it; and have dominion over the fish of the sea and over the birds of the air and over every living thing that moves upon the earth."

> (Genesis 1:27-28, RSV)

For almost four decades now it has been fashionable to point fingers at the Bible for teaching us to "have dominion over the fish of the sea, over the birds of the air and over the beasts of the field," to ìrule the earth and subdue it." The blame for the entire ecological problem of our day is commonly blamed on this message from the Judeo-Christian religious tradition.

It is an accurate yet primitive accusation. It may also be a crude case of scapegoating, akin to the way that Christianity scapegoats the theory of evolution as a cause for moral decay. The concept of humanity's literal "dominion over the earth" is more of a commentary on the way things are in this world than an ethical command. And are things not that way? One scarcely needs the Bible to make it apparent. We do rule other creatures. We have used them as beasts of burden, and we farm them for food. When we want to experiment with anything that might affect humans, we experiment with monkeys or rats. For entertainment we put them in cages and call a collection of such cages a zoo. As for the rest of earth, we farm it, mine it, manage it and pollute it. We are almost capable of doing anything we please with the earth and its creatures. The brain with which we are furnished, be it the result of a long period of evolution or an act more sudden and immediate than that, is so highly developed as to make us a little bit like God in our ability to rule other things and manipulate our environment. And that's the problem.

Because, what shall we do with the ability we have? Shall we do as we please, no matter the cost? Shall we destroy other creatures and each other? Shall we change our environment to match our wildest dreams?

The part of the biblical message we are prone to overlook is the part that holds us responsible for all that we do. To be placed in dominion is to be given the position of stewardship. We are stewards, not owners, of the earth and it is required of stewards to be faithful.

> Who, then, is the faithful and wise steward, whom his master will set over his household to give them their portion of food at the proper time? Blessed is that servant whom his master when he comes will find so doing. (Luke 12:42-43, RSV)

The point is simple but important. Much is required of us for much as been given. Much of earth is subordinate to us and that makes us responsible. We have the power to preserve or to destroy, to make good or cause evil. And our penalties are often of our own doing, for we must live with the results of all that we do.

Just as importantly, we should not use scripture to deceive ourselves about the material realities of this world. Pretending that we are "specially created" apart from nature is nothing more than a biblical fantasy, wishful thinking you might say. Yet it is common for people to lie to themselves that way. That is not the path to honest-to-goodness faith or a brand of Christianity that is healthy or sustainable in this world.

If we were so specially created there would be no need to rely on nature for our survival. Yet there are many ways in which we are related to the rest of nature. To some degree we are all consumers. As eaters of vegetables or meat, as users of wood and metal and rock, as creatures who drink water and breathe oxygen, we are all users of nature. Some of us are totally that. We are content to merely use whatever material resources are available to us and dump our refuse in whatever immediate environment we find ourselves.

Some of us are appreciators. We love to look at beautiful sunsets. We love to listen to the birds or observe the deer and the beaver. Some of us are such great appreciators that we make a profession of it as scientists or naturalists or artists. Perhaps there is no such thing as a person who cannot appreciate nature at least a little, though sometimes I fear that there are folks like that – even many.

Some become keepers of nature, by keeping a dog or a cat or a roomful of plants. Such people want to go beyond appreciating to nurturing – to sharing some of the secrets of the private life of another creature or a plant by participating in its breeding and feeding and growth. Some find satisfaction, alas, in the business of dominating and manipulating another. Some of us like dogs, for example, simply because we like to have something to train or just plain "boss around."

There are some who go so far in the domination of other species of life that they enjoy the role of destroyer. They hunt, but not for meat. They destroy for the love of destroying. Of such kind were the mighty men of money who rode the rails to the West for the sport of shooting the bison along the way. They nearly wiped out the species as a result. How is that in keeping with stewardship of God's creation? It is not.

There is a difference between the hunter and that so-called sportsman who merely shoots to get trophies or set a new record of body-kills. The true hunter is a survival of the primeval man who preyed upon other animals in order to eat. The true hunter is kin to the wolf and the panther. He is, in fact, a competitor for game with the wolf and the panther and this may explain our deeply-ingrained antipathy toward such animals. From time immemorial the human hunter has vied with the wolf for the same meat. But the true hunter realizes that the wolf has equal right with himself to the deer and the moose. He does not destroy for the sake of destroying, even if it be another creature who needs the same sustenance. The two are kin together.

It is a feeling of kinship with the rest of nature that we need more than anything else at this juncture of our human odyssey. Without it we may well destroy a good part of the natural environment upon which we so needfully depend. Without it we may become something worse than human, something demonic or machine-like that knows no passion or feeling. We must see ourselves as part of creation. We are as totally dependent upon it as the least of the bugs or the largest of wild beasts. But we must also see that we are that part of creation which possesses frightening power with which we can do great harm to other kinds of creatures. We must use that power with wisdom and respect and humility.

JESUS AND THE ECOLOGICAL CAUSE

At first thought it would seem that there is no necessary relationship between Jesus and a religious concern for our natural environment. One does not have to be a Christian in order to be concerned about the earth. One might even think that it would be better not to be a Christian if one wants to be concerned about the earth, for the most popular conceptions of the message of Jesus view him as a messenger of heaven rather than a messenger of earth. Again and again, we remind ourselves that his kingdom was not "of this world" and take "this world" to be the earth. But such conceptions are mistaken, for according to the New Testament gospels Jesus was much concerned about living on earth in fellowship with each other and with other creatures.

According to Matthew, Mark and Luke, Jesus' message was mostly about the Kingdom of God. (Kingdom of Heaven" is the phrase in

Mathew's gospel because Matthew was sensitive to pious Jewish habits of speech. It was the custom among Jews to avoid the use of the word God and speak with circumlocution instead. Jesus likely observed this himself and, therefore, Matthew's "Kingdom of Heaven" is likely as Jesus spoke it. When the Kingdom of God is defined, we find it to be a kingdom of mustard seeds, yeast in a loaf of bread, birds of the air, lilies of the field and little children. Its ways are the ways of nature and not always in accord with our sense of justice. It is a kingdom in which the sun and rain bless the good and the bad alike and seed is sown in the rocks and the weeds as well as on the cultivated land. In this Kingdom the laborers may receive the same wage, even though they worked a different sum of hours. It is a kingdom of grace and what we would call chance. It is in sharp contrast to our kingdoms and their rules. The kingdom of God of which Jesus spoke was surely the natural world of God's creation as over against the worlds that we construct for ourselves with boundaries, buildings, rules and defensive systems.

The vocabulary differs in John's gospel, where "this world" is the phrase that describes the realm in which most humans live. I take it to mean human culture. It is what we often call "the real world" but it is a world real only to ourselves for it is of our invention. Its systems of coinage, its governments, its commerce and trade are created by ourselves for ourselves and are of no particular use to any other creatures. In our kinds of kingdoms, we are satisfied to merely make use of other creatures of their value to us as food or hide or raw material for synthetic products. In our kinds of kingdoms, we live for ourselves and unto ourselves. We even make wars against other little kingdoms that are very much like our own.

Jesus appears as one who has come out of the world that is purely God's into our little worlds or kingdoms in order to reconnect us to that greater kingdom that is God's, that we may discover that we are supposed to be. And what are we supposed to be? Children of God. Not Americans, Germans, English or Japanese, or whatever other labels we can put upon ourselves to be distinctive, but simply children of God.

> See what love the Father has given us, that we should be called children of God; and so we are. (I John 3:1, RSV)

Jesus comes into our worlds as one who brings life. Yes, life. Simply and boldly and profoundly that. Nothing more, nothing less. He gives life by showing us the connections that flow from God to us and be seeking to reestablish the connections that have been broken. We are to know God as he knew God, as Father. In learning to think of God as Father we come to think of ourselves as God's children, and that is the central thrust of Jesus' message.

Throughout the gospel stories, Jesus seems to be in the business of reducing or elevating people in order to help them return to being naturally and simply human. To the mighty, the proud or the rich he said, "Sell what you have…; be willing to lose…; become as little children." Because they understood themselves to be more than they were, they needed to be reduced.

To the sick, the poor, the outcast of the society, he spoke the opposite message: "be healed…; your sins are forgiven…; follow me and have riches…; rise and walk…; come to me and I will give you rest." Because they thought themselves to be less than they were, they needed to be elevated. This is especially emphasized in the Gospel according to Luke, which often repeats this phrase: the first shall be last and the last shall be first. The words of mother Mary's magnificat summarize it beautifully.

My soul magnifies the Lord

and my spirit rejoices in God my Savior,

for he has regarded the low estates of his handmaiden.

For behold, henceforth all generation will call be blessed;

for he who is mighty has done great things for me

and holy is his name.

And his mercy is on those who fear him

from generation to generation.

He has shown strength with his arm;

he has scattered the proud to the imagination of the hearts;

he has put down the mighty from their thrones

and exalted those of low degree;

he has filled the hungry with good things

and the rich he has sent empty away.

He has helped his servant Israel,

in remembrance of his mercy,

as he spoke to our fathers

to Abraham and to his posterity forever.

(Luke 1:46-55, RSV)

One could say that Jesus was in the business of helping people to discover honest identity and worth. He corrected false images. One could even say that he was a natural man, helping others to be natural, too.

The problem that Jesus addressed has not disappeared from the face of the earth. We still have no shortage of people who think themselves more than they are and perhaps a greater number whose self-worth is too low in their own sight. We still need one to walk among us with words that will prick our balloons of inflated ego and with hands that will lift the lowly to their feet.

How does it happen that we can slip into false images of ourselves? Students of mine have discussed this and come up with some sensible suggestions. When one must play a certain role for too long, they suggested, the person can become the role and cease to be a person. Leaders seem especially vulnerable. One could imagine the president of a country coming to think that he was truly a special kind of human, as kings used to think. This could place his importance above that of other men. It could lift him above common morality and permit him to do what would be forbidden to other citizens. It could tell him that he deserves greater wealth and honor than other folks. He could fill his office so well that he could become that important office and never step out of it even when his term is ended.

Similarly, the reverse can occur. If one is dependent upon society for too long, one can become totally that to oneself as well as to others. One can become "just a housewife" or "just a worker" for so long that one is nothing else. One can be the criminal, the problem, the woman, the kid. These are not criticism of these stations in life, or any other. These are observations that it is possible to limit ourselves to being just "one thing," to the point where we lose sight of our own potential. When that happens one needs to be redeemed – which is to be reclaimed as someone of worth.

What can happen to individuals can happen to groups of people and even to entire nations. Traveling abroad I am often disgusted at how blatantly Americans or Europeans can show themselves to be of more worth than others. The rich tourist sauntering into a hotel lobby with a cartful of bags behind him says it so eloquently: I have money, importance and dignity. I will pay. You serve me. But remember that I deserve something better than you ordinary folk. In a similar way, a rich nation can think that because it has been lucky, it surely deserves more of earth's resources than other nations can have and enjoy. We Americans now think this way by habit. We simply assume that we deserve more of the "good things of life" than the rest.

Conversely, a little people can think themselves lowly and undeserving. Little people and little nations can be exploited by others for so long that they come to think of themselves as like a destitute woman who can only expect to be raped. Then there are nations or places that by nature their arrogance and greed, assume they have a right to abuse others at will. That was the case with the cities of Sodom and Gomorrah.

There are persons and nations that need to be judged, disciplined and brought down from their pedestals of self-esteem. There are persons and nations that need to be redeemed. Both works are the works that Christ came to do.

In a similar way, human beings can develop feelings of self-importance that say, "We are worth more than the wolf, the deer, the forest, the butterfly." Human beings can come to think that there is nothing more important in all creation than human beings. Or, on the other side, they can think themselves as nothing but slop and behave in manners that are beneath the dignity of other animals. It happens easily when too many people are crowded too closely into limited and sordid spaces.

What does it mean to redeem? It means to realize the value of a thing. We redeem rewards by cashing them in for goods that have value. There are still people who redeem goods at a pawn shop or what used to be called a hock shop. With a hock shop the sale coupon is presented to the proprietor, along with the appropriate amount of cash, and the property is redeemed in a transaction fashion. Redemption is for things that have been mere tokens of value for a time. After they are redeemed they are of real value again.

There are persons whose true value is lost. They are out of circulation, one might say. They need redeeming. Their lost value needs to be reclaimed. There are groups of people who are in the same category, whole groups of people who have been deemed worthless by the world around them. There are places where earth and its creatures are despised and rejected by men. Places and creatures that are raped and ravished for a value that is too narrow and too shortsighted. There are places where earth itself needs to be redeemed and there are many creatures of earth that are desperately in need of redemption.

If we would continue the work of our Lord Jesus Christ, we should be in the business of redemption. We should be redeeming all that needs to be redeemed. This surely includes the millions of persons who have been given a false sense of value or a sense of no value. Should it not also include the other parts of nature wherever they are treated without respect? Did not Jesus' sense of values include earth and all its creatures great and small? "Not one sparrow falls to the ground without your Father's will," he said. He valued the seed and the leaven and the rock as a pillow for his head. To follow Jesus is to value all that God has created. But neither do we need to plot control of every aspect of creation. Nor does God, really. Creation works because the universe operates on free will. That's why our choices matter. They have consequences, good or bad.

The identity of Jesus is also a matter to be considered. Buried in clichés as it is, the "original Jesus" is a bit hard to get at. He is there in the gospels, a Jew among Jews in a tiny land, available to our scrutiny as long as we keep the record unchanged. To a large group of the people of his time he was the prophet from Nazareth, one who spoke the word of God. To a group less large he was a savior, for he saved them from various ailments, from fear, from guilt and sin, from loneliness, from the straitjackets of roles overplayed. To a smaller group he was Master, Teacher or Rabbi. They gathered around him as disciples and learned his ways. To the smallest circle he was one who knew God as father with an intimacy that was awesome – as though he knew a secret that he could share in order that they might address God in the same terms and become sons and daughters of God in their own self-consciousness as well.

In time, Jesus became the property of the Church. For better or for ill, he became many things: a mascot or emblem for marching armies, but also the patron of hospitals and houses of mercy, the emblem and pride of princes and kings, but also the friend of the poor and the suffering. In the name of Jesus, the Church has performed both deeds of mercy and inglorious deeds of greed and violence. His armies of Crusaders brought suffering. His servants of the sick brought healing. Wherever the Church and its people have carried the cross, Jesus has become what we needed him to be.

In a mystery that he spoke of in some of his parables, Jesus is also one who walks in a million disguises over the face of the earth. At one moment he is the hungry child in need of food; at another, a naked man shivering in the street. In one place he comes to us asking for a drink of fresh water; in another he asks for our comfort. He is disguised in the needs of our neighbors and in whatever we do for the least of these we do it also for him.

Is he also disguised in the needs of the rest of creation? I fancy often enough that I see him there. I see him reflected in pools of polluted water. I hear him cry in the death of a forest that was dutifully cleaning our dirty air. (Did you know, dear reader, that healthy forests are nature's huge air filter systems?) I sense his pain as we ravage the earth with our missiles of war. Could it be that in serving any least part of creation that we might be serving this One?

THE COSMIC CHRIST

The apostle Paul had a particular vision of the resurrected Christ in which Jesus was the head of a cosmic body. The body was made up of believers – persons, that is – who heard the Gospel and responded. The unity of the body proceeds from the head and the parts of the body are knit to each other as in a true organism.

> For just as the body is one and has many members and all the members of the body, though many, are one body, so it is with Christ. For by one Spirit we were all baptized into the one body – Jews or Greeks, slaves or free – and all were made to drink of the one Spirit.
>
> I Corinthians 12:12-13, RSV)

As Paul saw it, each part of the body was joined to the other in both pain and pleasure and each part is obliged to serve the rest of the body, as the eye or the foot each serve the organism in a peculiarly useful way. Paul's complete code of ethics is rooted in this vision. It is because we are each parts of this common body that we are obliged to serve each other.

> For as in one body we have many members and all the members do not have the same function, so we, though many, are one body in Christ and individually members of one another... Rejoice with those who rejoice and weep with those who weep. Live in harmony with one another; do not be haughty but associate with the lowly; never be conceited.
>
> Romans 12:4-5, 15-16, RSV)

Nature also has something to do with this body, for it is out of nature's bosom that this body arises as Jesus rose out of her tomb. To the ears of Paul, creation was groaning in travail for the birth of this body, for the revealing of the sons of God." In this vision Paul saw the redemption of fallen mankind and, in a way, a redemption of earth as well, for in the birth of the worthy son the mother is also redeemed. It was a vision of humanity being redeemed to realize a value it had lost. This was to be a truly new form of humanity in which there was neither Jew nor Greek, bond nor free, male nor female. The divisions that are so often our causes for hatred or war are resolved by one whose power makes peace between person and person, between God and mankind.

In our time we feel a need to see this vision in larger scope, for we humans have become as estranged from the rest of creation as we are from each other. This body that is the unity in creation must include all that is created by God. It is still as needful as before to catch the vision of a single humanity that rises from the seed that Jesus planted as he committed himself to death and the hands of his Father. In addition to that we need now, more than ever before, to see the vision of earth redeemed together with a humanity healed by peace. The New Adam, like the first, must know that he is of earth's dust as well as of the breath of the Father.

I have had long discussions with many of my students about hope and vision. Hope can come in many forms, we agree. It can take the tangible form of a helping hand as a body sinks under the waves of the sea. It can take the form of encouraging words spoken by a friend in a time of distress. One of the most powerful forms it can take is the form of a vision and, when one is alone, that is apt to be the only form in which hope can come.

We have talked about how we live by visions and of how hard it is to live when there are no visions. We have talked of the case of a young man who lost his incentive to study and, in the extremities of his malaise, his incentive to live. Then one day it occurred to him that he could be a doctor and thus be of great use to others. All along he knew that he had much ability. Many had told him that, but they were also obliged to add, iif you can only get to work and do something with that you've got." Somehow he had not been able to do that – until he saw his vision. As he beheld himself in the vision he was clad in surgical gown, equipped with fine instruments and filled with the necessary knowledge. It put him in gear and fueled him for the years of study that had to be accomplished before the vision could be fulfilled. But he did all that and today he is where the vision showed him to be.

Mankind needs a vision as much as any individual does. Without such vision we flounder and perish. Will there ever be peace on earth unless there be in our minds a conception of what peace would be like? Can the world be better unless we see it as better? Can there be healing of the breach that exists between us and our natural environment? There can be only if we see the possibility in our vision.

Some people malign the song "Imagine" by John Lennon as being anti-religious or politically naïve. Yet within the lyrics written by Lennon there is a call to imagine a better, more peaceful reality than the one we typically create for ourselves or allow to exist. Some might claim that occurs because secular society has removed religion from the public sphere. But that claim depends on denial of all the horrible things religion has done in this world. So the answer to peace and a better world is not religion alone. It is a fusion of the better worlds wrought from the best human and moral values. These include both secular and religious principles.

The apostle Paul did share a vision that is realistic and important. *If we can believe it, it can become possible.* But only if we believe it. If we can believe that all persons are latently brothers and sisters, then and only then we can begin to act as though it were true and bring it about. If we can believe that we are at one with the earth who brings us forth in her travail, then and only then can we re-establish our connection with the environment.

The restoration and reclamation of the environment after the polluted devastation of the 1970s is proof that people caring about the world has great value. The earth has been redeemed in some ways, but the onslaught persists at a greater scale than we might have imagined due to anthropogenic climate change. We must begun by reconnecting what is important and what sustains us. It is important and necessary that we see clean waters and hear the wilderness singing. It is important that we know ourselves to be of the same substance as the stars. It is necessary that we know ourselves to be kin to the rest of the creatures on this planet. We have the power within us to shape much of our own future, but we will shape it in whatever direction we see it. We must have visions of what is good and wholesome and beautiful, or we shall not move to that kind of end. Without such vision we may find ourselves guided only by fear or greed. The bold and honest among us must embrace redemption for all.

Jesus left an ethic by which his followers should live. It was comprised of two components. One half of it was to be as concerned for the needs of a neighbor as for oneself. The other half was to apply oneself to the task of doing whatever dirty job needs to be done. It is epitomized by the scene in John's gospel in which Jesus washed the feet of his most intimate circle of disciples.

They were gathered for a feast, we remember. Unknown to them, it was to be Jesus' last gathering with them. They seem to have assembled around the eating mat with anticipation and joy. They were set for a celebration. In such a mood, all were expecting to be served. None thought of who might see to the amenities. They were a group of poor men who should have known that there was no money for servants, but poor men who anticipate a feast can easily act like rich men. It was Jesus who saw the simple task that needed to be done. He took a vessel of water and, with a towel wrapped around him, he washed and dried the feet of his guests. It was a lesson. They were to do as he did.

To learn the lesson and be his disciples in deed as well as in word, we must develop a sensitivity toward the dirty feet of this world, and we must set ourselves to washing them. Or if we see no dirty feet we must look to dirty air, dirty streams, dirty places of dwelling. There are a multitude of humble tasks that need to be done for the sake of earth and earth's creatures. A true follower of Jesus is one who gets to work at whatever dishonorable task needs to be done.

We commemorate Jesus and share his body ceremonially by celebrating the supper quite often. Should we perhaps be obliged to look around first and do a dirty task that needs to be done before enjoying the feast? Or should we notice that the feet of our neighbors are connected to us – that we who are gathered about the table are parts of that single body whose head is the Christ? Should we recognize that all dirty feet are our dirty feet, that all the troubles of earth are our troubles and that we are inextricably part of all that is around us?

It should be the chief business of Christian congregations to think like this and to do what such thinking requires. It is important that we pause to worship on Sunday or Sabbath. It is important that we teach our young and minister to our own. It is important that we be organized for those tasks. But most important of all is what we do to minister to the humble or difficult needs of the communities in which we are planted. A group of church people should be a sort of permanent clean-up committee that looks for dirty feet and pitches in to clean its part of the world. It should see itself as related to the community and the environment around it and not set apart in any way. It should be a miniature version of the cosmic Body of Christ.

PROPHETIC JUDGMENT ON OUR WAYS

The prophets of the Old Testament were men who heard and repeated the Word of God. Often as not the Word came directly out of nature and the warnings that it offered.

"I have you cleanness of teeth in all your cities

and lack of bread in all your places,

yet you did not return to me," says the Lord.

"And I also withheld the rain from you

when there were yet three months to the harvest.

I would send rain upon one city

and send no rain upon another city.

One field would be rained upon

and the field on which it did not rain withered;

so two or three cities wandered to one city

to drink water and were not satisfied.

Yet you did not return to me," says the Lord.

"I smote you with blight and mildew.

I laid waste your gardens and your vineyards;

your fig trees and your olive trees the locust devoured.

Yet you did not return to me," says the Lord.

(Amos 5:6-9, RSV)

What did the prophet mean by reporting such things as words of God? He meant that his people had forgotten the true God and were worshipping other gods by their deeds. Because they feared what the Assyrians might do to them, they did obeisance to the nation of Assyria and its gods. Because they hoped that the Egyptians might come to their rescue in the final pinch, they did the same to the god-king, the pharaoh of Egypt. And in their gullible desire for prosperity and profit, they had for some time been honoring the gods of Canaan that were less than God as they brought their offering to Baal and Asherah.

What Amos beheld in nature reminded him that God is still God and still in control of his world. Despite the rain dances to Baal, the rains did not come in their time. Why? Because something higher than Baal was in charge. At the very time when they were most respectful of the superpowers of their day they showed less respect for the God of nature on whom they had to depend for bread itself.

Amos was not the only one to sense the word of God in the messages of nature. Micah, for example, understood that nature was a special witness to God's covenant with the children of Israel. Therefore, he began one of his most well-known messages like this:

Hear what the Lord says:

Arise, plead your case before the mountains

and let the hills hear your voice.

Hear, you mountains, the controversy of the Lord,

and you enduring foundations of the earth,

for the Lord has a controversy with his people

and he will contend with Israel.

(Micah 6:1-2, RSV)

There was an ancient precedent for that manner of thinking. We find it in a tradition that is recorded in the Book of Deuteronomy. It is a tradition that records the establishment of the covenant.

Give ear, O heavens, and I will speak;

and let the earth hear the words of my mouth.

May my teaching drop as the rain,

my speech distill as the dew,

and the gentle rain upon the tender grass,

and as the showers upon the herb.

For I will proclaim the name of the Lord.

Ascribe greatness to our God!

Is not he your father, who created you,

who made you and established you. (Deuteronomy 32:1-3, 6, RSV)

If there is any single theme that runs through the messages of all the prophets from the earliest to the latest it is that God is God and in divine ways directs the nature of this world. His people do not always understand what his ways are about, for their sense of justice and propriety is too limited to allow for the many ways and times of God, but in all circumstances He is Lord over all nations as well as Lord of Israel. Psalmists reflected this message in striking ways.

The Lord thwarts the will of the nations;

he hinders the plan of the peoples,

but his own will endures forever;

the plans of his mind affect ages.

How happy the nation whose god is the Lord,

the people he chose as his own!

The Lord looks down from the heavens;

he sees the sons of mankind.

From the place where he sits he looks out

over all the inhabitants of earth.

The Creator looks into their minds,

he who observes all they do.

The king is not saved by great armies

nor the hero spared by great strength.

The horse is a vain hope for victory;

with all of its might it fails.

(Psalm 33:10-17, translation by the author)

Before the Kingdom of this God all kingdoms of men are shoddy and temporary affairs. They each parade for a time on the stages of history, but time and chance befall them all. Then comes their Day of the Lord and they solemnly walk to the land of the dead to join the great nations who had gone there before them.

A second theme, only slightly subordinate to this, is the theme of proper worship. Not rituals and proper procedures, say the prophets, but responsible living is what the Lord requires. Again, a psalmist has responded with this lesson.

God of Gods, the Lord,

has spoken and summoned the earth

from the rising of the sun to its setting.

From Zion, the perfection of beauty,

God shines forth.

God comes; let him not be silent.

Fire devours before him;

tempestuous winds surround him.

He calls to the heavens above,

to the earth, to judge his people:

"Gather my faithful before me,

who sealed my covenant with sacrifice!"

And the heavens declare his right,

for he, God, is the judge.

"Listen, my folk, while I speak!

O Israel, I testify against you,

I, who am God, yes your God.

For no lack of offerings I scold you,

for your fires are always before me.

I desire no bull from your temple

nor rams from your fattening pens.

I own all the beasts of the forest

and the cattle on the tribal hills.

I know every bird of the mountains

and the beasts of the field are my friends.

I would tell you if I were hungry,

for the world and its creatures are mind,

but do I eat the beef of the steers?

Do I drink the blood of the rams?

Offer to God some praise

and fulfill your vows to The Highest.

Call me in times of oppression:

I will help you and you will give glory."

God has said to the wicked,

"Should you recite my commandments

or speak with your mouth of my covenant?

--for you have despised my instruction

and thrown my words behind you!

When you see a thief you approve him

and you share the adulterer's fun.

You permit your mouth to speak evil

and fasten your tongue to a lie.

You sit and slander your brother,

finding fault with your nearest of kin.

You have done this and I have been silent,

while you thought that I was like you.

I accuse you; I put it before you.

(Psalm 50:1-21, translation by the author)

I rehearse this material because there are strong and consistent themes in the writings called The Prophets that speak a word of judgment that is as relevant to our time as it was to the times in which they first preached their messages to men. The judgment starts with the proclamation that there is one God who brooks no rivals. All gods less than this God are either subordinate powers or pure imagination. All national ideologies that pose as gods come to their various ends and crumble. Only this one rules as Lord of Creation forever.

And what happens when nationalistic ideologies fail and the nations they represent cease to be nations? They return to being purely and simply part of God's natural world. Their citizens become just plain people and the weeds grow in the ruins of their fine cities.

> And Babylon, the glory of kingdoms, the splendor and pride of the Chaleans, will be like Sodom and Gomorrah when God overthrew them. It will never be inhabited or dwelt in for all generations; no Arab will pitch his tent there, no shepherds will make their flocks lie down there. But wild beasts will lie down there and its houses will be full of howling creatures; there ostriches will dwell and there satyrs will dance. Hyenas will cry in its towers and jackals in the pleasant palaces. Its time is close at hand and its days will not be prolonged.
>
> Isaiah 13:19-22, RSV)

Zion will be plowed as a field;

Jerusalem shall become a heap of ruins

and the mountain of the house a wooded height.

(Micah 3:12, RSV)

Scripture foretells that God (and nature) has the last word in all human affairs, and his last word is wilderness. We are experts at taming the wilderness or wiping it out. But when we have finished doing our thing, then the Lord of Nature takes over again, and the wilderness returns with all its wild citizens. This is the judging action of God that goes contrary to human logic. This is the Kingdom that is not of the "this world" of our thinking. Its ways are too far beyond our ways to be comprehended. This is that Kingdom of God where the thistles grow with the wheat and where the thistles can even prevail. It is the Kingdom we battle as we create our cultures and countries, as we thrust about with our giant earth-moving machines and build mighty buildings that reach to the sky and challenge the gods, as we manipulate the genes of plants and animals to produce more food. We win many rounds of the contest and sometimes we seem to be ready to win for good – for our good, that is. But in the end, our accomplishments go the way that each of us goes: to the dust from whence we came. God represents the alpha and the omega, the beginning and the end. And the end, like the beginning, is wilderness. That is the message of the prophets of old.

And what does it say to us today? It says that we should not be overly proud or ambitious and that whoever is on the side of nature is one God's side. The largest of our kingdoms and accomplishments are only within the vastness of the realms that are God's and the worst that we can do in our efforts to be bigger and better than those who were before us is destroy ourselves. Our bombs of destruction are poised, one set against another, and with them we can do irreparable damage to much of the earth but, most of all, irreparable damage to ourselves.

The games we play as nations are quite ridiculous. Because the great powers of earth fear each other, they stockpile unbelievably destructive weapons and spend huge sums of money staying ready for an eventual mutual attack. In many respects, the United States of America is the worst of these hoarding villains. The whole affair is frightfully costly. But if one day we should unleash all of that stuff we shall find that whatever kind of enemies we imagined the others to be, the truth is that the weapons themselves are enemies of mankind and of nature. Because of our fear of each other we have become enemies of God and God's world. Yet we will not relinquish our weapons, for the gods of our national ideologies are greater gods to us than the God who created us all.

We would rather serve the gods that we create with our suspicion and fear than that One we confess as God in our religious creeds. These are the ways of legalists consumed by their own set of rules. We are fools beyond reason and that proves that our fear is greater than our power of reason. So people repress, and oppress, all instincts they fear. We are as hopelessly lost in the service of lesser gods as were the Assyrians or Babylonians or Greeks or Romans of old. We could turn it around, but will we? If we give it all up and destroy ourselves in our ultimate blast or the baking heat of climate change, then God who has been God from the beginning will prevail with some form of wilderness that few or none of us will be around to enjoy.

THE SEED OF THE FUTURE

So. what now? We are related to people who grubbed in the earth with sticks for bodily sustenance. They ate roots, certain insects, herbs and berries. We are related to communities who gathered, upon occasion, to prepare for hunting. They made sharp weapons, organized a plan of attack, assigned women and children to watching stations, found the game, pursued it, killed it in direct encounter, tore into the meat with hands and teeth and ate some of it raw if they were hungry enough. Then they cut it up for carrying, roasted some for immediate consumption, cured some for keeping, and generally reveled over what they had been given. We are related to primitive farmers who dug in the earth with sticks and stones, then harvested with a sickle of bone. Preparation of food was a daily task of starting with grains or vegetables raw and whole.

We are related to people who lived in tents and temporary shacks, available caves, huts of reeds or bark. We are related to stone-builders, mud-builders, stick-builders. Some of these relatives of ours still live in such ways in what we civilized folk call remote areas of the earth. We could move ourselves geographically to meet them. Or we can move our minds back through time to discover that our ancestors all lived in such ways. For some of us the journey back is only a few generations or a few hundred years. For others, a journey of thousands of years is required – but let not even ten thousand years seem long because once we get back that far, the primitive style of our ancestors moves back with barely perceptible changes for about five million years in all. Yet some people consumed by their own "rules" of scripture choose to deny that history. They do so on the shallowest of premises, and for the most selfish of reasons. To "control" the narrative as if that empowers them through the Word of God. It is as vain and ephemeral a worldview as any on earth, for it denies the depth of creation itself to claim human understanding above all.

There are some primitive ways and values retained in the Scriptures we know as sacred. The Torah, especially (the Old Testament) retains phrases and rituals that are quite obviously rooted in ways much older than the times of the storytellers themselves. Consider, for example, the rituals concerning blood. At the end of the story of Noah we find the basic concern for the sanctity of life in its animal form in these words: "Only you shall not eat flesh with its life, that is, its blood." It is the code of the ancient hunter and perhaps only one who has met an animal face-to-face and known the sight, smell and feel of the warm blood can understand the prohibition. A sacrifice takes place when the animal is killed and the human beings feast from the sacrifice. Life has been taken that life may go on. The beneficiaries knew this end, so they returned a token of the life that was taken by returning the blood to the ground.

In the blood was the life and therefore blood was sacred. In seed there was also life and for that reason seed was considered sacred. There were prohibitions against the mixing of seeds of grain in planting. There were rituals for the offering of bread that was made form the grain. There was still more respect and sanctity attached to human seed.

When Abram was ninety-nine years old the Lord appeared to Abram and said to him, "I am God Almighty; walk before me and be blameless. And I will make my covenant between me and you, and will multiply you exceedingly." Then Abram fell on his face and God said to him, "Behold my covenant is with you, and you shall be the father of a multitude of nations."

(Genesis, 17:1-3, RSV)

Now Abraham was old, well advanced in years; and the Lord had blessed Abraham in all things. And Abraham said to his servant, the oldest of his house, who had charge of all that he had, "Put your hand under my thigh and I will make you swear by the Lord, the God of heaven and earth, that you will not take a wife for my son from the daughters of the Canaanites, among whom I dwell, but will go to my country and to my kindred and take a wife for my son Isaac."

(Genesis 24:1-4, RSV)

In grasping the genitals of his master to take the vow, the servant touched what was sacred because it produced the seed of the future. The bearing of seed was central in the idea of God's covenant with Israel. Giving birth to children was a holy task that made matriarchs and patriarchs into heroines and heroes. There was no accomplishment of the biblical ancestors more important than that. Without this their stories would have ended shortly. So we celebrate the stories we know through scripture. Without this, Abraham and Sarah would have had no Isaac; Isaac and Rebekah would have had no Esau and Jacob; and Jacob would not have fathered (in a mannner of speaking) twelve tribes. Without ancestors there can be no descendants. Without our ancestors, none of us would be here. It is all very obvious. It is this realization that leads people to value the stories of ancestors and lists of genealogies. The sanctity of our own existence leads us to see the sanctity of seed. It is no wonder, but only logical, that the Bible should record blessings on human seed. Some of these perspectives are quite patriarchal and a bit anachronistic, but we can understand them in context with the times:

Sons are a heritage of the Lord;

the fruit of the womb, a reward.

Like arrows in the hand of a warrior

are the sons of vigorous youths.

Happy are those whose quivers are filled with such!

(Psalm 127:3-5, translation by the author)

But times have changed. Seed is no longer of such great value. In the long-ago times of sparse population it made sense to hope for much seed. Still more when chances of survival were slim and the mortality rate of the young was high. To guarantee their continuance into the future our ancestors had to place high value on seed and the births of many babies. In our time, by sharp contrast, we see the survival of most of our offspring and multiplication of populations that stagger us. There are clearly too many humans in many places already. More babies we do not need.

So it is that we now stand at the point in our history where we can easily undervalue babies and human life in general. Because there are so many of us, the life of one or even a few million does not matter much. Only such people as Jews, who saw their numbers decimated by nearly half during World War II, can see much value in population.

The current issue of abortion thrusts us into a consideration of the value of human life. At one extreme are people who see no need for any consequence beyond the pleasurable act of sexual intercourse, if that is all that was desired. Should abortion be permitted? Of course, they contend; any time a woman becomes pregnant against her intentions she should have the right to end the pregnancy. As for the life of the fetus, there is no value in it.

At the other extreme are those who oppose abortion no matter what the circumstance. Even if a young girl was raped by her father and pregnant with a child who cannot be welcomed, they would permit no removal of that which is conceived. A life is a life, no matter what and no matter how many there are in the world. (One wonders what they would do if it were so crowded that we had to crawl over each other like insects in order to move.)

As usual, there are in the middle sensible people who have a sound sense of values. On both sides of the argument are people who want to retain the value of human life. Some see it in terms of giving dignity to every life that is conceived even before it is born. Others see it in terms of limiting numbers precisely in order that every individual's life can be treated as important. They know that sheer numbers can cause devaluation and that a life that is not wanted can be harmed by that attitude.

Whatever decisions we make about this and similar issues, we must be concerned for the dignity of the lives of our children and of all children. Our ancient parents could be concerned about having enough children to guarantee survival in the future. We must be equally concerned for the quality of life possible for each child we help into the world. We need to have as much concern for seed as they had, but that same concern will lead us into different decisions. At some point we must limit human population. The danger point has long since been passed in the most congested areas of the planet. But while we seek to reduce or control population growth, we must be even more concerned to pass on to our descendants a world worth living in.

The greatest enemy of this cause is our own greed. If we insist on consuming all that our fancies desire, we shall leave precious little for those who come after us. Remember that in less than 150 years on the North American continent, the human population stripped off and lost some of the most valuable soil created in all the world's history. Water shortages are now staring us in the face as well. Without stewardship, we shall be robbing from our very own children. Likewise, if we use up or destroy all the last pockets of wilderness in our world, we shall leave nothing for anyone to enjoy. They will not even have the privilege (or the right...) of knowing what it was like. If we pollute our environment without restraint, we shall be poisoning the air that our own children must breathe. Whatever we do to this planet, we also do to our children. They shall inherit the results of all of our deeds. If we are not careful, we are the 'bad seed' that destroys the field even as it produces no crop for the future.

We hear much talk about the future in our time. What shall be the shape of the future, we ask ourselves again and again? And then we imagine all sorts of things by way of answer – fancy new gadgets of convenience, faster and faster forms of travel, knowledge of distant planets. Can people live on Mars? Occasionally we imagine the worst instead of the best, and we describe the ghastly aftermath of a nuclear war. But in either case we tend to leave out the obvious. There are, after all, some things that will be as much a part of the future as of the past or the present. For sure there will be the planet itself, and for almost as sure, there will be people. Who will those people be? They will be our descendants. Our seed is the seed of the future. We live on in our sons and daughters and in their children. That is a fact that will not change no matter what else changes about our way of life.

Knowing that, we must pause to question all that we undertake in the name of progress. If we use all the resources that area at our disposal, what do we leave to our children? Whatever we use of exhaustible materials, we take from our own descendants. Whenever we damage any part of the earth, we damage it for them. Dare we be so grossly selfish as some of us have been up to this point? Can anything be more immoral than to us and abuse all that we can, no matter what the consequence for those who continue our existence into the future? If nothing else should stop us in our tracks and compel us to act with a sense of responsibility, this should most of all.

None of us can afford to live solely for today, and we cannot truly live for the sake of the past. Only the future is ours to affect with our decisions and deeds. That future should be precious to us because it contains our children. For their sake we must act with wisdom. As surely as our acts of copulation produce them as people, all the rest of our acts produce consequences for the environment. Do we not want the best for our children? Then we must do our best in passing on to them an earth that is worthy of being home to countless generations. That world will not end tomorrow, no matter what the predictions of high-powered preachers of doom. Our little worlds will end – frequently enough and from time to time. But God's is the world without end, and earth is part of that world.

A WAY OF RETURN: ST. FRANCIS OF ASSISI

There is every possibility that we humans can destroy so much of our natural habitat and even the air we breathe that the quality of our lives will be considerably diminished in the future. Which is to say that life for our descendants would not be as good as it has been for us. What can prevent that? A turning, I have suggested. But to what can we return and what is the nature of our turning? The turning cannot simply be aimless. Such turning is nothing more than confusion. To merely turn away from where we were going to be lost. There must be a vision for turning back as much as there must be a vision for going forward. We must turn to something we can see as real.

One way of turning is the way of St. Francis of Assisi, whose story has been part of the tradition of the Church since the thirteenth century. Francis, as the story goes, was born into a wealthy family. His father was a dealer in fine dry goods and Francis could well have followed his father into that profession and into wealth. His future was assured, so to speak. He had it good. But while still a youth, Francis caught a vision of something called poverty. (To him it was a someone; Dame Poverty" he called her.) It was part of the message of Jesus and Francis followed it to the full. He did as the Master once said. He sold what he had and gave it to the poor. And when his father objected, he stripped himself naked, presented his clothing to his confused and irate father, and took to the life for which he became famous.

In his poverty St. Francis made some new discoveries about himself and all of us who call ourselves human. He discovered his relationships to the rest of the creatures of earth. He learned to commune with the birds and the beasts and with all the elements around him. The wind became Sister Wind to him; the sun, Brother Sun. He discovered that all the realities of nature were his kin. He discovered that we live in a world of big and little sisters and brothers. There are legendary stories of how Francis was able to speak to the wolves that haunted the forest – that the wolf, whom all Europeans held in dread, was his friend – and of how the birds would come to his hands to be fed

A changing of ways of behavior begins with and follows a changing of our feelings. As long as we dread the elements of the wilderness about us, we treat them with hostility. As long as we think of the wolf as an enemy we shall pursue all wolves until the last one is dead. So have we done with many species before and so we continue to do. The only living specimens of certain kinds we will tolerate are those imprisoned in the cells of zoos where we can ogle at them in safety. That is a diminished world to occupy.

What if we should learn that the beasts are our friends? What if we should learn that there are many ways in which we depend upon them and that there is such a thing as a totally balanced ecosystem in which each part needs the other for a life of the fullest happiness? What if we should learn that there is a kind of natural Body of Christ in creation and that we, ourselves, shall be better off if we allow all parts to live and discover that we can feel their parts with them? What if we should discover that the wolves and also their prey, the moose, are our sisters and brothers?

If that should happen, we will begin to treat all of nature with respect and honor. The change of attitude will change our behavior. Once we see the values of all species of life and all the elements upon which all species of life depend, then we shall get on nature's side and seek to preserve all that we can.

There are prophets in our time who have shown us the way to such respect. Loren Eisely and George Wald are two whose messages are well-known through numerous books. Lesser-known folks are greater in number. There is a small but growing population of people who are seeking a new lifestyle based on communion with nature. They dress in other people's cast-off clothing and move to vacant farms where they learn to walk in the meadows and woodlands, grow vegetables as the mainstay of their diets, and bake their own bread. They have found food better than what the supermarkets can sell and a set of values that makes the commercial values of our society look shabby. The society typically calls them Kooks, but I say that they are prophets for our time.

Dare we stop and consider the shabbiness of what most of us in the affluent part of the world call wealth? The prepackaged foods that we buy are largely small variations of a few limited natural food sources that are heaviest on starches and sugars. Under the disguises of ever-new packaging that promises another New Product, we eat less variety of foods in our diet than did our farming forefathers in the nineteenth century. And much of what we do to improve or preserve the products turns out to be harmful to health.

Or consider that necessity called the automobile. If we could be satisfied with safe and economical transportation, we could ride in rugged, durable machines that would last a lifetime. But because we want style and convenience more than anything else, we buy cars that are destined for the junk heap. Some within a few years, others longer. But all, eventually. Most of us are so gullible that we follow the pied piper call of sales gimmicks into whatever late model promises some new twist of the body line or some new gadget to make riding more entertaining. And when our government has the gall to require something like greater fuel efficiency in our vehicles, or to convert them to electric power, there always seem to be cynics and opponents of those laws whose selfish ideals think nothing about the future.

The consumer society in which we live is a very sick society if measured by some kinds of values. The majority of its citizens want nothing more than to try something new that they fancy to be better simply because nothing has ever satisfied them before. The whole system depends on our dissatisfaction. Without that dissatisfaction there is no progress,- no chance for further sales. Because we have more than we need of the necessities of life, we must be persuaded to buy on the basis of our petty dissatisfactions. Sales is the point of it all. Those at the helm of our ship have one aim in mind: to sell us more and more no matter what the cost.

What if any one of them should stop and discover the immense satisfaction of being part of a natural system in which every dawn does bring new delights without our mad efforts to produce it? That would be the end of the person's interest in being merely a consumer or a peddler of consumable goods. We have, in other words, sold off our sense of wonder. Has it been sold for too cheap a price?

We must consider what we have done to ourselves by believing in the values of the market above all other values. We have cheapened life for ourselves and we have blinded our eyes to the value of natural realities around us. We can slaughter birds and small beasts on the highways without a thought of regret because we value only the speed of the vehicle in which we are moving our fat asses. We can litter the roadsides of our movements with smelly junk because we have never bothered to value the lovely natural smells that we blatantly blank out with the fumes of our exhaust and our refuse. By rushing and thrusting ourselves forward into what must be newer or better, we shut ourselves off from a myriad of beautiful sights and sounds and scents around us.

As I write these words I am sitting at the level of treetops in my home. The windows are open. I hear the morning calls of a dozen breeds of birds and smell the freshness of June foliage. In the distance I hear the traffic of the highway and the streets. What if my position were reversed? What if I were sitting beside the highway instead of here? The sounds of its traffic would overpower the sounds of the birds and the fumes of the motors would blanket all-natural smells. Where one sits make quite a difference.

Many of us are so much surrounded by the fumes and racket of our culture that we cannot know the smells and sounds of God's world. We can take trips in our cars, of course, to look at the scenery." But even that is scarcely enough to pull us out of our muddled worlds of junk. Riding in the vehicle we shall look at the passing scene as one looks at the moving pictures on a screen. We shall see nothing in detail and nothing of the intricacy of the natural world beyond the edge of the highway. Worst of all, its sounds and scents will escape us completely, for our ears will hear only the sounds of the engine and the radio, while our noses are treated only to the smells of the machine and the spray can odors of the people inside it. We will not hear the birds and the trees. We will not smell the meadows of whatever else is swept by the breeze. Even as we behold the passing sights of nature we cheat ourselves of most of what is there. What poverty of values! We multiply our exposure to a severely limited number of goods and services but cheat ourselves of exposure to the infinite variety of experiences that are available to us in the natural world that is God's.

To follow St. Francis of Assisi we need to cast off the clothing our culture demands, if even for a few moments, and take to our feet. With feet and nothing more for conveyance, we need to walk in places where wild things grow and discover their beauty – the beautiful form of a cobweb at morning, the beautiful fragrance of honeysuckle or a wild rose, the beautiful sounds of brooks and insects. We must begin by giving ourselves an opportunity to fall in love with the elements of wilderness.

For those of us who live in country places the trip is convenient. We only need to take the time to try it. For those whose lives are surrounded by city, it is extremely difficult most of the time. And those surrounded by city are the majority of people these days. But even in these places, there is the wilderness of light, a resource that comes to us free from the sun and glance off human inventions to attract our eye.

Granted, only domesticated nature is readily available to people in cities – the nature of the park or the greenhouse or the zoo or whatever is natural in the people round about them. To encounter more than that they must leave the city. For that they have only the automobile or the airplane and either of these ways is less than adequate. Sealed inside the machine they see only a mirage that disappears in the journey back into the city. What is needed is a chance to stop in the midst of a place that is natural – to stop and strip down enough to feel the wind and smell the earth, to go barefoot in running water and to look with unshaded eyes at the little things that grow from the soil.

As we replan and rebuild our cities, we must incorporate pieces of wilderness into the plan. By way of example, the City of Chicago, Illinois, has set aside and restored essential natural areas along the Lake Michigan lakefront. These include acres of wood on the South Side adjacent to Jackson Park that provide critical habitat for migratory and breeding birds within the city limits. On the north side at Montrose Harbor a section of the park includes a zone call the Magic Hedge attracts migrating birds. On a stretch of beachfront a pair of endangered Piping Plovers has now bred for three consecutive years. Nature comes rushing back if we give it a place to thrive.

We have already gone too far for that in most urban areas, of course, but there will be more replanning and rebuilding in the future. It is not fair to cheat huge populations of people of the opportunity to meet nature directly. We must allow piece of wild land into the landscape of every populated area in order that all people may find the connection between themselves and the rest of creation. The rewards are too great to forfeit; the penalties for not knowing this experience are too severe.

We need this connection for the sake of our survival and health. As Isaiah nobly suggests:

> Why do you spend your money for that which is not
>
> bread and your labor for that which does not satisfy?
>
> Hearken diligently to me and eat what it good
>
> and delight yourself in fatness.
>
> Incline your ear and come to me;
>
> hear, that your soul may live…
>
> Seek the Lord while he may be found,
>
> call upon him while he is near;
>
> let the wicked forsake his way
>
> and the unrighteous man his thoughts;
>
> let him return to the Lord, that he may have mercy on him,
>
> to our God, for he will abundantly pardon.
>
> For my thoughts are not your thoughts,
>
> neither are your ways my ways, says the Lord.
>
> For as the heavens are higher than the earth,
>
> so are my ways higher than your ways
>
> and my thoughts than your thoughts.
>
> (Isaiah 55:203, 6-9, RSV)

THE WAY OF WISE MANAGEMENT: ST. BENEDICT

There is a way to which we can turn that could be called the way of wise management – or the way of St. Benedict, for it was the Rule of Benedict which introduced this way within Christian tradition.

Benedict was a monastic leader of the sixth century. Like Francis of Assisi who came seven centuries later, he, too, started by living in poverty. In that poverty he studied himself and others like himself and found wise limits within which to live. Against the value of fasting, for example, he discovered the value of good food in moderation, of adequate shelter and adequate rest. Against the value of ascetic prayer and meditation he discovered the value of labor. The communities that followed the rule of St. Benedict became model communities that helped Europe to avoid repeating some of the sad mistakes made by earlier civilizations.

In the Benedictine communities there was planning and organization that gave to each member a significant task to perform for the sake of the whole. There were those who farmed the fields, those who tended the stock, those who prepared the food, those who studied and wrote books and those who devoted themselves to contemplative prayer. All tasks were held to be equal. Wherever these communities function well they were miniature models of the Body of Christ that was envisioned by the apostle Paul. They were true communities in that there was room for the place of each individual as part of a single organic society.

In their husbandry of the land they worked with similar plan and organization. They did not put all land under the plow. Certain areas were cleared for the planting of crops. Other areas were left as forest or swamp. There was place for the wild flora and fauna as well as for that which was domestic. There was a bit of wilderness along with every human settlement, and there are areas in Europe which are still managed in the same way. Despite centuries of civilization, the Benedictine way has been followed enough to preserve nature as is alongside what we humans can develop- and shape by our manipulation.

To see the importance of this, one can travel in the ancient world of the Middle East either before or after a tour of the European countryside. There in the Middle East, where great civilizations began and lived out their years, land that was once lushly productive is now barren wasteland. Once wooded slopes are now denuded heights and what humans call wasteland covers the sites of former great cities. The only wilderness one finds in most of the Middle East is wilderness that has overtaken and replaced what mankind once mismanaged.

In America we are now tugged in two directions. Thanks to the natives who made important treaties too often broken since and thanks to farsighted conservationists of the past, we still have large areas of pristine earth. But greedy profiteers have been gnawing into these areas for the past several decades and the press of high population threatens them even more. Increased demand for raw materials eats into these areas a little more each year. If no one defends them, they shall soon be gone. For every nature freak who stands up to fight for a swamp or a forest, there are ten who want to develop it for industry or housing or military defense. We are engaged in an important struggle with very high values at stake.

Even at local levels we can see the struggle played out. In the laws that governed homesteading, every homesteading farmer had to promise to leave one quarter of his land in forest where the land was forested. So came about the forty-acre woodlots of Wisconsin and the rest of the Upper Midwest. But time has gone by and farmers now struggling for more income against inflationary costs clear the remaining forest or plow to the fencline and all is converted to cropland. The promises of the past are forgotten. Old laws are forgotten. Desire for profit rules. Farmers frequently don't even own the seeds that they plant each year. They cannot keep any of it for the future. It is owned by corporate agriculture. Farmers can sell their product, but not truly own it.

I know two farmers who represent two radically different ways to farm their land. One is a mite old-fashioned. He does not buy every new labor-saving machine that appears on the market. He does not pour larger quantities of commercial fertilizer on his field in order to increase the yield to higher and higher records. He is concerned for the soil, he tells me. He wants to leave his son a farm that is better than the farm he took over in his youth. He seeks to build and improve the soil. He saves fencerows for wild birds and small game. He enjoys the beauty of his place and reaps an adequate return for a good living. He lives as a steward who is committed to improving what he holds in trust.

The other farmer I have in mind is a truly "with it" kind of guy. He is ambitious, imaginative and energetic. He has found ways to double or triple the yields of his fields and he now feeds hundreds of livestock where his father raised tens. He is heavily indebted at the bank because of the expensive machinery he owns, but with those machines he can do by himself the work that employed several men in his father's time. He is tough and profit-minded. A short time ago his neighbors began to complain that the run-off from his stock feeding concern had polluted their wells. Thanks to him, they now have to dig deeper for drinkable water. But that is none of his business, he claims. He watches out for himself; they must solve their own problems. He has stripped all but a little of the woodlot that he inherited through his father's name. He has enlarged his tillable acreage to what he calls the maximum. To me, he shows no concern for the future. To him, the future is immediate and to be measured in profit and loss.

The difference between these two is apparent, is it not? One sees value in the land itself and he sees himself as servant to it. He makes his living, and moderate it is, but his chief pleasure comes from the task itself and not from beholding the environment he controls. The other sees value in profit above all else. Oh, to be sure, he gets a kick out of the gadgetry of his new enclosed tractors or the lines of a fine beef animal. He even takes pleasure in vacation trips that treat him to new scenic views and faraway places. But above all else he values the profits he can make as he pits himself against the elements of a highly competitive system. He devotes the best of his energy to this and sacrifices whatever is necessary to achieve it.

Cities and countries can be compared in a similar way. Some give an impression of beauty and balance. Others sprawl themselves over the landscape with rapidly-built buildings and industrial mess.

Wise management is what we exercise when we look at all the values of what we held in trust and plan for the future in terms of preserving all that is good. The nation that sells its soul solely to technological progress or a higher and higher GNP is shortsighted and foolish. In its greed for a narrow range of values it will get just those things and nothing more but, along with them, all their by-products. We can have as much atomic energy as we want, but we then also have the problem of atomic waste. We can burn as much coal as there is at our disposal, but we will also have to breathe the smoke that comes out of our smokestacks. We can farm as much land as we are able to plow, but in doing so we shall destroy the habitat of living creatures and alter the terrain. We cannot have both what our greed demands and what good judgment advises. Whatever we do, we shall have the reward we have chosen. We reap what we sow.

Wise management is what happens when we count the cost of everything we undertake before we set out to undertake it. Wise management is management based on a richly and widely informed set of values. Wise management feels concern for the land and for other forms of life, for the Owner's demands upon us as stewards and for the people who will pick up and do with whatever we leave when our days are done.

The concern of St. Benedict might seem to be old-fashioned and out-of-date, but to many it is not. There are an important number of people of this bent today. They are people who have saved for us much of what we now have to enjoy. St. Benedict, who lived his life way back in the sixth century, produced a band of followers who believed in God and in living life with a sense of responsibility. If that ever becomes out-of-date, we are lost. After all, nature is still ruled by the same forces that St. Benedict respected and regarded as God's. Nature has not changed. Even we have not changed that much. We still live by the same needs as our forefathers and mothers.

As for our traditions, some of us might be turned off by the mention of "saints" of any kind. But these wise people were not so much "men of religion" as they were "men of wise existence." Like John the Baptist and Jesus, they broke the mold in order to live closer to the earth and with God.

SALVATION

The minds of most of us operate most conveniently with clichés of speech. We read a book like this and judge it upon whether or not it contains the familiar clichés of our own religious vocabulary. The more there is of the familiar, the better we like it. Unfamiliar jargon frightens us. I suppose that the dearest of all familiar words in our religious vocabulary is the word salvation. Salvation is what it is all about, say the preachers of the gospel. Believe in the Lord Jesus Christ and you shall be saved.

But the term itself begs a question: salvation from what? Salvation from death? Salvation from war? Salvation from disease or drunkenness or distress? There are many dreadful things from which a person might want to be saved.

The preachers of the fundamental gospel have a ready response to our question. Salvation from sin and Hell, they will shout. What else? According to the theologies most popular in America today it is still the medieval realities of sin's punishment that are the problem. Eternity is a long time, they say, and where you spend eternity is the matter of greatest importance.

By now it must be apparent that we have been addressing this fundamentalistic theology throughout this treatise Religion From Earth. We could have addressed more sophisticated theologies, to be sure. We choose to address this subject only because it is so popular. It is the brand of theology so familiar to many Christians in America today and the stereotype of Christian theology that is most well-known to outsiders. It is by such theology that the largest single group of Christians think.

This theology needs to be challenged, we believe, because it fails to cope with the most significant problems of our time. It assumes that it is from a hell of the hereafter that we need to be saved and overlooks the large and real dangers around us from which both we and the earth need to be saved. Its offer of salvation is legitimate for those still living in the fears of the Middle Ages. It fits the fears of other people only because it creates those same fears in the first place, and in creating those fears it binds people to real dangers that are already doing destructive work.

To get at what we conceive those real dangers to be, let us review some of what salvation has meant in the past. In the ministry of Jesus, it meant more than one thing. In some cases, the problem was guilt. In other cases, it was a bodily malady. The stories of Jesus' healing ministry present us with a range of various threats or problems from which Jesus saved people in his time. Never once is it explicitly said that he saved one from Hell's damnation, however. In the sermon of Peter that is recorded in the Book of Acts we find this interesting exchange.

> Now when they heard this they were cut to the heart and said to Peter and the rest of the apostles, "Brethren, what shall we do?" And Peter said to them, "Repent and be baptized every one of you in the name of Jesus Christ for the forgiveness of your sins; and you shall receive the gift of the Holy Spirit. For the promise is to you and to your children and to all that are far off, every one of whom the Lord our God calls to him." And he testified with many other words and exhorted them, saying, "Save yourselves from this crooked generation."
> (Acts 2:37-40, RSV)

There were two problems from which these people needed to be saved, according to Peter. One was their sins and the other was "this crooked generation" in which they lived. Their own culture was the danger that engulfed them, not the threat of a hell beyond the grave.

In the Old Testament we find the concept of salvation repeatedly. And what was it from which Children of Israel were saved or needed to be saved? Most often, from enemies. Sometimes from death or sickness or a natural disaster. Occasionally from guilt or some other consequences of their sins. In short, there were a number of situations and predicaments from which they were saved. Most important of all, they were saved from slavery in Egypt.

> You have seen what I did to the Egyptians, and how I bore you on eagles' wings and brought you to myself."
>
> (Exodus 19:4, RSV)

It was in Western European Christianity that the concept of Hell as a place of punishment for sinners reached its full development. In Latin Christianity, if not in European culture-at-large, people really did fear what might happen to them as a penalty for their sins after they died. Salvation from such a fate was extremely important to them. When church leaders withheld that salvation, the people were in distress, and when Martin Luther and other reformers announced that salvation is a free gift from God there was genuine relief and rejoicing.

There are far fewer people today who live in dread of going to Hell when they die. There are people who dread death itself because it seems to be the end. There are also a great many people who feel worthless because of their failures and their guilt. There are people who feel unloved and lonely. The Gospel of Life, of God's love and forgiveness, is still valid and effective, but not because there is some connection to punishment after death. Men and women do need salvation from guilt in our time, but not with the same fears as those of the Middle Ages. More often they need salvation from a sense of failure or of loneliness. Much of the world needs salvation from hunger, from disease, from political oppression, from violence and crime. There are far more situations than one that cry out for salvation. If we want to preach a gospel that is convincing it shall have to be a gospel that deals with dozens of human dilemmas. But to concentrate solely on one's personal salvation, claiming it before all else, is salvation greed.

Scripture cries out to us to provide salvation for all that we can see, hear and feel. Earth itself needs salvation in our time. There are poisoned lakes and rivers, plundered forests, unclean breezes, eroded hillsides that need to be saved. In the places where humans live more crowded together there are jungles of crime and disease that infects the body of earth. Earth has many ills that we and our fathers have caused. For our fathers, it is too late to help. For us, now is the time.

There are possible and even probable disasters of the future from which we need to be saved before it is too late – the disaster of nuclear war or an earth altered by deadly chemicals, packaged germs, and yes, viruses springing from nature thanks to our abusive, often thoughtless and consumptive penetration into every crevice of the earth. When we rape the earth, guess what? It tends to rape us right back. Climate change and global warming are already here, and denying it does nothing to alter the fact of its effects on our planet, and us? If selfish people have their way and humanity does nothing to ameliorate its collective effect on our atmosphere, it is hell on earth we need to be concerned about, not some remote place we might be sent someday.

We also cannot afford to be selfish about salvation. The saving of our immortal souls is not the ultimate event of life and not the end of the matter. We must not be so selfish as to think that "finding myself" through the strictures of religion is the final goal of existence. There are many others in need and many other kinds of need in this world. That is what Jesus tells us to focus upon.

Nor should we forget that we are to be instruments of salvation to each other. If one is drowning and I can swim, I must save him. If one is lonely and I can be a friend, I must save him. If one is sick and I can heal, I must save him. If some are starving and we have food, we can save them. If some are in fear and we possess the might that they fear, we can save them. If some are in poverty and we possess wealth, we can save them. If people and other creatures are suffering from the fumes of what we burn, we can save them. If we possess tracts of unspoiled land within our borders, we can save it, if we will. If we have power on the high seas and the seas are being plundered without thought of conservation, we can save the seas. There is redemption. And there is salvation.

There is much more to salvation than avoiding the penalties of our individual sins. In God's world, God saves many things in many ways. God saves air with regenerating forests. God saves water with filters of soil and sand and rock. God saves species of life from death by the process of birth. In the cycles of creation, salvation occurs at all times and in multitudinous ways. It is we alone who try to stop parts of the cycle and cause damnation. If we can learn to live in harmony with God's world we shall be saved and we shall perform a part in the salvation of the earth itself.

There are those who will object to such a loose and free interpretation of salvation as this. "So you are caught in the material world alone." they will perhaps counter. "You don't know the difference between life in the ordinary sense and spiritual life."

But we come back with this: the term spirit is used about life in all its ordinary dimensions in the Bible. The word, after all, is a single word for things that we divide, whether in the Hebrew of the Old Testament or the Greek of the New Testament. In one and the same utterance, the biblical term means all of what we mean by the three words, spirit, breath and wind. There is no difference between such terms in the Bible. The breath we breathe is God's spiritual gift to us. Life in the literary sense is ours because God breathed into Adam's nostrils the breath of life. When Jesus wanted to pass on the essence of his life and power to his apostles, he breathed on them, says the evangelist John, and he said, iReceived the Holy Spirit (Holy Breath, Holy Wind)." There is no line of difference between ordinary life and spiritual life. All life is spiritual. All dimensions of life are the gifts of God. What we sometimes call ordinary is as much a miracle and wonder as is a person filled with the Spirit and speaking tongues.

I suppose the very point of coining a phrase like earth religion for Christians is this, that we do not separate life into two realms. We were not made to live here for a while and then in heaven. Heaven is colloquially known as the realm of the stars and we are made of the same stuff as the stars. (Scientifically that is true.) We were made to live here and die here and the breath of life that is ours for a while and taken by God is given back here whenever and however the Giver of all life pleases. We must submit to that. There really is no choice in the matter.

OF PURPOSE AND REASON

"What is our reason for being here?" I heard a preacher ask in my youth. I thought it a wise question at the time. So did the preacher. He waxed eloquent on the theme and allowed as to how it was the most important question a person could ask and of how everybody must ask it sooner or later. Then he proposed his important answer: "God put us here because He needed something to love." The answer bothered me as I thought about it in the time that followed. Does God not love the rest of creation? I thought to myself. I can love it. It is beautiful. It is masterfully and intricately conceived. Or are we somehow more lovable than the rest of it? I could not imagine humans being more lovable than some of the creatures I knew. I had a dog that was hard to surpass for sheer lovableness. I was fond of most of our domestic beasts on the farm and loved what I knew of the wilder creatures. I could easily imagine people to be less lovable than some of those creatures. What other creatures do so much violence and killing as we? What other creatures make war as we do? What other species would produce an Adolph Hitler or an atom bomb? If God created us because He needed something to love, he played a nasty trick on himself for sure!

I have encountered people of various purpose in life. I have met some high-powered individuals who felt that the purpose of life is to succeed. They are people of energy and wit and admirable drive. Climbers is what I would call them, and I notice that they take pleasure in the climbing itself – so much, I have noticed, that when they succeed with one ascent, they are all the more ready to start the next. If there were a single top to get to they might be disappointed, for it is the climbing that they enjoy.

There are people who pursue pleasure as a purpose, I am told. But then, who doesn't? To some degree at least, we all need pleasure from time to time. In the great critique of human purposes and goals known as the Book of Ecclesiastes, the person who pursues it exclusively is named as an example of the vanity of life, but the person who would be wise, writes, the author, should eat and drink and find pleasure in the labor at which he toils beneath the sun through the days of his life.

Is it possible to live for self-gratification alone? Perhaps so. There are psychologists who believe that nothing else is possible but that there are many different ways in which we can each pursue our pleasure. It becomes a way of explaining all human behavior in one neatly-packaged theory. I can understand how it works as a way of explaining our curious ways, I must say, but I also find that it seems pathological when I behold a grown person who strives only for immediate gratification of all sensual needs – sex for sex's sake, gourmet eating and drinking for appetite's sake, expensive adult toys for the sake of thrilling rides, files or piles of music to titillate the ears with new sounds, and the like. If a person spends all available energy and income for obvious gratification, the purpose of life seems dreadfully trite.

There were generations of elders who taught that work is the purpose of life. Along with it went frugality and orderly life. And cleanliness which was second only to godliness, they said. They were a bit like the climbers, except that they felt it was somehow sinful to achieve overly much with their efforts. It was not the thrill of the climb so much that impelled them, but the very virtue of their labor.

Noble causes are the drumbeats that are followed by many admirable achievers. They become great by accomplishing things for others. What would we do without them? Without Florence Nightingales or Clara Bartons or Booker T. Washingtons, the world would be far grimmer than it is. May God give us many such persons for the sake of it all.

We've addressed the issue that there are those who say that the only purpose in life is to get to Heaven when we die. This life is a testing ground, as they see it. The real show comes later. What we believe and how we believe and what we do about it are the things that matter because getting to heaven depends on that. In the end we are judged and if we are deemed worthy then… well, at this point we are faced with two ways. If we stick to biblical terminology, the rest of the sentence finishes with "then we enter the Coming Age." In Christianity of Medieval times and in much of popular Christianity today, the sentence ends with, "then we go to Heaven and be with God."

As I think about it, there are many possible purposes to life. People differ very much as people by the different purposes that they find. There are even people who distinguish themselves by finding no purpose at all. They fall into two categories, it seems. Some are persons suffering from depression to whom the purposelessness is one more reason for their depression. The others are nonchalant characters who simply relax and live without thinking of purpose. They are pleasant for company. Think of the Jeff Bridges character in the movie, The Big Lebowski. Thd Dude Abides.

I have wondered for myself whether there is some single divine purpose for us all – or, to use more naturalistic terms, whether nature has a way that is best or most proper for all humans. Some things seem apparent. One thing most clear to me is that we are an integral part of the whole natural system. Putting it in biblical phrases, it seems clear that we are of the dust of the earth, that the breath of the beast and our breath are the same, that we are members of a mighty chorus of praise-singers that includes all parts of the earth and the universe. Thinking more scientifically, we know that we are made of the same elements as all other creatures and even the same basic elements as the living stars. We cannot divorce ourselves from the natural system. We are undeniably and totally part of it. This must be by purpose if there be anything at all of purpose in creation. Those claiming that human beings enjoy a status of ìspecial creation" are typically either ignorant or arrogant about the matter out of fear or trying to make themselves feel superior in some way. That is tribal at best and beastly petty at worst.

For a time of a certain kind of exile we thought ourselves to belong to another realm. In a time before that exile we thought of the heavens as the place of God while earth was the place of all creatures. It was a way of recognizing that God is not like us. By thinking of the heavens as God's place and earth as ours, we could say that God and God's ways are above us. It was helpful. At the time.

Then we came to think of ourselves as partly of both realms. Our bodies belong here on earth, we reasoned (it was, after all, quite obvious); our minds belonged to the heavens. That was the age of popular Greek philosophies that may have been responding to thoughts from the Far East, and of the Gnostic religions that thrived in the Mediterranean world. We became increasingly uncomfortable with the part that belongs to the earth and began to think of ourselves as strangers here. This was the beginning of our exile, we sought to find ways to leave the earth, to condemn it and to condemn the part of ourselves that is too obviously wedded to it. We thought ourselves to be creatures of the heavens and we saw salvation in becoming totally that.

We were rescued from that thinking in part by the scientific revolution that is still going on because it has been through a scientific exploration of reality that we have discovered the unbroken continuity between the heavens and the earth together with the unity of all that is. As we study stars and galaxies alongside the minutest phenomena of our planet we affirm the oneness that our ancient forebears dared to call God.

In this unity there seems to be something also of purpose. If it is an accident, then it is an accident more colossal than any purpose that ever existed. Everything we can observe or study is bound to everything else. So true is this that we can study nearly inaccessible stars by virtue of the fact they shine with the same lights as nearer bodies of space. Nothing in all reality is isolated. Nothing exists by itself

Is this not a powerful lesson to us? It forces us to consider that no human creature should live solely for the sake of the isolated self. The self must identify with others and link to others. To say that no man is an island is to say something that must be profoundly true. The great inventor Buckminster Fuller arrived at a similar conclusion through secular introspection. "You do not belong to you," he is quoted. "you belong to the universe." On that basis he proceeded to create great inventions to help the human race, and by proxy, all of creation.

This exciting concept is what the apostle Paul proposed to the world in his vision of the Body of the Christ. In a time in which death was overcoming old cultures and systems, Paul said this certain resurrection – a body rising out of the belly of a travailing creation to declare the possible unity of the future in which people could live as simply people who are neither Greek nor Jew, slave nor master, female nor male.

Binding this body together is what the New Testament writers call agapé, the greatest of the gifts of God. We translate the word as love in modern English, but that is somewhat unfortunate for the word love has become all too small a word for us. "I love you" and i"I love pizza" we say in the same breath. What do we mean? What we mean has something to do with feeling good. I feel good when I am with you; I feel good when I eat pizza. What is the difference? Or how much of ìgood feeling" is at the center of our word comes out in the phrase, ìmake love." It is a word about self-gratification much of the time. With these connections in mind, how does the world hear such phrases as "love is the answer" or "God is love" or "let's all love each other right now"? Let's learn to gratify our sensual needs is what much of our culture hears!

The New Testament term, agapé, has to do with meeting and giving. It was a word of the Greek vocabulary that was not much used until Christians used it. It was a word to describe a genuine and kindly greeting to another person and the hospitality that good people show to others. To treat another person with agapé is to treat that one with kindness and respect no matter who that other person be. Hence it was possible to love an enemy. Not possible to like the enemy, to be sure, or to feel good about persons who mistreat us. Only possible to treat that enemy with kindness and respect despite the hostility that the enemy shows.

What a powerful thing to do! – and that is precisely the power of agapé. The person who lives by agapé does not permit the behavior of the enemy to determine his behavior, too. You may curse me, but I will bless you, says agapé. You may persecute me and mistreat me; I shall still bless you. Agapé-people are people who believe in the unity of humankind despite all division and hostility. They believe in the single body and therefore they are able to bear all manner of things and endure all. The vision by which they live gives them strength. It is their purpose for living.

Are all purposes of life equally legitimate? Is it all right to see no purpose? Are purpose and meaning matters that we must discover or figure out for ourselves? Perhaps there are hierarchies of purpose and reason. There is a level at which we must each find out own. And finding it is to be found, for without a sense of purpose, most of us feel lost. Above that there is a purpose for all of us in the relationship and the unity that beckon us out of creation itself. It is that relationship and that unity which produce the sounds of praise to which ancient psalmists exhort us in the Bible and this raises our sense of purpose yet one step higher. Those poets felt that the very purpose of existence is to sing such praise. "Let all living things praise the Lord!" they cried, and thus summoned the world to what they felt was its highest calling.

Is that what moves us to assemble for worship on Sabbaths and Sundays, or any religious gathering? Our assembling would be a thrilling experience if that were so. What exuberant pleasure we might find in meeting if we met to rediscover our unity with each other and our relationship to all in God's kingdom and if, in the rediscovery, our words and acts of worship expressed that.Let's do that. What a great weekly reality check that could be.

I once heard a person say that the purpose of life is faith. At first I thought he was merely delivering religious rhetoric devoid of substance, for I took him to mean that faith is the acceptance of certain doctrines and traditions. But then I discovered that by faith he meant the attitude and acts of receiving all and whatever God has to give and I began to perceive the sense of what he said. It scarcely seems a purpose, does it, to say that we are meant to be receivers? It is so passive a role. In that there is no achievement. Not even any doing. But what else can we be –we and all creatures of earth?"

To be born is to receive life and to grow is to continue to receive. Is there any other way to live but by receiving constantly what the Giver has to give? It is by grace alone that we live and that means much. To live by grace is to live despite all sins and failures, all weakness and want, all fear and doubt and all depression.

We humans have done many things badly. The times in which we now live may not be the worst of times, but neither are they the best. What makes these times crucial is the size of the evil and damage we can now do. All violence and crime and destruction of the past look petty compared to the scale on which we now commit such acts of folly. We can now destroy more than we have ever destroyed before. The evils of World War II passed all prior evils. What could happen in a World War III would be still worse. Yet life goes on and that means that we are tolerated despite our madness. That is what I mean by grace, and to willingly believe it is to believe. We might be tempted to quit. Perhaps some of us are. We might long for an escape from what appears at times to be an accursed planet. But let us not succumb to that temptation and rely simply on this claim, that the Giver of life continues to give us life.

I heard once of a man who went to the top of a high bridge to jump from there to end his life. He had failed so many times over that he felt himself to be utterly unworthy. Subtly and gingerly he had checked out his friends and acquaintances with hints and leading questions that sought some genuine sign of approval from them. He received none. Now, deep in distress, he climbed the bridge and stood over the bay. He was ready to jump and die. In a last gesture of hope he cried out into the teeth of the wind, "O God, whoever you are and if you can hear me, answer me now: should I live or should I die?"

Did God answer? Not with words of human speech. But with the peculiar language of God that is the very movements of creation God answered. With the breath that entered that man's lungs in response to his cry, God said to him, "Live!" The man hadn't decided to breathe. The man hadn't commanded his heart to beat. Nature alone gave that command and nature spoke for God. Her word was yes.

CHAPTER 21

Reconciliation

As we've now discovered, a God of symbolic richness is available to us through scripture. When we engage at that level, the corrupting influence of religious legalism falls away, because it cannot gain a foothold. When the metaphorical fullness of scripture is embraced, we can speak of faith in this world without fear of false dichotomies ruling our minds. Science and material knowledge are no longer the enemy of our religion. The secular world is no longer a perpetual threat to our faith. We can view all of nature and humanity as equals, without judgment. We are restored to oneness with all of creation and God.

A religion no longer consumed by defending its own territory and authority is far more able to reconcile itself to other faith traditions, and to the world at large. It is even time to move past the notion that a Middle Eastern religion with roots from six thousand years ago holds the key to the entirety of the world's knowledge and its sense of history. A world freed from the pain and fury of religiously legalistic bickering and conflict would be a far better place in which to live. The thought of it makes you want to ask, "Why do we cling so often to sources of anachronism and falseness that only lead to conflict?"

Of course, the legalistic side of Christianity resists such instincts with all its might. The legalists of Christianity tell us not to love this world or anything in it under the cynically shallow claim that we shouldn't worship rocks or trees or the oceans. But they are applying their literal and limited mindset to the issue at hand. They base their understanding of the Bible on a rigid, self-perpetuating tautology that denies the organic core scripture in all its metaphorical glory. That same mindset insists that we're a "specially created" race of living things that exists separate from nature. But they're wrong. And instead, we should be reconciled to the fact even that the Lord's Prayer tells us to bring the Kingdom of Heaven to life here on earth. In that spirit, God is with us and all around us. That is our personal connection to God and to the universe. It is special indeed.

The problem remains that so many people still claim that getting into heaven is the only thing that matters. But God expects more of us than indulging our selfish spirits in that kind of salvation greed. It a simple fact that we don't get to go to heaven if we don't take care of what we have here in this life, especially others.

The Christian religion should focus on the priorities of respecting creation and loving others because these are the principles by which Jesus Christ himself taught during his time on earth. His primary purpose was bringing God's grace to life in this world. That's where all the "goodness" to be found in Christianity resides. We can legitimately substitute the word "goodness" for the word "kingdom" in the Lord's Prayer and arrive at a more honest take of what Christianity is supposed to be about. The whole "kingdom" thing is an anachronistic concept suitable to the past, when kings and queens ruled the world. But things have changed in developed countries that aren't consumed by religious laws. Government by the people is what rules democratic nations. Now it is time for Christianity by the people as well. The two leading principles in that approach to faith and religion are pursuing 1) Honesty and 2) Goodness.

Imagine what a reputation the Christian religion could earn if it replaced all its anachronistic prejudices with an active appreciation of grace, goodness, and acceptance in this world. Far more people would respect that approach, and as a religion, it might yet grow again. Embarking on this more honest approach to Christianity requires us to break with traditions that have grown and persist through legalism. Jesus told us to do that through his words and action.

Breaking free from "the rules" of tradition

It may seem counterintuitive for many Christians to accept that Jesus and his disciples "broke the rules" or religion. So did the apostle Paul by reaching out to Jews and Gentiles alike. Those actions weren't popular at the time, but they were the right thing to do. We are long overdue to break the rules again, and in particular were need to resist people insisting that fealty to anachronistic rules and laws are core tenets of. the faith. We also need to resist branding Christianity the one true faith. There is too much evidence that humanity is far older than the Bible depicts, and that even Christianity borrowed or stole plenty of its history from other faith traditions. It is certainly a false claim that the Bible contains all of human history dating back to Adam and Eve. Paleontology, archaeology and the science of human genetics now trace the origins of human ancestry back to Africa, from where it expanded across the Middle East, then European and Asia. During periods of immense climactic change, the human race crossed over to the North and South American continents, over to Australia and across oceans to far-flung island chains. These migrations took place over tens of thousands of years, and account for the human diversity we find today.

The cultures that grew from these populations date much farther back than the origin tales contained in Genesis. There were advanced Asian and Meso-American cultures building socially complex and intellectually capable cultures thousands of years before the Book of Genesis and its version of Jewish history was written down. It is arrogant to assume that the Judeo-Christian version of culture and history trumps all other advanced cultures. We've learned how these culturesdeveloped highly accurate calendars, sophisticated languages, complex agricultural systems, progressive forms of architecture, and effective forms of warfare. Human history is bigger than the Bible, and earth history is even bigger than that.

The more honest approach to religion is to place the Judeo-Christian religious tradition in its accurate historical context. If six thousand years is all that it covers, then it is both prudent and necessary to stop making claims beyond the scope of time covered by the Bible. Knowing the process of human migration around the world, it is an embarrassment to suggest that the Book of Genesis story and its creation narrative constitute an absolute record of the earth and human history. Anyone that holds to that literal account should be ashamed of their blatant prejudice against the truth. There is no goodness in that approach, only selfishness and naivete.It does not good to lie to ourselves about the past.

We need to break free from traditions anchored to anachronistic falsehoods such as creationism and Dominionism. These only hold people back from a greater appreciation for knowledge and human culture the world over. If Jesus is the "one truth path" then that should be self-evident from the good done by Christians, not by arrogantly anachronistic claims that their religious savior is a king. Let the world know Christianity by its beneficial actions rather than through tribal words too often uttered in the name of God. Though many have tried, it has never worked to shove religion down other peoples' throats. In the long run, the world rebels at such religions, and rightly so.

Culture wars

Nor does it help Christianity to trump up culture wars over false pretenses such as the "War On Christmas." That is just one of the gaslighting themes pumped through conservative media channels to make a common enemy of those who choose to say Happy Holidays rather than Merry Christmas. It's tribal nonsense at best. Jesus would mock such petulant efforts at cultural control, especially since the entire notion of a winter holiday was effectively stolen from other cultures long ago. He'd have a good laugh at that too.

If we're being honest about Christmas, we'd acknowledge that it was Christianity that drove the commercialization of the holidays. No one else brought Santa Claus into the mix or welcomed a whole host of other characters and traditions into our living rooms. Along the way, some Christians have complained that the world has forgotten the "reason for the season.". No one can blame secular society for a problem created by Christianity itself. The so-called "War On Christmas" basically began with Christians trashing their own holiday. Blaming others is an obvious hypocrisy. Anyone claiming a secular "War On Christmas" should be told to STFU. It's bad theology.

Religious liberty

The same standard of hypocrisy exists among people whining that their 'religious liberty' is restricted when they can't impose their religious beliefs over the civil rights of others. So, let's be clear: persecuting gay people by refusing to bake them a wedding cake does not make anyone a better Christian. The honest-to-goodness truth must be stated plainly. Religious beliefs do not take precedence over civil law in the United States of America. Christian nationalism is an ugly farce of self-perpetuating lies about both religion and the democractic form of government so many claim to cherish. Christian petulance does not change the fact that the United States Constitution guarantees freedom from religion as well as freedom of religion. There is no favored faith tradition in a nation where the Establishment Clause specifically bans a state-sponsored religion. Any other interpretation is a lie.

The same standards apply to public education, where no religion has the right to demand that its belief system be taught as science. While the Book of Genesis delivers a creation account valued by generations of Christians, the obvious lack of detail serves no purpose beyond the traditional framework of religion. Engaging in speculation and making up lies to compensate for these shortcomings is bad theology and in no way constitutes anything approaching a field of science.

The honest-to-goodness path of faith

An honest-to-goodness path of faith does not force us to lie about the world or act like spoiled jerks using religion to persecute others and claim special privileges for ourselves. Nor should we spend time fretting about how the world will end. Speculation about the End Times and concocting prophecies from the Book of Revelation only make Christians look selfish, stupid and blockheaded. The brand of bad theology that leads people to engage in End Times speculation and predictions about the end of the world is vengeful folly. None of that activity ever brought anyone closer to God.

> "But about that day or hour no one knows, not even the angels in heaven, nor the Son, but only the Father.

Matthew 24:36 *New International Version*

The entire genre of End Times prophecy is rife with conflicted reasoning. Either Jesus himself was wrong about predicting the end of the world within a generation of his earthly life or he was speaking figuratively. We should learn from that. Recall that Jesus told the religious authorities that he could tear the temple down and rebuild it in three days. He was speaking symbolically, not literally. These rhetorical examples free us from viewing the Bible as any form of literal instruction manual.

Rather than trying to predict or even bring about the end of the world, we ought to be trying to achieve a more honest path to helping Christianity find its true place in the world. An honest-to-goodness, we should add. That way is paved with gratitude, discernment, and appreciation of grace. It embraces the future and provides a sustainable way of life for future generations. That is the gift we ought to be offering our children, and our children's children.

The Italic Letter Bible

The starting point in achieving an honest-to-goodness Christian faith is to clearly identify all aspects of scripture that are chained to the past by outdated cultural context and anachronism. These ancient prejudices, laws and superstitions can and should remain in scripture where they were originally placed. But these should be fully identified and explained as evidence of bygone days. We've seen Red Letter Bibles to highlight the words of Jesus. We've seen Green Letter Bibles to highlight the presence of nature throughout scripture. Both have their purpose, but they stop short of calling religious legalism to account. Now it is time for a Italic Letter Bible to identify aspects of scripture that are anachronistic and no longer serve a useful purpose in modern society, much less a role in serving the Kingdom of God. They are the product of bygone days, and should be relegated to that status.

Once identified, these anachronistic aspects of scripture still provide instructional value. They can help us educate the world about how God's people have grown in spirit and understanding over the ages. With this exegesis in place, we can help Christianity find its honest-to-goodness place in the world.

It is unnatural and frankly unbiblical to suggest that the human race has not been able to achieve some degree of social progress over the last 2000 years. That notion is absurd, and dangerous. Scripture shows God demanding change from humanity time and again. The symbolic truths about the need to change or repent are everywhere in scripture. When people refuse change, really bad things happened. Before the flood, Noah was mocked for telling people to change. When Abraham begged God to spare Sodom and Gomorrah if one righteous person could be found, he knew that there was little hope among that population of despots and brutes. The cities met their end. Even in the Garden and Eden, when Adam and Even breach God's trust by following the Serpent's seeming shortcut to salvation, they find themselves separated from God. How many times do we have to be told that change is both good and necessary?

We're in that position again. Yet we're stuck battling with people whose legalistically oriented worldview resists the very legacy and lessons Jesus sought to teach. God wants us to change. Jesus called for change, and Christianity ignored him. His words on the cross were both reactive and prophetic: "Father, forgive them, for they know not what they do."

We disrespect Jesus by acting with impunity toward the need to change. He ardently challenged the religious authorities that refused to change. Yet here we are, facing the same problems that religion faced two thousand years ago. It's inexcusable. It is the product of stiff-necked and stubborn idiocy, to be frank and honest.

Goodness knows, change is good

There is no dismissing the fact that change is good. When John the Baptist called for repentance, he sought a change of heart. When Jesus called people to follow his path of compassionate love for all, he also sought a change of mind and culture. When scripture tells us that God cares about humanity, that does not mean we are not supposed to care for each other, and creation. Most of all, we are not supposed to sit around wishing hell on the supposedly sinful while hoping the world will come to an end so that we can all be swept up into heaven. That is nothing but greed and selfish tripe.

Dispensing with the legalistically bad habits of creationism and End Times theology would also be liberating to the Christian religion and the world at large. We'd no longer be caught between the bookends of outright lies about creation and the seemingly endless (and always wrong) predictions about the world's final days. Nothing good has come from either of these traditions.

We must shake free from the binds of anachronism found throughout the Bible. Those that cling to these repressive instincts must learn the truth, and we must state it emphatically, "You do not own the Word of God." That's effectively what Jesus told the religious authorities of his day. We must speak those words to the legalists, the fundamentalists, and the apologetics that seek to dominate the Christian religion today.

It is also time to rid the Christian world of religious originalists claiming that the Bible is inerrant and infallible. Our goal must be to revise and improve our interpretation of the Bible in much the way that the United States of America has revised and amended its Constitution through amendments. That's how real freedom has come about. That's what true religious liberty would deliver.

Protecting creation

On yet another front, the world is engaged in a fight to preserve its natural resources for future generations. Here again the anachronistic worldview of Dominionism stands in opposition to a more sustainable way of life. The selfish outlook that views the earth as a dispensable commodity to be used up and replaced by Jesus must be overcome. It is, after all, nothing more than human arrogance and a self-fulfilling prophecy to claim that God grants humanity unrestricted control over the world. This shortsighted worldview shows hubris to an extreme and exhibits a profound lack of respect for creation and responsibility to God. It is also ironic, given how many times scripture shows God's displeasure with how the human race manages things here on earth.

By contrast, Jesus humbly placed creation at the center of spiritual insight. He shared examples from nature and everyday life to teach us about the Kingdom of God. That method resounds in scripture from beginning to end. All of God's Word depends on the foundation of creation. It is the mortar holding the building blocks of truth together. If we separate creation from the rest of scripture, it tumbles down in a heap of human detritus and falsely constructed traditions. That seems to be what the End Times folks are literally praying for. It will be a perverse form of self-fulfilling prophecy if it does come true.

In the face of these threats from within the religion, Christianity needs an intervention to find its honest voice as a source of morality and truth in the world. Rather than allow religious legalism to impact the world in cruel and irresponsible ways, we should be honest with ourselves about what the Bible and Christ want us to do. We must intervene and call legalism to account. We must fight for truth over selfish, self-fulfilling doctrine.

The right path

An honest Christian will at this point ask themselves, "What are we supposed to do with all this information? Didn't you just make it ten times harder to be a Christian?

The truth of the matter is that being a Christian of consequence is never easy and was never meant to be. Being true Christians means we don't settle for shortcuts that typically turn out to be most deceiving and misleading paths of all. We should have learned that from the Serpent in Genesis. Some people just can't get that through their thick heads.

It is a far more honest-to-goodness path to pursue a Christian faith in context with the realities of the present world than it is to pretend that we should live in some oversimplified version of the past. We have nothing to fear from modern knowledge when we dispense with anachronisms that bind us to a blinded past.

Instead, we need to think and act like Jesus did by welcoming signs of God in creation and sharing love in this world. Like Jesus, it is also our job to challenge evil where we find it by calling sources of deception to account whenever possible. We should follow the example of Jesus by asking questions rather than concocting rules and laws to control others and then engaging in constant accusations of heresy and sin. If we're honest with ourselves, it is far easier to find out whether people are being honest in life or acting selfishly in their beliefs and actions. That is the honest-to-goodness method of seeking the truth in this world. That is the way of Jesus, who was first and foremost an honest person.

The way of a contrarian

Jesus was famously both a contrarian and brutally honest in his teaching methods. His advice often seemed counterintuitive or cryptic to those that received it, yet he held nothing back when it came the "fixes" required to get back on the right path in life. The woman at the well1 with the sordid past was urged by Jesus to stop lying to herself about the damage her behavior was doing. He shared with her a promise of "Living Water" and the restorative power of the spirit. She did not immediately understand that symbol as an invitation to follow Jesus. Ultimately, her mind awakened to his meaning. She was "woke" in that moment, and ready to receive the truth he offered. It was simple, "Go, and sin no more," he told her. Both methods of engagement revealed the truth that she needed to hear. That is how the entirety of scripture works.

In keeping with the example of Jesus, what follows is a mind-opening path to religious liberty. We don't need a full-on creed or confessional statement of faith to bind us together. We do need some guideposts to help us know what to avoid and stay on the path to honest-to-goodness faith.

Resist...

Letting legalism automatically define your faith.

Allowing anachronism to define biblical understanding

Fearing facts that contradict closely held ideas.

Denying legitimate forms of knowledge outside of scripture

Letting your religion become a tool of discrimination

It is important to have objectives and focus as well.

We should all try to...

Challenge scripture that leads to the persecution of others.

Work to reconcile scripture with material knowledge.

Do what you can to appreciate God's grace in the world.

Respect and sanctify nature in appreciation of creation.

Do our best to be honest with ourselves in all things, especially in our faith.

Awaiting on you all

I've always loved the lyrics of George Harrison's song Awaiting On You All because it communicates the fact that God wants us to action in this world, and not by traditional methods alone.

You don't need no church house
And you don't need no Temple
You don't need no rosary beads or them books to read
To see that you have fallen
If you open up your heart
You will know what I mean
We've been kept down so long
Someone's thinking that we're all green

This might be a different take on Mr. Harrison's lyrics, but yes indeed, we are all "green" in spirit if we allow ourselves to grow. In that light, let us add two important principles by which to guide your Christian faith.

The first of these is trust. In a world filled with often dishonest, even abusive people, keeping a faith alive and learning to trust is a difficult thing to do. It is even harder to trust in a God that we cannot literally see, and about which there seems to be little proof at times other than the words in scripture.

By those accords, God doesn't seem to reach us much by way of material reality. That's partly because legalistic religion has kept God cooped up in a cage of its own making. It is hard to find God when our access is blocked by the brand of bad theology focused on owning the narrative rather than helping people find the spirit within themselves. Christian apologetics love to claim, in soft and warm voices, that they hold the key to the kind heart of Christ. But when their theology persists in persecuting others based on age-old prejudices and fears, they are lying to us all. Their voices are like those of the hissing Serpent, eager to control and only telling half the truth.

That's why having a faith more broadly founded in the depth of all creation is the best way to find and manifest trust in this world. It opens us up to a world of discernment and marvel. It looks at the human condition as part of all creation, rather than divided up into tribes and races, genders, and orientations. An honest-to-goodness faith has foundations in nature that we can see and understand through the symbols in scripture. We can trust that the world will continue to revolve and evolve. We know that it will bring day and night, just like the Book of Genesis says. That is the constancy side of scripture. We also trust that the sun will shine on us, yet when it doesn't, we know that cloudy days and precipitation are necessary for all of life to thrive. Nature has its constants.

But it also changes in a minute, and over long periods of time. Learning to embrace change is vital to our relationship with God. Think of all the surprises that the people we find in scripture received. Even the God of scripture changes in mood and interaction with humanity and creation. These lessons teach us that while God is eternal, that aspect of a deity does not necessarily need to remain fixed in our minds.

The hard part in all this is finding ways to trust that God cares for us in highly personal ways. Some people despair at the thought that they might be alone in this world, which can be a cruel place. Their trust in God sustains them in the face of dishonesty and deceit. But here's the most important thing to remember: Don't let your religion deceive you first.

Despite all the great religions of the world, we make our own paths to God. There is both comfort and challenge in that reality. How do we know if we are being heard, or that our prayers are being answered? All we can do is look for evidence, and when we find it, be grateful for those answers in whatever form they arrive.

Prayer perceptions

Allow me a few moments of personal testimony. When my late wife was going through repeated cancer treatments over an eight-year period, I sometimes needed to stay home from work to take care of her. Sometimes that was by choice. But I was also dismissed from jobs because the owners of small companies were afraid their healthcare costs would rise due to my wife's cancer. They found ways to cut me from the payroll. If you want to talk about stress and confusion, try being unemployed when your wife has cancer.

In any case, there were points where our finances dwindled. At those moments, we'd sit together at the dining room table adding up the bills. "We need $3500," she told me one evening. To which I replied, "It will be okay. Something always comes along." I freelanced whenever I was staying home with her or was out of a full-time job. We said a short prayer that night and I helped her to bed.

I arose early in the morning to make her oatmeal. Standing in the kitchen, I heard the squeaky mail slot in our front door open and slam shut. Our caregiving group often dropped off cards and other bits of encouragement. But that morning, there was a fat envelope on the floor behind the door.

Inside was $3700 in cash.

We had not spoken to anyone about our financial needs, yet here was the seemingly literal answer to our prayer from the night before. Some might call that $3700 in an envelope a miracle or a direct answer to a prayer. I have no objection to that if someone likes to believe that way. It is much more likely that our patent vulnerability in our situation was evident to others. Certainly, it could also have been a coincidence. Yet there were other times when we needed money and it somehow came our way. That convinced me that something is at work in this world. I wrote a book titled The Right Kind of Pride about that survivorship journey. It is a chronicle of Character, Caregiving and Community. The primary message is accepting vulnerability is the right kind of thing to be proud about. That is, having humility to admit that you need help is a form of honesty in this world. We were genuinely blessed with help of many kinds over those years. I viewed that as God taking care of us too.

The voice of God

Yet as we know, life isn't all favors and joys. During one period in my career, I'd worked hard in sales for a newspaper and put together a proposal to open a new position as director of promotions and creative services. The company had just built a new building and was looking forward to growth in circulation and revenue. My proposal was accepted, but it came with a catch. I'd be reporting to a former director of the advertising department who'd essentially gotten a demotion to run a specific wing of sales, and he would be my boss.

Fearing for his job, that man pulled me aside with an appeal that felt like manipulation. "Put all your work through me...I'll take care of you." I wasn't interested in having him represent my efforts, because frankly, I'd seen enough from his management style the previous three years to understand that he wasn't always forthright or honest. There was a definite trust issue, and I was angry at him for trying to control my every move.

I was so angry, in fact, that coming home to my family that afternoon proved difficult to control my temper. Upon entering the house, I told my wife that I needed to go out for a walk. She read my face and understood.

It was an overcast night, and dusk was approaching. I walked over to the high school track where I always did my running workouts. I could hear those words from my 'new boss' ringing through my head, "Put your work through me...I'll take care of you..."

At the track, I flopped down on the high jump pit and took off my glasses. Without clear vision, the cloudy skies above seemed to press down on me. At that moment, I heard the word "forgiveness" as if someone had spoken to me out loud. I sat up, looked around, and wondered if another person had wandered onto the track. No one was there. I sat there for a moment thinking about the word forgiveness. It suddenly made sense.

On the way back home, I needed to repeat the word out loud to fully quell my anger. By the time I got home, a feeling of peace came over me. That next day at work, I did exactly what my new/old boss asked me to do. I put all my work through him, and worried not about whether I'd get credit or not. Removing that need for recognition was in some ways liberating. I engaged in daily forgiveness.

Two weeks into that new relationship, I was pulled into the office of the Publisher who informed me that my new/old boss was being dismissed as part of even more realignments in the sales department. From then on, I reported directly to the Publisher. Honestly, that did not make life all that easier. In some ways, I was taught a lesson that you need to be careful what you wish for.

My former boss landed a job with another newspaper and went on to have many years of success. I grew in my new position and later accepted a role as the marketing manager for a much larger newspaper. That worked well for seven years. Then the entire industry stumbled for lack of a will to change. The digital age had arrived, and most newspapers initially stuck with their old ways while revenue channels slipped away. Looking for a way out, I took a job with a marketing agency for a much larger salary, but my wife's cancer came back within weeks of my new role. She had an emotional breakdown and I wound up needing to stay home for a while and direct all her care. We struggled at times, but somehow things always worked out. Our motto was "It is what it is," when it came to medical treatments and the bills. The rest we often turned over to God in prayer.

No control freak

As a lifelong participant and believer in the Christian faith, my personal experience is that there is a caring God at work in the universe. I don't view that deity as a control freak running our lives like we are machines. It is much more likely that the God we find in the Bible views things the other way around. When we abide in trust, accept grace, and appreciate it to others, it seems returns to us in some form of grace. It may not always be the exact answer to our prayers, but that's the learning part of prayer. Sometimes we're supposed to grow in understanding by what comes around in life.

I shared these stories because they illustrate two things. One, we do have to be proactive in our intentions. It is often said that "God helps those who help themselves." That is not a tautology so much as it is a practical reality. God doesn't do everything for us. Nor does Jesus. That's just not how it works. If we are honest with ourselves about our means and our needs, and trust that we are supported in spirit according to those priorities, things often do happen to help us along.

As you are blessed, be a blessing to others

At another point in time the leader of our caregiving group delivered a literal Money Tree to help us along. But by then, we'd gotten back on our financial feet and decided to find others in need that could use that money. As my wife often stated, "As we are blessed, we should be a blessing to others." That perspective brings us to the final topic of this book, which is love.

The meaning of love

For all the time people spend obsessing about control over the message and meaning of scripture, it seems that the main message of God and Christ is too often lost on those that are legalistically religious. When Jesus tells us to "love one another" that is no idle statement. Yet when laws and rules, doctrines and dictates are all we must live by, they too easily take precedence over loving others. All that is godly is truly lost.

There are many kinds of love in this world. They all count when it comes to God's directive to love one another. The most difficult kind of love is perhaps the communal love we are asked to share toward all those we encounter. Too many people find reason to ignore this calling to love others, choosing paths of fear or prejudice or tribal instincts over acceptance and love.

That is because people too often have a lack of gratitude toward their own circumstance and behave in selfish ways as a result. Again, this lack of gratitude reaches all the way back to creation, because if people take the frail state of humanity in this universe for granted, they are too easily drawn into dismissive and abusive behaviors that harm others, and creation itself. They become dismissive and unkind. That is not what God or Christ wants from any of us.

The reality of pain

To put the importance and reality of love into perspective, imagine one of the most painful moments in your life. It may be the loss of a loved one, or some other tragic event. Emotional pain is real. It affects us just as much as the sun and rain or food and water affect our bodies.

If emotional pain is real, so is love. Thus, to claim that "God is real" is not some falsely religious statement. The God of Love touches us in much the same way that the sun strikes the surface of the earth. We can hide from it or ignore it if we choose. We can also let it burn our skin or drive us to thirst, even death, which is how the notion of sin works in our lives. It is often the appetite for things that on the surface appear good or harmless that lead to overindulgence and selfish behavior. These can cause our downfall and are by no coincidence the opposite of love.

Religion slaps the name "Original Sin" on the downfall of humanity that led to loss of inherent trust and love in our lives. Many blame this loss of conscience on Satan or the devil. Too few realize that the devil really is in the details of scriptural legalism and religion that leads us into deception, willful ignorance, and moral decay. That's what happens when those in charge of religious tradition embrace power and authority over the humble causes of trust in God and loving others. As history demonstrates, the love of money is the root of all evil, but the determination to rule over others and claim selfish dominion over the world runs a close second.

Stand up for God

The solution to this misappropriation of God's trust and love is to stand up to those whose priorities have gone askew. They may garb themselves in the robes and language of religious piety, or host consoling programs on a multitude of media and claim to speak for God and Christ. But we can measure their credulity easy enough by thinking back to the way the Serpent in the Garden of Eden approached Adam and Eve with an offer that appeared to be too good to be true, and it turned out that it was.

It is our calling to avoid that fate and hearken to an honest-to-goodness faith based more on trust and love than ruling the world according to the "traditions of men."

Solutions

Many of us were raised to think literally about the creation story and other Bible stories. It seems hard to replace that comfortable narrative with a faith that invites one to reconcile the Bible with science and other seemingly complex subjects that don't seem to have much to do with God or the meaning of Christ in a spiritual sense. But good relationships require honesty in all its forms. That's true as well in a relationship with God. While scripture calls us to be "children of God," that does not mean that we should be naïve or immature about our most meaningful beliefs.

As Paul wrote in 1 Corinthians 14

> But in the church I would rather speak five intelligible words to instruct others than ten thousand words in a tongue. ...

That is a call to honesty,and forthrightness. That is how God wants us all to be. Honest with ourselves. Honest with others. Honest in heart and soul. Honest-To-Goodness.

BIBLIOGRAPHY AND REFERENCES

Foreword

1. Campus Life: The organization states, "Every day at thousands of community centers, high schools, middle schools, juvenile institutions, coffee shops, and local hangouts, YFC staff and volunteers meet with young people who need Jesus. Our focus as a movement is on multiplying fruitful and sustainable ministry sites across the nation and around the world. https://www.yfc.net/campuslife.

2. Luther College. The website states: In the reforming spirit of Martin Luther, Luther College affirms the liberating power of faith and learning. As people of all backgrounds, we embrace diversityand challenge one another to learn in community, to discern our callings, and to serve with distinction for the common good. As a college of the churchLuther is rooted in an understanding of grace and freedom that emboldens us in worship, study, and service to seek truth, examine our faith, and care for all God's people. As a liberal arts college, Luther is committed to a way of learning that moves us beyond immediate interests and present knowledge into a larger world—an education that disciplines minds and develops whole persons equipped to understand and confront a changing society. https://www.luther.edu/about/mission/

3 Albert Camus: https://www.nobelprize.org/prizes literature/1957/camus/biographical/

4.Jean Paul Sartre https://plato.stanford.edu/entries/sartre/ First published Thu Apr 22, 2004; substantive revision Mon Dec 5, 2011Sartre (1905–1980) is arguably the best-known philosopher of the twentieth century. His indefatigable pursuit of philosophical reflection, literary creativity and, in the second half of his life, active political commitment gained him worldwide renown, if not admiration. He is commonly considered the father of Existentialist philosophy, whose writings set the tone for intellectual life in the decade immediately following the Second World War.

5. Candide, Voltaire https://plato.stanford.edu/entries/voltaire/François-Marie d'Arouet (1694–1778), better known by his pen name Voltaire, was a French writer and public activist who played a singular role in defining the eighteenth-century movement called the Enlightenment.

6. Plate tectonics: Plate tectonics is a scientific theory that explains how major landforms are created as a result of Earth's subterranean movements. ... In plate tectonics, Earth's outermost layer, or lithosphere—made up of the crust and upper mantle—is broken into large rocky plates. National Geographic.

7. Evolution: In biology, evolution is the change in the characteristics of a species over several generations and relies on the process of natural selection. ... Evolution relies on there being genetic variation? in a population which affects the physical characteristics (phenotype) of an organism.

8. Blood on your hands, Bible Citation: "David said to Solomon: "My son, I had it in my heart to build a house for the Name of the LORD my God. But this word of the LORD came to me: 'You have shed much blood and have fought many wars. You are not to build a house for my Name, because you have shed much blood on the earth in my sight. 1 Chronicles: 22"

9. Parables. The use of symbols or allegory to relate more lessons.

10. Anti-Semitism: hostility to or prejudice against Jewish people.

11. Scripture used to justify slavery:

12. The Genesis Fix: How biblical literalism affects politics, culture the environment, by Christopher Cudworth, 2007, Human Nature Publishing. The book dissects the how biblical literalism has been used to justify the discrimination and abuse of other people and nature.

13. Professor Richard Simon Hanson. https://nordic.luther.edu/?p=collections/findingaid&id=1445&q=&rootcontentid=83470Dr. Richard Simon Hanson, Professor Emeritus of Religion, Luther College, Decorah, Iowa.

14. Dominion; ibid

15. Hypocrisy; ibid

16. Anachronism: This is a good description of the source and damage of anachronism in scriptural study. https://www.patheos.com/blogs/messyinspirations/2019/10/anachronism-distorts-scripture/

Chapter 1: Practical Realities

1. History : Early history of Christianity: https://www.worldhistory.org/article/1205/early-christianity/ Emerging from a small sect of Judaismin the 1st century CE, early Christianity absorbed many of the shared religious, cultural, and intellectual traditions of the Greco-Roman world. In traditional histories of Western culture, the emergence of Christianity in the Roman Empire is known as "the triumphof Christianity." This refers to the victory of Christian beliefs over the allegedly false beliefs and practices of paganism. However, it is important to recognize that Christianity did not arise in a vacuum.

2. Legalism : Scriptural legalism: https://www.openbible.info/topics/legalism. Samples of scripture dealing with the topic of legalism.

2. *Reformation* https://www.history.com/topics/reformation/reformation The Protestant Reformation was the 16th-century religious, political, intellectual and cultural upheaval that splintered Catholic Europe, setting in place the structures and beliefs that would define the continent in the modern era. Protestant : Protestant: https://www.britannica.com/topic/The-Protestant-Heritage-1354359 The Protestant Heritage, Protestantism originated in the 16th-century Reformation, and its basic doctrine, in addition to those of the ancient Christian creeds, are justification by grace alone through faith, the priesthood of all believers, and the supremacy of Holy Scripture in matters of faith and order.

4. *Inerrancy Biblical infallibility and inerrancy*: For reference; https://spectrummagazine.org/views/2019/god-inerrant-and-infallible-bible-neither. The terms biblical infallibility (the Bible cannot contain errors) and inerrancy (the Bible contains no errors) are close cousins of the same idea, one that scriptural religions – Christian and Muslim fundamentalists most especially – prize and promote. While individual Christian apologists have posited an infallible and inerrant Bible for millennia, it is only recently – 1970s and early 1980s – that entire Christian denominations have advocated for this position, a phenomena that peaked with the 1978 Chicago Statement on Biblical Inerrancy. This statement grew out of a conference attended by over 200 global evangelical/fundamentalist leaders who were reacting to modernism and its critique of biblical historicity, accuracy, and literalness.

5. *Infallibility* ; Ibid

6. *Literalism*: the interpretation of words in their usual or most basic sense."biblical literalism". Dictionary.com: adherence to the explicit substance of an idea or expression, https://www.nytimes.com/roomfordebate/2013/08/15/should-creationism-be-controversial/the-risk-of-biblical-literalism. This article is by The Rev. Wil Gafney, whose doctorate is in Hebrew Bible, is an associate professor of Hebrew and Old Testament at The Lutheran Theological Seminary in Philadelphia. A quote: "We must ask about the intent and genre of the text. Biblical literalism requires reading all of the Bible as being intended to relay a series of historical (and theological) facts. This ignores what we know about language, that there are many kinds of speech and writing, which we use in combination to make our points: irony, exaggeration, puns, sarcasm, riddles, proverbs, quotes in and out of context, etc. Insisting on biblical literalism flattens out the richness of the text and its multiple contributors. And even among Christians, there is no single Bible: there are different books in different sequence in Orthodox, Catholic, Protestant and Anglican Bibles."

7. *Apologetics* : Here's an apologetic for apologetics. https://seminary.grace.edu/what-is-apologetics/

8. *Parables* : a simple story used to illustrate a moral or spiritual lesson, as told by Jesus in the Gospels.

9. *Religion and health*

10. *Tautology* : the saying of the same thing twice in different words, generally considered to be a fault of sty

11. *End Times* : Here's a creepy take from Focus on the Family about how some evangelicals view the End Times https://www.focusonthefamily.com/family-qa/preparing-for-the-end-times/

12. *Squabbles* : A treatise on why Paul and James disagreed on some issues. https://www.vision.org/james-and-paul-why-conflict-312

13. *Jesus Beatitudes* : Matthew 5 : 1-12

14. *Gnostics*: The Gnostic Gospels: The 52 texts discovered in Nag Hammadi, Egypt include 'secret' gospels poems and myths attributing to Jesus sayings and beliefs which are very different from the New Testament. Scholar Elaine Pagels explores these documents and their implications.https://www.pbs.org/wgbh/frontline/article/gnostic-gospels/

15. *Civil rights* : Protecting civil rights is an essential part of thedemocratic values of the United States; and despite the country's legacy of slavery and continued racial inequities, people's individual rights and freedoms are considered sacred. Additionally, most people realize that interfering with another individual's civil rights is a violation that can trigger a lawsuit. The term "civil rights" stimulates intense emotions that get to the roots of morality -- but what are civil rights? It's a broad term with many connotations, but has a specific meaning in U.S. law. https://www.findlaw.com/civilrights/civil-rights-overview/what-are-civil-rights.html

16. *Sinful* : wicked and immoral; committing or characterized by the committing of sins.

17. *Science* : the intellectual and practical activity encompassing the systematic study of the structure and behaviour of the physical and natural world through observation and experiment.

18. *Civil liberties*: Civil liberties are the "basic rights and freedoms guaranteed to individuals as protection from any arbitrary actions or other interference of the government without due process of law." Simply put, they're the basic rights and freedoms guaranteed by the Constitution—especially, in the Bill of Rights.

19. *Scripture:*

20. *LA Times*:

21. Sexual Abuse : Sex abuse scandals continue in the Catholic Church https://www.bbc.com/news/world-44209971

22. Catholic : Controversies over protection of priests accused of sexual abuse have resulted in litigation and settlements with thousands of victims. .

23. Roman history: https://www.pbs.org/empires/romans/empire/christians.html The spread of Christianity was made a lot easier by the efficiency of the Roman Empire, but its principles were sometimes misunderstood and membership of the sect could be dangerous. Although Jesus had died, his message had not. Word of his teachings spread to Jewish communities across the empire. This was helped by energetic apostles, such as Paul and by the modern communications of the Roman Empire.

24. Sex: (chiefly with reference to people) sexual activity, including specifically sexual intercourse."they enjoyed talking about sex" …either of the two main categories (male and female) into which humans and most other living things are divided on the basis of their reproductive functions

25. Genesis Fix: How biblical literalism affects politics, culture the environment, by Christopher Cudworth, 2007, Human Nature Publishing. The book dissects the manner in which biblical literalism has been used to justify the discrimination and abuse of other people and nature.

26. 2016 Election: A full list of the 2016 election results is available online at: https://www.nytimes.com/elections/2016/results/president

27. Climate Change: Predictions of climate change and global warming have been issued by an overwhelming majority of climatologists for several decades. Resistance to these predictions and even the identifiable outcomes of those predictions are still "debated" by skeptics from the political and religious right. Political objections to the concept of climate change are primarily based on economic and legislative concerns about what the costs of combatting climate change could be. Religious objections primarily center on doubts about science in general along with the belief that only God would affect the climate on a global scale. Both of these worldviews appear to center around a desire to control the narrative rather than revealing the truth and considering what to do about climate change.

28. Originalism US law : a legal philosophy that the words in documents and especially the U.S. Constitution should be interpreted as they were understood at the time they were written

29. Bad behavior: specific to the Christian Church, the "bad behavior" of the past includes inquisitions, genocide, anti-Semitism and persecution of other religions.

30. Long Line of legalists: The point of this book is simple. It has been legalism that has corrupted the Word of God from the beginning, starting with the Serpent in Genesis and extending through the religious authorities who indicted Jesus through to the Catholic Church and Protestant apologetics of this day and age.

31. Spiritual greed: Spiritual greed is the belief that earning and claiming eternal salvation trumps all other priorities in an earthly life.

32. Addiction: a compulsive, chronic, physiological or psychological need for a habit-forming substance, behavior, or activity having harmful physical, psychological, or social effects and typically causing well-defined symptoms (such as anxiety, irritability, tremors, or nausea) upon withdrawal or abstinence : the state of being addicted

33. Hypocrites: Both John the Baptist and Jesus called the religious authorities they encountered "hypocrites" for focusing so much on law and tradition they refused to extend care or compassion to the people most in need of it.

34. Practical realities: These can be defined as plainly evident facts as determined by insights from basic science.

35. Parables: For reference, a complete list of parables in the teaching of Jesus. Note the considerable use of organic symbolism in these messages. https://www.thecharaproject.com/parable.

36. Religious : adjective relating to or believing in a religion.

37. Theology of Work: https://www.theologyofwork.org/ A fascinating website examining the intersection of faith and work life.

38. End Times: There are many sources and perspectives on the issue of the "End Times," but this Mother Jones piece on how it relates to modern politics is particularly revealing.https://www.motherjones.com/politics/2020/01/evangelicals-are-anticipating-the-end-of-the-world-and-trump-is-listening/

39. Forced conversion: https://christianhistoryinstitute.org/magazine/article/interview-converting-by-the-sword From the article: There's no sense in pretending this was an exceptional missionary tactic; for many centuries, it was the method of choice among Christian rulers and missionaries. The conversion of much of Europe and of Latin America is unimaginable without the sword. It is not a pleasant aspect of our heritage, but one that nonetheless teaches us a great deal about human nature and what, in fact, solidifies Christian faith."

40. God: (in Christianity and other monotheistic religions) the creator and ruler of the universe and source of all moral authority; the supreme being. 2. (in certain other religions) a superhuman being or spirit worshiped as having power over nature or human fortunes; a deity.

41. Luther College: Private Lutheran College in Decorah, Iowa. The college website says of its mission, Asking Tough Questions: Martin Luther was both a pastor and a professor. The reformation of the church he sparked in 1517 began with a heated debate on a university campus. Perhaps this start in an academic setting is one reason Lutherans have always given education a high priority. In fact, because of our Lutheran tradition, we want you to wrestle with challenges in economics, biology, or literature, while exploring deep questions about faith and values. To do this, we encourage conversation with people of diverse backgrounds and with differing opinions. In this way, you come to better appreciate and understand your own beliefs.

42. 67th book: In this instance, we refer to the idea that "nature is the 67th book of the Bible." This notin is specifically resisted by creationists, including the Institute for Creation Research, who rail against the notions of materialism the claim represents. https://www.icr.org/article/unity-worthy-of-our-creationist-heritage

43. Antoni Gaudi: https://www.biography.com/artist/antoni-gaudi The son of a coppersmith, Antoni Gaudí was in 1852 and took to architecture at a young age. He attended school in Barcelona, the city that would become home to most of his great works. Gaudí was part of the Catalan Modernista movement, eventually transcending it with his nature-based organic style.

44. Legalism: https://www.ligonier.org/blog/3-types-legalism/ Basically, legalism involves abstracting the law of God from its original context. Some people seem to be preoccupied in the Christian life with obeying rules and regulations, and they conceive of Christianity as being a series of do's and don'ts, cold and deadly set of moral principles.

45. *Jewish*: https://www.britannica.com/biography/Jesus/Jewish-Palestine-at-the-time-of-Jesus "Jewish Palestine at the time of Jesus," Brittanica.com. Palestine in Jesus' day was part of the Roman Empire., which controlled its various territories in a number of ways. In the East (eastern Asia Minor, Syria, Palestine, and Egypt), territories were governed either by kings who were "friends and allies" of Rome (often called "client" kings or, more disparagingly, "puppet" kings) or by governors supported by a Roman army. When Jesus was born, all of Jewish Palestine—as well as some of the neighbouring Gentile areas—was ruled by Rome's able "friend and ally" Herod the Great. For Rome, Palestine was important not in itself but because it lay between Syria and Egypt, two of Rome's most valuable possessions. Rome had legions in both countries but not in Palestine. Roman imperial policy required that Palestine be loyal and peaceful so that it did not undermine Rome's larger interests. That end was achieved for a long time by permitting Herod to remain king of Judaea (37–4 BCE) and allowing him a free hand in governing his kingdom, as long as the requirements

of stability and loyalty were met.

46. Literalism: the interpretation of words in their usual or most basic sense.

47. Roman states: Ibid Jewish

48. Legalism: excessive adherence to law or formula, dependence on moral law rather than on personal religious faith.

Chapter 2: The Call of Segrada Familia

1. Segrada Familia: in Spanish, "Holy family." Also the name of the basilica designed by Antoni Gaudi I Barcelona, Spain.

2. Time.com: An online article referring to the history of Sagrada Familia. https://time.com/sagrada-familia-barcelona/

3. Culture Trip: A website devoted to travel information.

4. Symbols: Tree of life: https://bibleproject.com/learn/tree-of-life/ In the opening pages of the Bible, humanity is portrayed as God's royal partner, his divine image. God orders a sacred space where heaven and earth are one, and then he makes eternal life available to humans by means of a tree. While many throughout history have imagined the tree of life as a magical tree that imparts eternal life, the biblical story paints a bigger picture. Sacred trees that offer divine life were a major theme in the religious art of ancient Egypt and Babylon. But in the garden of Eden, the tree is located at the center of the sacred space, the "holy of holies" of this heaven and earth place. River of life or "water of life" Referencing the point in the Bible where God God transforms a desolate wilderness into a garden through a stream that waters the ground and brings life wherever it goes. Water of Life develops throughout the biblical story as wells, cisterns, rain, and rivers. Living water https://www.christianity.com/wiki/christian-life/what-does-living-water-mean-in-the-bible.html

5. Jesus answered and said to her, "If you knew the gift of God, and who it is who says to you, 'Give Me a drink,' you would have asked Him, and He would have given you living water" (John 4:10). God as "the Rock" https://bible.knowing-jesus.com/topics/God,-The-Rocke.g.: Psalm 78:35 And they remembered that God was their rock, And the Most High God their Redeemer. Source: https://bible.knowing-jesus.com/topics/God,-The-Rock

6. *The Spirit as the Dove* https://www.christianity.com/wiki/holy-spirit/why-is-the-dove-often-a-symbol-for-the-holy-spirit.html. The Dove is a symbol for the Holy Spirit inspired by Jesus's baptism. The dove has been used among many Christian denominations as a symbol for the Holy Spirit as well as a general symbol for peace, purity, and new beginnings. Jesus as the Lamb https://www.biblestudytools.com/

bible-study/topical-studies/what-does-it-mean-that-jesus-is-the-lamb-of-god.html
The names of God tell us important information about who God is. So do the names of Jesus, and we hear about Jesus being the Lamb of God a lot, especially at Easter. Keep reading to learn more about why Jesus is called that and the incredible implications it has for us even today. Most of us picture lambs as downy white animals frolicking in rolling green meadows or carried tenderly in the arms of their shepherd. Lambs represent gentleness, purity, and innocence. Though it is one of the most tender images of Christ in the New Testament, the phrase "Lamb of God" would have conjured far more disturbing pictures to those who heard John the Baptist hail Jesus with these words. Hadn't many of them, at one time or another, carried one of their own lambs to the altar to be slaughtered as a sacrifice for their sins, a lamb that they had fed and bathed, the best animal in their small flock? Hadn't the bloody sacrifice of an innocent animal provided a vivid image of the consequences of transgressing the Mosaic law? Surely, John must have shocked his listeners by applying the phrase "Lamb of God" to a living man. When we pray to Jesus as the Lamb of God, we are praying to the One who voluntarily laid down his life to take in his own body the punishment for our sins and for the sins of the entire world.

7. *The Holy Trinity, Father, Son* and Holy Spirit: https://www.christianity.com/god/trinity/god-in-three-persons-a-doctrine-we-barely-understand-11634405.html

8. *Quote from the article on Christianity.com*: "All Christians believe the doctrine of the Trinity. If you do not believe this—that is, if you have come to a settled conclusion that the doctrine of the Trinity is not true—you are not a Christian at all. You are in fact a heretic. Those words may sound harsh, but they represent the judgment of the Christian church across the centuries. What is the Trinity? Christians in every land unite in proclaiming that our God eternally exists as Father, Son, and Holy Spirit. Those who deny that truth place themselves outside the pale of Christian orthodoxy." This harsh statement illustrates the problems with legalism and the doctrinal approach to Christianity.

9. *Legalism*: https://theblazingcenter.com/2018/12/legalistic.html Five signs your a legalist (and probably miserable) Specifically; Legalism is any attempt to gain acceptance or forgiveness from God through your own works or merits.

10 *Religious authority* https://www.cambridge.org/core/journals/new-testament-studies/article/abs/religious-authorities-in-the-gospel-of-mark/9BF67DFC9981C8AC28BF6C210DEC883A Within the story-world of Mark, the religious authorities — the scribes, Pharisees, Herodians, chief priests, elders, and Sadducees — form a united front opposed to Jesus61 and therefore constitute, literary-critically, a single, or collective, character. If Jesus is the protagonist, they are the antagonists, and both Jesus and they exhibit a 'root character trait', that is, a character trait from which all other traits spring.

11. Corrupt authority https://www.cambridge.org/core/journals/new-testament-studies/article/abs/religious-authorities-in-the-gospel-of-mark/9BF67DFC9981C8AC28BF6C210DEC883A In contrast, the religious authorities are characterized as being 'without authority', which is to say that they 'think the things of men' and view reality from a purely human perspective. Consequently, the conflict between Jesus and the authorities in Mark's story is an extended clash over 'authority'. Instead of receiving Jesus as God's Messiah and Son, they oppose him throughout his ministry.

12. Stumbling block Romans 14:13-23 English Standard Version Do Not Cause Another to Stumble 13 Therefore let us not pass judgment on one another any longer, but rather decide never to put a stumbling block or hindrance in the way of a brother. 14 I know and am persuaded in the Lord Jesus that nothing is unclean in itself, but it is unclean for anyone who thinks it unclean. 15 For if your brother is grieved by what you eat, you are no longer walking in love. By what you eat, do not destroy the one for whom Christ died. 16 So do not let what you regard as good be spoken of as evil. 17 For the kingdom of God is not a matter of eating and drinking but of righteousness and peace and joy in the Holy Spirit. 18 Whoever thus serves Christ is acceptable to God and approved by men. 19 So then let us pursue what makes for peace and for mutual upbuilding.

13. Pharisees: a member of an ancient Jewish sect, distinguished by strict observance of the traditional and written law, and commonly held to have pretensions to superior sanctity.

14. Law and tradition https://www.britannica.com/biography/Jesus/The-relation-of-Jesus-teaching-to-the-Jewish-law Jewish law is the focus of many passages in the Gospels. According to one set, especially prominent in the Sermon on the Mount (Matthew 5–7), Jesus admonished his followers to observe the law unwaveringly (Matthew 5:17–48). According to another set, he did not adhere strictly to the law himself and even transgressed current opinions about some aspects of it, especially the Sabbath (e.g., Mark 3:1–5). It is conceivable that both were true,

15. 4th Century AD https://www.christianity.com/church/church-history/centuries/4th-century-11631963.html The fourth century, like the sixteenth, and perhaps our own twentieth, is one of those periods in church history when momentous changes take place that stand out as pivotal turning points in the history of God's people.

16. Reach Dominion theology https://digitalcommons.liberty.edu/cgi/viewcontent.cgi?article=1073&context=pretrib_arch This excerpt from a Liberty University document suggests the chilling nature of Dominion Theology. Titus DEFINING DOMINION DT advocates believe that dominion over every area of life has been restored by the first coming of Christ. Since we are now in the Kingdom (this is where the synonym for DT "Kingdom Now" arose), they believe the present task of the Church is to call believers to reclaim the rule of Christ on planet earth by whatever means their particular brand of DT advocates

17. Rebuke authorities:

Chapter 3: On the Nature of Judgment
Jeremiah 7:5-7
Matthew 7:1-5
John 8:1-11

1. Radically Christian, Wes Macadams. https://radicallychristian.com/do-not-presume-to-have-the-authority-of-jesus-when-rebuking-others

2. Jesus Returned:

3. Jewish heritage: Jesus was well-schooled in Jewish tradition and law.

4. Father forgive them: "for they know now that they do…" Luke 23:24

5. Killing Jesus: The literal claim that the Jews "killed Jesus" served as an excuse to persecute and kill people of Jewish heritage for centuries.

6. Roman authority: PBS. Org. Over time, the Christian church and faith grew more organized. In 313 AD, the Emperor Constantine issued the Edict of Milan, which accepted Christianity: 10 years later, it had become the official religion of the Roman Empire.

7. Legalistic: concerning adherence to moral law rather than to personal religious faith.

8. Dominion: A theocratic movement hiding in plain sight.

9. Fix it all: The belief that Jesus will come back some day to "repair" the world and install an entirely new one.

10. Gaslighting: The name comes from a '30s play called Gas Light in which the main character attempts to drive his wife crazy by dimming the lights in their home, which were powered by gas, and then denies the lights are changing.https://www.domesticshelters.org/articles/gaslighting/what-is-gaslighting

11. NBC5. A Chicago affiliate of the NBC media network

12. God's own Word in the Bible. The website Bible.org delivers a set of "proofs" that the Bible is the Word of God. In hundreds of passages, the Bible declares or takes the position explicitly or implicitly that it is nothing less than the very Word of God. Some thirty-eight hundred times the Bible declares, "God said," or "Thus says the Lord" (e.g. Ex. 14:1; 20:1; Lev. 4:1; Num. 4:1; Deut. 4:2; 32:48; Isa. 1:10, 24; Jer. 1:11; Ezek. 1:3; etc.). Paul also recognized that the things he was writing were the Lord's commandments (1 Cor. 14:37), and they were acknowledged as such by the believers (1 Thess. 2:13). Peter proclaimed the certainty of the Scriptures and the necessity of heeding the unalterable and certain Word of God (2 Pet. 1:16-21) ohn too recognized that his teaching was from God; to reject his teaching was to reject God (1 John 4:6).17

Chapter 4 Straight Out of Purgatory

1. Purgatory: noun (in Roman Catholic doctrine): a place or state of suffering inhabited by the souls of sinners who are expiating their sins before going to heaven.

2. Belief: an acceptance that a statement is true or that something exists.

3. Catholic: including a wide variety of things; all-embracing.

4. Public:

5. Indulgences An 'indulgence' was part of the medieval Christian church, and a significant trigger to the Protestant Reformation. Basically, by purchasing an indulgence, an individual could reduce the length and severity of punishment that heaven would require as payment for their sins, or so the church claimed. Buy an indulgence for a loved one, and they would go to heaven and not burn in hell. Buy an indulgence for yourself, and you needn't worry about that pesky affair you'd been having.

6. Martin Luther https://www.history.com/topics/reformation/martin-luther-and-the-95-theses Born in Eisleben, Germany, in 1483, Martin Luther went on to become one of Western history's most significant figures. Luther spent his early years in relative anonymity as a monk and scholar. But in 1517 Luther penned a document attacking the Catholic Church's corrupt practice of selling "indulgences" to absolve sin. His "95 Theses," which propounded two central beliefs—that the Bible is the central religious authority and that humans may reach salvation only by their faith and not by their deeds—was to spark the Protestant Reformation.

7. European Reading Room: https://www.loc.gov/rr/european/

8. Anti-Semitism: hostility to or prejudice against Jewish people.Blaming the Jews, Jewish deicide: https://www.bibleodyssey.org/en/passages/related-articles/crucifixion-of-jesus-and-the-jews

9. Gentiles:

10. Blaming Jews: including a wide variety of things; all-embracing.

11. Adolf Hitler: https://www.history.com/topics/world-war-ii/adolf-hitler-1 Adolf Hitler, the leader of Germany's Nazi Party, was one of the most powerful and notorious dictators of the 20th century. Hitler capitalized on economic woes, popular discontent and political infighting to take absolute power in Germany beginning in 1933. Germany's invasion of Poland in 1939 led to the outbreak of World War II, and by 1941 Nazi forces had occupied much of Europe. Hitler's virulent anti-Semitism and obsessive pursuit of Aryan supremacy fueled the murder of some 6 million Jews, along with other victims of the Holocaust. After the tide of war turned against him, Hitler committed suicide in a Berlin bunker in April 1945.

12 ChurchandState.com: March, 2019 website article.

13. Nazi Party: https://www.history.com/topics/world-war-ii/nazi-party. T*he National Socialist German Workers' Party, or Nazi Party*, grew into a mass movement and ruled Germany through totalitarian means from 1933 to 1945 under the leadership of Adolf Hitler (1889-1945). Founded in 1919 as the German Workers' Party, the group promoted German pride and anti-Semitism, and expressed dissatisfaction with the terms of the Treaty of Versailles, the 1919 peace settlement that ended World War I (1914-1918) and required Germany to make numerous concessions and reparations. Hitler joined the party the year it was founded and became its leader in 1921. In 1933, he became chancellor of Germany and his Nazi government soon assumed dictatorial powers. After Germany's defeat in World War II (1939-45), the Nazi Party was outlawed and many of its top officials were convicted of war crimes related to the murder of some 6 million European Jews during the Holocaust.

14. Counterpunch: https://www.counterpunch.org/"Christian churches, the master race and American exceptionalism," https://www.counterpunch.org/2016/02/22/christian-churches-the-master-race-and-american-exceptionalism

15. Evolution: LiveScience https://www.livescience.com/474-controversy-evolution-works.html

16. Eugenics: Excerpt from "On The Jews and Their Lies, Martin Luther. Numerous resources share these quotes from Martin Luther. https://www.iwu.edu/history/constructingthepastvol9/Paras.pdf

17. Aryan: The Aryan race is a debunked historical race concept which emerged in the late 19th century to describe people of Indo-European heritage as a racial grouping. The theory has been widely rejected and disproved since no historical or archaeological evidence exists.

18. Materialism: the doctrine that nothing exists except matter and its movements and modifications.

19. *Scapegoating:* the history of; a goat upon whose head are symbolically placed the sins of the people after which he is sent into the wilderness in the biblical ceremony for Yom Kippur

20. *Hitler Quote*: Hitler *quote*s: https://www.inspiringquotes.us/quotes/EdHB_lGJT9bojAlso:https://www.goodreads.com/quotes/892840-my-feeling-as-a-christian-points-me-to-my-lord

21. *Twisted cross*: https://www.amazon.com/Twisted-Cross-Occultic-Religion-Hitler/dp/0910311226*22. Blood libel*: The "blood libel" refers to a centuries-old false allegation that Jews murder Christians – especially Christian children – to use their blood for ritual purposes, such as an ingredient in the baking of Passover matzah (unleavened bread). It is also sometimes called the "ritual murder charge." The blood libel dates back to the Middle Ages and has persisted despite Jewish denials and official repudiations by the Catholic Church and many secular authorities. Blood libels have frequently led to mob violence and pogroms, and have occasionally led to the decimation of entire Jewish communities. https://www.adl.org/education/resources/glossary-terms/blood-libel

23. *Bonhoeffer*: German theologian who was assassinated by Nazi Germany two weeks before the work camp where he was asigned was liberated during WWII.

24. *Brittanica*: As described on Britannica.com Also: The Cost of Discipleship:

25. *NPR*

26. *Zionism*: a movement for (originally) the re-establishment and (now) the development and protection of a Jewish nation in what is now Israel. It was established as a political organization in 1897 under Theodor Herzl, and was later led by Chaim Weizmann.

27. *CNN*: May 14, 2018 CNN article

28. *Shrinking Church attendance* https://news.gallup.com/poll/341963/church-membership-falls-below-majority-first-time.aspx

29. *Source: Gallup 2021*: WASHINGTON, D.C. -- Americans' membership in houses of worship continued to decline last year, dropping below 50% for the first time in Gallup's eight-decade trend. In 2020, 47% of Americans said they belonged to a church, synagogue or mosque, down from 50% in 2018 and 70% in 1999. U.S. church membership was 73% when Gallup first measured it in 1937 and remained near 70% for the next six decades, before beginning a steady decline around the turn of the 21st century.

30. Secular society. Study.com In a secular society, the powers of the church and the state are separate. Basically, this means that the state's governing cannot be the result of the policies and beliefs of any organized religion and that no religious leader has automatic political authority.

25. Facebook: Excerpted from Progressive Christianity, Facebook Group, January, 2021.

31. Wedding cake: Christian baker: The Supreme Court ruled in favor of Jack Phillips, as described on NBC.com: "The decision was a victory for Jack Phillips of Masterpiece Cake in Denver, who has said that his cakes are works of art and that requiring him to bake them for same-sex weddings would force him to express a view that violated his religious beliefs. He runs his business guided by religious principles, closing on Sunday and refusing to make cakes containing alcohol or celebrating Halloween."

32. Religious liberty: Numerous court cases were brought in which dispensing birth control to employees was considered a breach of "religious liberty." Religious liberty: As defined onBJC.com (Baptist Justice Center): "Religious liberty" is the freedom to believe and exercise or act upon religious conscience without unnecessary interference by the government.

33 Slavery: Religious burden Slavery: https://www.history.com/topics/black-history/slavery

34. Genocide: Of Indigenous peoples. From the Holocaust museum website. https://hmh.org/library/research/genocide-of-indigenous-peoples-guide/ When European settlers arrived in the Americas, historians estimate there were over 10 million Native Americans living there. By 1900, their estimated population was under 300,000. Native Americans were subjected to many different forms of violence, all with the intention of destroying the community. In the late 1800s, blankets from smallpox patients were distributed to Native Americans in order to spread disease. There were several wars, and violence was encouraged; for example, European settlers were paid for each Penobscot person they killed. In the 19th century, 4,000 Cherokee people died on the Trail of Tears, a forced march from the southern U.S. to Oklahoma. In the 20th century, civil rights violations were common, and discrimination continues to this day.

35. Fascist groups: Quote on fascism: The ultimate source of this quote remains unknown. It persists because it appears to be true.

36. 2016 Trump Election: NPR. Trump led controversy before he ever got elected. https://www.npr.org/2016/11/05/500782887/donald-trumps-road-to-election-day

37. Forbes

38. Flag

39. Michael Flynn: Trump's key advisor and former Cabinet member indicted and then pardoned for his illegal actions related to the presidential campaign. https://www.csmonitor.com/USA/Politics/2022/0428/Disgraced-general-to-far-right-hero-Michael-Flynn-rides-the-next-wave

40. Benjamin Franklin as Quoted on Forbes.com, https://www.forbes.com/quotes/9010/

41. Christian dominion theology: Dominionism is the theocratic idea that regardless of theological camp, means, or timetable, God has called conservative Christians to exercise dominion over society by taking control of political and cultural institutions. https://www.politicalresearch.org/2016/08/18/dominionism-rising-a-theocratic-movement-hiding-in-plain-sight

Additional References:

Dispensationalism: belief in a system of historical progression, as revealed in the Bible, consisting of a series of stages in God's self-revelation and plan of salvation. Oxford Languages.

Hal Lindsey: A graduate of the Dallas Theological Seminary, a prominent Christian Zionist and dispensationalist, he expresses this theology in his writings. He is best known for his best-selling book The Late Great Planet Earth. https://www.biblio.com/hal-lindsey/author/490

Left Behind: A book series published by Tyndale House that also spawned a video catalog. The Left Behind series was authored by Tim LaHaye and Jeremy Jenkins. The Wikipedia description summarizes the lot: Left Behind is a multimedia franchise that started with a series of 16 bestselling religious novels by Tim LaHaye and Jerry B. Jenkins that dealt with Christian dispensationalist End Times : the pretribulation, premillennial, Christian eschatological interpretation of the Biblical apocalypse. The primary conflict of the series is the members of the Tribulation Force, an underground network of converts, against the NWO-esque organization "Global Community " and its leader, Nicolae Carpathia, who is also the Antichrist.End Times Theology: Millennialism, premillennialism and dispensationalism are all theories of the end of the world. https://www.bbc.co.uk/religion/religions/christianity/beliefs/endtimes_1.shtml

Salvation greed: As defined in this book, caring so much about gaining salvation in the afterlife that concerns and caring for others in this life are regarded as unimportant.

ACLU: https://www.aclu.org/ *From its About page on the website.* "The ACLU dares to create a more perfect union — beyond one person, party, or side. Our mission is to realize this promise of the United States Constitution for all and expand the reach of its guarantees."

Manifest Destiny: the 19th-century doctrine or belief that the expansion of the US throughout the American continents was both justified and inevitable.

1 Timothy

Matthew 25

Chapter 5 : All Apologetics. No Apologies.

1. Commercial temple, see Cleansing of the Temple, Bible Odyssey, https://www.bibleodyssey.org/en/passages/main-articles/jesus-and-the-moneychangers

2. Christian right: see National Humanities Center, http://nationalhumanitiescenter.org/tserve/twenty/tkeyinfo/chr_rght.htm

3. Apologetics : Dictionary.com; a branch of theology devoted to the defense of the divine origin and authority of Christianity

4. Moody Bible Institute, see https://www.moody.edu

5. Paul: see St. Paul the Apostle, https://www.britannica.com/biography/Saint-Paul-the-Apostle

6. IBS see International Bible Society, https://www.biblica.com/

7. Michael Kruger, President of Reformed Theological Seminary, RTS: see Reformed Theological Seminary https://rts.edu/

References

Matthew 7:5, "Hypocrite! First get rid of the log in your own eye; then you will see well enough to deal with the speck in your friend's eye."

Chapter 6 : What John the Baptist Taught Us

1. Voice Crying Out in the Wilderness, https://www.biblegateway.com/verse/en/John%201%3A23, NIV John replied in the words of Isaiah the prophet, "I am the voice of one calling in the wilderness, 'Make straight the way for the Lord.'"

2. Religious authorities: https://www.cambridge.org/core/journals/new-testament-studies/article/abs/religious-authorities-in-the-gospel-of-mark/9BF67DFC9981C8AC28BF6C210DEC883A

3. Rebellion: See, The Jewish Revolts, https://www.thattheworldmayknow.com/the-jewish-revolts. Jewish people of Jesus' day had a passionate desire for freedom from the domination of the pagan Romans and the oppressive Herod dynasty that had ruled them for many years. Revolt seethed continuously, mostly underground, for more than 100 years from the time Herod became king (37 BC) until the Romans destroyed Jerusalem and the Temple (AD 70).

4. Bible interpretation: James Charlesworth, bibleinterp.com3

5. Franklin Graham testimonial: Axios.com

References:

John 14:6 – "I am the way, the truth, and the life. No one comes to the father except through me."

Salvation greed: Author's term.

Biblical Jesus information: BiblicalJesus.org http://www.biblicaljesus.org/index.cfm/fuseaction/basics.tour/ID/13/In-Presence-Enemies.htm

Chapter 7: The Serpent's Legacy

1. Salvation Greed: This is the author's term for people so consumed by getting to heaven they relegate events in this life to insignificance.

2. Real Problems:

3. Franklin Graham: His ministry is called Samaritan's Purse. https://www.samaritanspurse.org

4. Grace: "You see that the grace of God is more than salvation but also everything we need for life and godliness. The definition of grace could be "God's life, power and righteousness given to us by unmerited favor." It is through grace that God works effective change in our hearts and lives." https://www.marionstar.com/story/life/2019/01/19/pastor-what-grace-god-does-us/2569447002/

Chapter 8: Jesus in the Wilderness

1. Wilderness: Luke 4:3

Chapter 9: The Lord's Prayer

1. Lord's Prayer Our Father, who art in heaven, hallowed be thy name; thy kingdom come; thy will be done on earth as it is in heaven. Give us this day our daily bread; and forgive us our trespasses as we forgive those who trespass against us; and lead us not into temptation, but deliver us from evil. Amen.

Chapter 10: Releasing Tradition's Grip

1. Patriarch: the male head of a family or tribe, or; any of those biblical figures regarded as fathers of the human race, especially Abraham, Isaac, and Jacob, and their forefathers, or the sons of Jacob.

2. John 1, 1-14: In the Beginning was the Word…

3. Archetypes: a very typical example of a certain person or thing."the book is a perfect archetype of the genre" an original that has been imitated. "the archetype of faith is Abraham"

4. Ten Talents Parable: Matthew 25: 14-30

5. Good Samaritan Parable: Luke 10, 25-37

6. Pope Francis: November 19, 2019 article on the Jesuit review website.

Chapter 11: Creationism and the Science of Denial

1. Creationist website: Institute for Creation Research

2. Creationism: https://www.lexico.com/en/definition/creationism The belief that the universe and living organisms originate from specific acts of divine creation, as in the biblical account, rather than by natural processes such as evolution. Also: 'Intelligent Design creationism is bad theology, bad politics, bad education, and bad science.'

3. Henry Morris: Institute for Creation Research. https://www.icr.org/article/in-loving-memory-of-dr-henry-m-morris-iiiDr. Henry M. Morris III has been at the heart of ICR's ministry work for decades, using his gifts as a leader, speaker, and writer to proclaim the truth of God's Word and how science affirms creation. Some might say a passion for creation ministry has run in his family. His father, Dr. Henry M. Morris—widely known as the father of modern creationism—founded ICR in 1970, and his brother Dr. John Morris served as ICR President from 1996 to 2014 and as President Emeritus after that

4. Ken Ham: https://answersingenesis.org/bios/ken-ham/ Biography of Ken Ham on the Answers In Genesis website.

5. *Answers In Genesis*: https://answersingenesis.org/The organization that eagerly promotes the biblically claim that the earth is just 6,000 years old and "kinds" of living animals, including dinosaurs, were on board an ark that rescued them from a worldwide flood.

6. *Ark Encounter*: https://arkencounter.com/

7. *Creation Museum*: https://creationmuseum.org/

8. *Dr. Gary Parker*: https://www.icr.org/article/from-evolution-creation-personal-testimony e.g.: "All of us can recognize objects that man has created, whether paintings, sculptures, or just a Coke bottle. Because the pattern of relationships in those objects is contrary to relationships that time, chance, and natural physical processes would produce, we know an outside creative agent was involved. I began to see the same thing in a study of living things, especially in the area of my major interest, molecular biology."

9. *Gallup Survey*: https://news.gallup.com/poll/261680/americans-believe-creationism.aspx40% of Americans believe in creationism.

10. *Live Science*: 2011 survey of high school science teachers. https://evolution-outreach.biomedcentral.com/

11. *The Real Deal* by Ken Ham and Britt Beamer, 2011.

12. *Christian denial of the Holocaust*, The Failure of Christian Love in the Holocaust, Andrew Tix, May 4, 2106 https://cct.biola.edu/failure-christian-love-holocaust/

13. *Legalistic*: adjective adhering excessively to law or formula.

14. *Addiction*: Addiction is an inability to stop using a substance or engaging in a behavior even though it is causing psychological and physical harm.

15. *Crazy shit*: https://www.salon.com/2015/07/14/9_horrible_things_the_christian_right_does_because_god_said_so/

16. *Geological history*: Young earth creationism, https://ncse.ngo/young-earth-creationism

17. *Young Earth Creationists* adopt a method of Biblical interpretation which requires that the earth be no more than 10,000 years old, and that the six days of creation described in Genesis each lasted for 24 hours. Young Earth Creationists believe that the origin of the earth, the universe, and various forms of life, etc., are all instances of special creation. The doctrine of special creation involves direct divine intervention, suspending the laws of nature to achieve a given result. This doctrine contrasts with a view common among theistic evolutionists that God can work through natural laws.

18. *Resurrection* see JesusOnline.com, Did Jesus Really Rise From the Dead?

19. *Gaslighting;* also, gaslight. See, Betterhelp.com..Gaslighting... "is the act of manipulating someone using psychological efforts to make them question their own sanity. It is a severe form of emotional abuse that often leads them to question their own memories, thoughts or events that have happened. If the behavior is not stopped, it can result in a victim doubting and losing their own sense of identity and self-worth." Politically or religiously, the most famous form is to repeat a lie often enough that it becomes a sort of accepted truth. That lie is adopted and repeated ad hominem to make all others feel as if they are experiencing some sort of personal belief crisis.

20. *Intervention*: From Verywellmind.com: "In the context of substance use and recovery, an intervention involves an organized attempt to confront a loved one with an addiction about how their drinking, drug use, or addiction-related behavior has affected everyone around them." Interventions also occur for other addictive and destructive behaviors.

21. *Irreducible complexity*: (IC) is the argument that certain biological systems cannot have evolved by successive small modifications to pre-existing functional systems through natural selection, because no less complex system would function.

22. *Intelligent Design Theory*: The theory of intelligent design holds that certain features of the universe and of living things are best explained by an intelligent cause, not an undirected process such as natural selection.

23. *Reason to Believe*, "Can Science Identify the Intelligent Designer?" https://reasons.org/explore/publications/articles/can-science-identify-the-intelligent-designer?

24. *Fossil reconstruction*: Why are birds the only surviving dinosaurs? https://www.nhm.ac.uk/discover/why-are-birds-the-only-surviving-dinosaursBirds evolved from a group of meat-eating dinosaurs called theropods. ... These ancient birds looked quite a lot like small, feathered dinosaurs and they had much in common. Their mouths still contained sharp teeth. But over time, birds lost their teeth and evolved beaks. https://ourworldindata.org/life-on-earth

25. Abiogenesis: https://www.britannica.com/science/abiogenesis

26. Microevolution vs. macroevolution: In young Earth creationism and baraminology a central tenet is that evolution can explain diversity in a limited number of created kinds which can interbreed (which they call "microevolution") while the formation of new "kinds" (which they call "macroevolution") is impossible. Here's an interesting take from the perspective of the creationist community. https://www.scriptureoncreation.org/macro-vs-microevolution.html - variation within the Biblical kind. Macroevolution - the changing of one Biblical kind into another kind.

27. Neanderthals: https://www.nhm.ac.uk/discover/who-were-the-neanderthals.html

Chapter 12: Why the Easier Paths lead to difficulty

1. Heliocentrism: Heliocentrism, a cosmological model in which the Sun is assumed to lie at or near a central point (e.g., of the solar system or of the universe) while the Earth and other bodies revolve around it. https://www.britannica.com/science/heliocentrism

2. NYT: 1992 story

3. Catholic: CatholicAnswers.com,

4. Flat Earth Society: https://www.tfes.org/

5. You.gov: Article on acceptance of Flat Earth Theory by even people that aren't religious by nature.

6. Live Science; Flat Earth, What Fuels the Internet's Strangest Conspiracy Theory?https://www.livescience.com/61655-flat-earth-conspiracy-theory.html

7. Noah Flood: Is a Global Flood Scientifically Possible? by Jeff Zweerink https://reasons.org/team/jeff-zweerink

8. September 21, 2015 Also: https://ncse.ngo/yes-noahs-flood-may-have-happened-not-over-whole-earth"Yes, Noah's Flood may have happened but not over the whole earth."

9. Genocide: https://www.theguardian.com/science/punctuated-equilibrium/2011/jan/09/1 Noah's Ark, God, Giraffes &

10. Noah/Grace: https://www.simplybible.com/f30j-grace-and-noah.htm How did Noah find grace in the eyes of the Lord?

11. Genesis 7:2

12. Nathan Jeanson: The Origin of Species After the Flood. https://answersingenesis.org/noahs-ark/origin-of-species-after-flood/ "Modern science is giving us even more windows into this enigma of antiquity. The more we learn about the origin of species, the more hints we gain into Noah's vistas. The stamp of the Flood reverberates all the way down to the present day—in the form of genetics."

13. AIG: https://answersingenesis.org/dinosaurs/

Chapter 13: Lessons in Bad Theology

1. Victor Scott…bad theology: "What makes bad theology?" Jeremiah's Vow, 2012

2. Anachronism: a thing belonging or appropriate to a period other than that in which it exists, especially a thing that is conspicuously old-fashioned. Oxford dictionary.

3. Demons: Stop blaming 'demons' for bizarre delusions or behavior! https://www.mdedge.com/psychiatry/article/106097/schizophrenia-other-psychotic-disorders/stop-blaming-demons-bizarre

4. Founding Fathers: Eight Founding Fathers and how they shaped America. https://www.history.com/topics/american-revolution/founding-fathers-united-states

5. Establishment clause: the clause in the First Amendment of the US Constitution that prohibits the establishment of religion by Congress. Oxford Dictionary.

6. Manifest Destiny: the 19th-century doctrine or belief that the expansion of the US throughout the American continents was both justified and inevitable.

7. Christian Nation: Is America a Christian Nation? https://www.au.org/resources/publications/is-america-a-christian-nation. Is the United States a "Christian nation"? Some Americans think so. Religious Right activists and right-wing television preachers often claim that the United States was founded to be a Christian nation. Even some politicians agree. If the people who make this assertion are merely saying that most Americans are Christians, they might have a point. But those who argue that America is a Christian nation usually mean something more, insisting that the country should be officially Christian. The very character of our country is at stake in the outcome of this debate.

8. Theocracy: a system of government in which priests rule in the name of God or a god. Oxford languages

Chapter 14: Playing God and Imposing Tradition

1. Bible Study: BibleStudyTools.org, Tower of Babel.

2. Genesis 11 **Genesis** 18, 20-21, 22-25, Sodom and Gomorrah

3. *Rape*: https://reformationproject.org/case/sodom-and-gomorrah/

4. *Shawshank Redemption*, dialogue discussing Bull Queer

5. *Ezekiel 16*: 49-50

6. *Lot and his daughters*: https://www.bibleodyssey.org/en/places/related-articles/lot-and-his-daughters

Chapter 15: From Repression to Oppression

1. *Repression*: the action of subduing someone or something by force.

2. *Hyperbole*: exaggerated statements or claims not meant to be taken literally.

3. *Pluck out*: Matthew 5:29, If your right eye causes you to stumble, gouge it out and throw it away. It is better for you to lose one part of your body than for your whole body to be thrown into hell.

4. *Repressive laws in scripture*: The Repressive Laws in Leviticus don't apply to Christians https://reformationproject.org/case/levitical-prohibitions/

5. *Gay Lifestyle*: Why the term gay lifestyle offends and is hurtful http://www.schools-out.org.uk/?news=why-the-term-gay-lifestyle-offends-and-is-hurtful

6. *Sins of Scripture*, Bishop John Shelby Spong.

7. *Transgender*: Transgender people have a gender identity or gender expression that differs from the sex that they were assigned at birth. Some transgender people who desire medical assistance to transition from one sex to another identify as transsexual.

8. *Oppression*: Goodtherapy.org

9. *Chocolat:* Movie. When mysterious Vianne and her child arrive in a tranquil French town in the winter of 1959, no one could have imagined the impact that she and her spirited daughter would have on the community stubbornly rooted in tradition. Within days, she opens an unusual chocolate shop, across the square from the church. Her ability to perceive her customers' desires and satisfy them with just the right confection, coaxes the villagers to abandon themselves to temptation -- just as Lent begins.

Chapter 16: In Originalism We Cannot Trust

1. Originalism: a type of judicial interpretation of a constitution (especially the US Constitution) that aims to follow how it would have been understood or was intended to be understood at the time it was written. Also: the principle or belief that a text should be interpreted in a way consistent with how it would have been understood or was intended to be understood at the time it was written.

2. Americans United for a Separation of Church and State: https://www.au.org/

3. Gun violence by the numbers: Brady organization website. https://www.bradyunited.org/key-statistics 363M guns

4. Chicago Tribune, Sept 25, 2021 By JEREMY GORNER, ANNIE SWEENEY and ROSEMARY SOBOL

5. Larry Pratt: Larry Pratt, the executive director emeritus of Gun Owners of America. https://www.gunowners.org/alert062817/

6. Daily Beast article: 2018 Jan 6, 2021 How one of America's ugliest days unraveled inside and outside the Capitol https://www.washingtonpost.com/nation/interactive/2021/capitol-insurrection-visual-timeline/

7. NBC.com: More Americans kills by guns since 1968 that all US wars combined https://www.nbcnews.com/storyline/las-vegas-shooting/more-americans-killed-guns-1968-all-u-s-wars-combined-n807156

8. ABC News: https://abcnews.go.com/US/federal-government-study-gun-violence/story?id=50300379 13th Amendment" Passed by Congress January 31, 1865. Ratified December 6, 1865. The 13th Amendment changed a portion of Article IV, Section 2 https://constitutioncenter.org/21st Amendment https://constitutioncenter.org/Passed by Congress February 20, 1933. Ratified December 5, 1933. The 21st Amendment repealed the 18th Amendment and Prohibiton

9. 18th Amendment https://constitutioncenter.org/ After one year from the ratification of this article the manufacture, sale, or transportation of intoxicating liquors within, the importation thereof into, or the exportation thereof from the United States and all territory subject to the jurisdiction thereof for beverage purposes is hereby prohibited.

10. Abolitionist movement: https://history.com/topics/black-history/abolitionist-movement

11. Conference

12. Living doc: Why the late Justic Scalia was wrong: The fallacies of constitutional textualism. https://digitalcommons.law.lsu.edu/cgi/viewcontent.cgi?article=1411&context=faculty_scholarship

13. Christianity as a Justification for Slavery https://historyengine.richmond.edu/episodes/view/3535 "Abolitionists Use Scripture to Support Their Cause Rebecca Graf."Medium https://medium.com/@rebeccagraf_63084/abolitionists-used-the-bible-to-support-cause-31824d8de221

14. Jim Crow laws: https://www.history.com/topics/early-20th-century-us/jim-crow-laws

15. KKK: Washington Post, "A White Preacher Used the Bible to Revive the Klu Klux Klan" Also: Readex.com https://www.readex.com/blog/religion-and-rise-second-ku-klux-klan-1915-1922-kelly-j-baker

16. Torture the action or practice of inflicting severe pain or suffering on someone as a punishment or in order to force them to do or say something.

17. MLK quotes: History.com https://www.history.com/topics/black-history/martin-luther-king-jr

18. Nixon: A 2018 article in The Guardian https://www.theguardian.com/commentisfree/2008/apr/04/thelegacyofthe1968riots

Chapter 16 Echoes of Manifest Destiny

1. Chief Pontiac: Quote sourced from History.com

2. Treaties: Broken treaties with Native American Tribes: Timeline https://www.history.com/news/native-american-broken-treaties

3.Gold Rush: https://www.greenbiz.com/article/long-toxic-tail-gold-rush#:~:text=During%20the%20U.S.%20gold%20rush,an%20estimated%2010%20million%20pounds

4. Bison: millions of American bison were extirpated within a 50 year period in the late 1800s.

5. Passenger pigeon: Recommended reading, A Feathered River Across the Sky, by Joel Greenberg, https://www.amazon.com/Feathered-River-Across-Sky-Extinction/dp/1620405342

6. NPR soil: A February 2021 story on NRP.org titled "New Evidence Show Fertile Soil Gone from Midwestern Farms"

7. Cattle grazing: GlobalRangelands.com

8. Water: USDA, irrigation and water use. https://www.ers.usda.gov/topics/farm-practices-management/irrigation-water-use/ 50%

9. Mercy for Animals: mercyforanimals.org https://mercyforanimals.org/animal-agriculture-wastes-one-third-of-drinkable

10. Dust Bowl: Foundation for Economic Education, https://fee.org/articles/the-great-dust-bowl-of-the-1930s-was-a-policy-made-disaster/?gclid=CjwKCAjwz_WG BhA1EiwAUAxIcc66l5cfk3B3vCSiUIoewcRuU2UfSXnAa3uOumPXvfdvSj28YL7 nCBoCIp0QAvD_BwE

*11. Our Rabbi Jesus*1 and Lois Tverberg

12. Nine plagues: Exodus 10:21-22 https://ourrabbijesus.com/plague-of-darkness/

Chapter 17: Cause and Effect

1. Act of God: an instance of uncontrollable natural forces in operation (often used in insurance claims).

2. Anthropogenic: (chiefly of environmental pollution and pollutants) originating in human activity.

3. Rush Limbaugh: August 2019 blog.

4. NCEI: https://www.ncei.noaa.gov/https:// and www.ncei.noaa.gov/news/weather-vs-climate

5. CNN.com, James Inhofe report https://www.cnn.com/2015/02/26/politics/james-inhofe-snowball-climate-change/index.html

6. Pew Review climate: Pew Research study "Religion and Views On Climate and Energy, https://www.pewresearch.org/science/2015/10/22/religion-and-views-on-climate-and-energy-issues/

7. Newsweek: Kashmira Gander article

8. Robin Veldman: book The Gospel of Climate Skepticism: Why Evangelical Christians Oppose Action on Climate Change

9. Grist: What evangelical Christians really think about climate change https://grist.org/article/what-evangelical-christians-really-think-about-climate-change/

10. Argus: https://www.argusmedia.com/en/news/1937457-republicans-struggle-to-unite-on-climate-message

11. Presidential approval ratings: https://news.gallup.com/poll/203198/presidential-approval-ratings-donald-trump.aspx

12. Privatize the profits, socialize the losses : Privatizing profits and socializing losses refers to the practice of treating company earnings as the rightful property of shareholders and company losses as a responsibility that society must shoulder. In other words, the profitability of corporations are strictly for the benefit of their shareholders. But when the companies fail, the fallout—the losses and recovery—are the responsibility of the general public.

13. EPA Environmental Justice: https://www.epa.gov/environmentaljustice

14. Beatitudes: Matthew 5: 3-11

15. Trickle down economics: https://fee.org/ Trickle-down economics (the critics said) was based on the theory that tax breaks given to the rich would multiply investment, provide jobs, and eventually create increased income for everyone in the economy. In other words, by "giving" the rich more after-tax income, the government would foster economic growth, because the rich are more likely to invest than the poor, since any additional money in their hands would not have to be spent on necessities.

16. CBSNews: https://www.cbsnews.com/news/tax-cuts-rich-50-years-no-trickle-down/ Tax cuts for the wealthy have long drawn support from conservative lawmakers and economists who argue that such measures will "trickle down" and eventually boost jobs and incomes for everyone else. But a new study from the London School of Economics says 50 years of such tax cuts have only helped one group — the rich.

17. 1970s : The Cuyahoga River caught fire at least a dozen times, but no one cared until 1969 https://www.smithsonianmag.com/history/cuyahoga-river-caught-fire-least-dozen-times-no-one-cared-until-1969-180972444/Despite being much smaller than previous fires, the river blaze in Cleveland 50 years ago became a symbol for the nascent environmental movement

18. Bald eagle/DDT National Fish and Wildlife Service, https://www.fws.gov/midwest/eagle/Nhistory/biologue.html : Shortly after World War II, DDT was hailed as a new pesticide to control mosquitoes and other insects. However, DDT and its residues washed into nearby waterways, where aquatic plants and fish absorbed it. Bald eagles, in turn, were poisoned with DDT when they ate the contaminated fish. The chemical interfered with the ability of the birds to produce strong eggshells. As a result, their eggs had shells so thin that they often broke during incubation or otherwise failed to hatch. DDT also affected other species such as peregrine falcons and brown pelicans. In addition to the adverse effects of DDT, some bald eagles have died from lead poisoning after feeding on waterfowl containing lead shot, either as a result of hunting or from inadvertent ingestion. By 1963, with only 487 nesting pairs of bald eagles remaining, the species was in danger of extinction. Loss of habitat, shooting, and DDT poisoning contributed to the near demise of our national symbol.

19. Free market is god: literally, "godonomics." https://theceme.org/wp-content/uploads/2020/04/Part-1-1.pdf The free-market is God's market, which may be surprising for some. It is a God given institution1 for our economic prosperity for which we should be truly thankful.

20. EPA website: Clean Air Act

21. Greenwashing: from Investopedia, Greenwashing is the process of conveying a false impression or providing misleading information about how a company's products are more environmentally sound. Greenwashing is considered an unsubstantiated claim to deceive consumers into believing that a company's products are environmentally friendly.

22. Clean Air Act: The Clean Air Act (CAA) is the comprehensive federal law that regulates air emissions from stationary and mobile sources. Among other things, this law authorizes EPA to establish National Ambient Air Quality Standards (NAAQS) to protect public health and public welfare and to regulate emissions of hazardous air pollutants. https://www.epa.gov/laws-regulations/summary-clean-air-act

23. Locked down: https://www.pbs.org/wgbh/pages/frontline/shows/religion/why/legitimization.html From the article: One of the first things Constantine does, as emperor, is start persecuting other Christians. The Gnostic Christians are targeted... and other dualist Christians. Christians who don't have the Old Testament as part of their canon are targeted. The list of enemies goes on and on. There's a kind of internal purge of the church as one emperor ruling one empire tries to have this single church as part of the religious musculature of his vision of a renewed Rome. And it's with this theological vision in mind that Constantine not only helps the bishops to iron out a unitary policy of what a true Christian believes, but he also, interestingly, turns his attention to Jerusalem, and rebuilds Jerusalem just as a righteous king should do.

24. Acts 9: 1-6

Chapter 19: Scriptural Inventory

Chapter 20 Religion From Earth

This book is a self-referencing series of chapters written by Dr. Richard Simon Hanson. The scripture contained within is translated from Hebrew by the author himself, a scholar on the subject and a Professor of Religion (Emeritus) of Luther College. This essay was written in the 1980s and shared with Christopher Cudworth for inclusion in a future work after Professor Hanson read The Genesis Fix: A Repair Manual for Faith in the Modern Age (2007, Human Nature Publishing)

Chapter 21: Reconciliation

Acknowledgements and Notes:

I'd like to thank Dr. Richard Simon Hanson for providing his treatise Religion From Earth. Our thoughts and beliefs, though drawn from different histories, bear strong resemblance in seeing the connection between Creation and God.

I thank my wife Suzanne Astra for believing in the value of this work, and for listening to plenty of car conversations about its topics.

My thanks always go to my son Evan Paul Cudworth, for his willingness to push his father to be authentic, motivated, and true to himself. And to my daughter Emily Cudworth, whose talents and path in life always reveals things new to my awareness, and the value of family.

I say "Gracias" to my faithful Mac Powerbook, for trusting my fingers and my mind through millions of keystrokes. Also, to Grammarly, for pointing out casual errors in text. The remaining mistakes are due to a lifelong struggle with ADHD, and they are all mine. This is a collaborative venture on many front. Please feel free to send me any corretions or suggestions at cudworthfix@gmail.com. The great thing about Amazon is that I can upload a corrected version.

Thank you to Laurie Stephans for transcribing Dr. Hanson's original manuscript from typewritten copy to Word files. Note that the single-space after periods rule was not in effect during this transcription. I have left it in its original form because it breathes better. Thank you to Luther College for the liberal arts education that encouraged us all to engage in critical thinking to the best of our ability. I do thank the ELCA for its ministry to my family and I for many years of care and concern for our family.

About the Authors

Christopher Cudworth

Christopher Cudworth is a freelance writer whose interest in religion and natural history goes back to early childhood. Raised out East, he roamed the hills of New York and Pennsylvania with a sense of wonder and rich imagination. By age twelve, his ardent interest in birds blossomed into an avocation of painting birds and wildlife, and his writing talents took off from college into a publishing career producing articles and columns for newspapers and magazines. He earned a role as Editorial Writer for the Daily Herald, Illinois' third-largest newspaper, where he edited the columns of syndicated national writers from a broad spectrum of political perspectives. He also engaged with the public through editing Op-eds, Letters to the Editor, and responses to his own columns. As national politics mixed with religion ini the early 2000s, he embarked on an essay project that resulted in his first book, The Genesis Fix, A Repair Manual for Faith in the Modern Age, How Biblical Literalism Affects Politics, Culture, and the Environment. He is a frequent blogger who produced a memoir of his wife's cancer survivorship journey in a book titled The Right Kind of Pride, Character, Caregiving and Community. His work also earned him honors such as Article of the Year on Yahoo! Associatedcontent.com and numerous public relations awards for his work in that field as well. Honest-to-Goodness is his second book on religion and natural history. Another book titled Nature Is Our Country Club is in the works as well. Website: ChristopherCudworth.com Blogs: Werunandride.com, Therightkindofpride.com. Genesisfix.com

Dr. Richard Simon Hanson

Dr. Richard Simon Hanson grew up in rural Wisconsin with a love of farm life that has led a journey of learning, teaching, and sharing. He was ordained, received his Ph.D. from Harvard University, and is a Professor Emeritus of Religion at Luther College where he taught for almost 40 years. He and his wife, Rita, were married for over 55 years and had four children throughout their life's adventures. A highly respected storyteller, Chaplin, caregiver, mentor, and educator, Richard Simon now spends many days a week volunteering and visiting with those giving and receiving skilled, nursing home, and hospice care. He was a member of the Dead Sea Scrolls archaeology and translation team and was awarded the Carnegie Foundation 'US Professor of the Year Award' for Iowa in 1998. He is the author of several theological and related works, including his own translation of the Book of Psalms. Hanson is also featured in the eight-part DVD series "How the Bible Happened" which was hosted by the NE Iowa Unitarian Universal Fellowship. Dr. Hanson biography excerpted from: https://www.iloveinspired.com/probituaries/richard-simon-hanson/

The Path of Legalism in the Judeo-Christian Tradition

OUTCOMES		OUTCOMES
	Original SIN **SERPENT IN GENESIS** Advent of Legalism	
CHRISTIAN		**POLITICAL**
Biblical Canonization	Religious Authoritarians **JEWISH TRADITION**	Love of Law
Anti-Semitism	Roman Catholicism **INSTITUTIONAL RELIGION**	Purgatory Indulgences
Anachronism	Protestant **REFORMATION**	Repression
Dominionism		Oppression
Creationism	Biblical Literalism **INFALLIBILITY AND INERRANCY**	Constitutional Textualism/ Originalism
Anti-Modernity	Evangelicalism **FUNDAMENTALISM**	
Anti-Science		Conservative Alliance
Zionism	Political Religion **CONSERVATISM**	
End Times Theology	Theocracy **NEO-LEGALISM**	Political Activism
Culture of Denial	Christian Nationalism **RELIGIO-FASCISM**	Anti-abortion, Anti-Gay
		Culture Wars

The impact of legalism within the Judeo-Christian tradition has deep roots traceable to its first scriptural evidence in which the Serpent tempts Adam and Eve using God's Word to take them under its authority. Legalism grows with Judaism's love of law, an attitude inherited and expanded upon as Christianity consolidates its power through political alliances. The Reformation challenges this dynamic, but in turn spawns new forms of legalism through biblical literalism, infallibility and inerrancy. These instincts lead to fundamentalism and resistance to modernity along with corresponding denial of other forms of turth. Together with literalistic takes on prophetic symbolism, Christian legalism claims authority over the beginning and end of time... and asserts that its brand of truth is superior to all others.

$3700.^{00}$ answer to prayer

The impact of Tradition

Legalism – serpent desired control

"Gas lighting" – Reformation –

Organic symbols – John the Baptist - baptism